Dog Collar Diary

Memoirs of the Vet in the Vestry

Dog Collar Diary

Memoirs of the Vet in the Vestry

ALEXANDER CAMERON

Author of
Vet in the Vestry and *Poultry in the Pulpit*

To my wife Janet,
the dearest helpmeet any man ever had,
whose love, understanding and total sharing of everything
have made life such a joyous journey.

"Thy bield should be my bosom; to share it a'"

British Library Cataloguing in Publication Data
A catalogue record for this book is available from the British Library.
ISBN 1-899863-03-6

Typeset by XL Publishing Services, Nairn
Printed in Great Britain
by BPC Wheatons Ltd, Exeter
for House of Lochar, Isle of Colonsay, Argyll PA61 7YP

Contents

Foreword vi

Part One: The Boy - The Vet - The Minister

1 A Long, Long Day 3
2 The Rescuer 14
3 The Scotch Vetnary 19
4 The Essential Ingredient 28
5 Veterinary Vignettes 40
6 "Change Course!" 51
7 True Greatness 61
8 "Go to the Country" 67
9 "A Correspondence fix'd wi' Heaven" 78
10 The Real Person 90
11 A Chat with a Friend 95
12 One of These Days 101
13 The Right Kind of Medicine 107
14 Persistent Lawbreaker 112
15 The Dream 118

Part Two: The Border Years... and Lockerbie

16 Return to our Roots 127
17 Happy Valley 136
18 Weathering the Storm 147
19 Crossed Lines 155
20 The Moderator! 161
21 Wonders Beneath our Feet 166
22 Memories are Made of This 172
23 Hands Across the Sea 185
24 When the Curtain Parted 198
25 Goin' Home 202
26 When Day's Work is Done 210

Foreword

Ever since my two books *Vet in the Vestry* and *Poultry in the Pulpit* were published and did far better than an ordinary person like me could ever expect... in Britain, Australia and most of all America, I have been asked frequently when the next one was coming. I constantly answered "No more! I haven't another book in me" and I meant it. However, since retiring, various experiences as vet or minister have come back to me, and I decided to try just once more.

The first two books were fairly equally divided between my two "lives" with animals and people, the ministry part being in what I called Moorton... in reality the lovely little church of Fenwick in Ayrshire, and Aldermouth, easily recognised as the huge church of Nairn Old in the Highland Region.

My latest effort is not quite on the same lines, but more of a diary, which, like all diaries, has the happenings of a particular day, and a place where one can make one's views known on certain topics.

My latest effort is in two distinct parts; the first still concerned with my work amongst four- and two-legged animals, and still based, in general, in Devon as a vet, and my two Scottish churches. The second part, however, takes us to the lovely Border country and my ministry in four peaceful little country churches. But it includes the very terrible Lockerbie Air Disaster and the part one of my little churches played in this, for the nose cone and part of the fuselage of the giant plane came down just 100 yards from our little church, the picture always shown been taken from just in front of the church.

Seventy percent of the victims were found in our parish, and hundreds of relatives came from all over the world to our church, some three miles from Lockerbie and many found, in the peace of an old place of worship, a measure of comfort and healing, and my successor tells me many are still coming. I felt something should be said about the trauma of these days, and the part our little Scots Kirk played.

There is one difference I should mention between the other two books and this one. In the first the characters were given names that were not their own… including the author! Likewise with the second book, but in my latest offering, writing about sparsely populated country, this was not feasible, so the folks of the Borders are being denied the "fun" I am told Fenwick and Nairn folk had playing "spot the person"! This book then, completes the trilogy of churches where I have ministered.

Since this will certainly be my last effort, I want to express in my old age, thanks to a number of people, whose lives have touched mine and enriched my life in a variety of ways. I am fortunate in having had many friends, but to name them all would be a book in itself.

First, my appreciation of my parents who were poor in this world's goods, but rich in their love for us, and gave my brothers Graham, Fergus and myself the inestimable blessing of a Christian home, and planted sound standards for living which have stood the test of time. Then Major Ian Thomas DSO, still, well into his seventies, preaching the gospel, and who has founded a veritable empire of bible schools and Christian conference centres. He it was who first showed me that to be a real Christian was not the boring, long faced business I thought… not a duty, but a joy. He planted a real faith in me, something personal, vibrant, thrilling… like falling in love.

I turn to my vet life and another Major, Ken Davis, though called Davidson in the books. Ken took me on as a partner and I saw in him that a deeply committed Christian could also be successful in his profession, and be respected by all, regardless of faith, or none. The only thing I have against him was that he first thrust me into a pulpit, which was to lead years later to me wearing a dog collar! But of course, Ken, I speak in jest. He was followed by, as my next partner, Bernard Phillips, not Paterson, as the books said. He was… and is, a very fine vet, a superb surgeon, and the most humble, modest, generous and kind man I know. The warm friendship of Bernard and his wife Ann mean more… much more than I can ever express.

I must mention our four sons, and also their wives and our grandchildren who have all been, and are, our pride and joy and I want, probably to their embarrassment, to record how much happiness and pride they have given us in their careers, prowess at many sports, but most of all just the kind of people they are. But of course, surpassing all the many other blessings is the lass I have loved for fifty years, whose patience with an impatient man, constant support and total sharing in everything in life, have meant, as my dedication states, just everything. I have been a very lucky man.

I turn to my publishers, especially Neil Wilson and Michael de Luca of Lochar, who first took a chance with an unknown writer and published my first two books. Thanks go also to Penguin and St Martin's, New York, and my gratitude goes now to Kevin Byrne and Partners in House of Lochar, my new publishers, for their faith in me, and David St John Thomas for his encouragement when I felt sometimes like giving up on this one. My gratitude goes also to the editor of *The People's Friend* for allowing me to publish one or two pieces I had contributed to that magazine.

So, dear reader, I set out this late lark singing, my final effort. I hope you will find what I have tried to convey; things that will interest, inform, amuse, maybe challenge, and most of all find that to have the greatest Friend in the world is the greatest blessing in the world.

Happy reading

Alexander Cameron

PART ONE

The Boy - The Vet - The Minister

"In all your ways acknowledge God...
and He will direct your paths."

ONE

A long, long day

7am on a September morn in 1950, and the Cameron household was stirring for the duties of another day, still not fully dressed, half listening to the early morning radio news... when suddenly, in an instant we were all transfixed as if turned to stone. Father, mother, my twin brothers Graham and Fergus, and myself all looked at each other in deep dismay and anxiety, for the news reader had just announced to the nation that there had been a major mine disaster at Knockshinnoch Colliery in New Cumnock. One hundred and twenty-nine men had been entombed by a massive fall, and New Cumnock had been home for all of us until quite recently. There we had all been born and grown up, and almost certainly amongst those trapped miners would be perhaps relatives, certainly friends and acquaintances.

We now lived some thirty miles away where father had a job that no longer exists – that of station master in two little country stations, our home being actually on the station platform, where every door and window shook when "Paddy", the Irish boat train thundered through on its way to Stranraer. As a young man father had wanted to be a minister, and was a far more worthy man than me, who eventually wore the cloth, but in the early years of the century there were no grants or bursaries to finance him through University, and he had gone to the railway instead. But he did as much for the Church as many a minister, being at different times Sunday School superintendent, treasurer, elder, choir member much in demand as a solo singer with his fine baritone voice. He was also a church organist, having studied at something else that does not now exist, the Tonic

Sol Fa College. Mother? Well, she was just mother, typical of millions of women of her era who saw her full time task in life to be caring for home and family. In fact, I cannot remember ever coming in from school and mother not being there. However, she had started a poultry farm with six hens, paying she thought, the exorbitant price of five shillings each. Now there were hundreds of hens, ducks, turkeys, geese, guinea fowl reared on the free range system, for we had masses of ground. Father started with one skep of bees, and rose to ten, all this effort being to help the budget and educate the family, for father's salary, like most railwaymen, was pathetically minute.

My brother Graham, who in time was to become managing director of a timber firm, was at that time an apprentice joiner. We had a goat which was regarded as Graham's, for which he made a harness and cart, and as a boy collected the cut grass by the roadside for nest boxes. He was the handyman of the family, while his twin, Fergus, not without skill in his hands, was more bookish, aiming to be a teacher, but after gaining his MA, felt the pull of his beloved trains and in time became manager of passenger services in Scotland.

But all that was future. On that September day, I was in the early stages of my Vet career, being assistant to Ian Buchan at Mochrum, three miles from our home.

I could picture these men in Knockshinnoch Colliery, for as a boy I had been down a pit and remembered vividly the horror and fear that gripped me as I saw the narrow, long tunnels, some only about three feet high, many running with water, and in these workings men lay on their backs, sides or knelt to chip away the coal, the roofs of the tunnels held up by the old, wooden pit props. I shivered as I recalled the rats, to my boy's eyes seeming to be hundreds, which scuttled about, especially round the stalls of the pit ponies, and as I remembered, I committed to God in a little prayer the trapped men, and their anxious relatives, for it seemed initially only God could somehow get the men out again into His fresh air and sunshine.

New Cumnock then was a large village that straggled for miles, much of it made up of the old miner's rows of Victorian times, primitive in the extreme, with no bathroom or even toilet, most still lit by gas. Those who were fortunate (including us) had a council house which at least had a bathroom, in time electricity, and a small garden. Life was hard in every way. Very few of the mines had baths (oddly enough Knockshinnoch was one of the few which did) so most men came home filthy and wet each day, the clothes were thrown into a heap to be washed and dried in front of the fire for the next day. The climate too was harsh, the village sitting under the shadow of towering Black Craig, while the river Afton, of which Burns sang so beautifully "among thy green braes", flowed down from the hills, and a walk up Afton was the favourite with most people. Just up from the river was a sanatorium, a relic of the days of tuberculosis, then latterly converted into a geriatric hospital. Almost everyone worked in the mines or pits, the only other jobs being on the railway, surrounding farms, or in shops; those not in the pits regarded, and perhaps regarding themselves as a cut above the miners. I doubt if any miner ever saw the inside of a bank or played on the golf course, which was only used by those in some higher station in life, like teachers, bankers or shop-keepers. There was a Drama Club, with the plays of Joe Corrie the favourites; there were several reasonably attended churches and a wonderful community spirit: neighbours rallying round if a family was in trouble or need, with the breadwinner ill or injured.

Roughly speaking, there were two main areas... the Bank and the Toon (town), each with its school, and tremendous rivalry existed between the two, especially on the football field. School games in those days were watched by hundreds of vociferous spectators, for there was very little in the way of sport and no recreational facilities whatever. One of my earliest memories was a cry "Run! Here's the fermer!" Near our council estate was a farmer's field with a distinct slope, by no means ideal for playing football, but it was all we had. So when we thought the farmer was busy with the milking, we would climb the dyke, put our jackets or jerseys down for goalposts and if in funds, play with a bona fide size 3 football... if not "rich" at the time, we stuffed a leather cover with newspapers. I remember getting a football for my birthday, and the news spread like wildfire, so that almost every evening, boys would be at the door enquiring hopefully... "can we ha a len (loan) o' the ba'?" When the farmer's dread form was seen approaching, we grabbed our precious football, and if possible our garments, and ran for it, hotly pursued by his dogs. Many a boy had a skelping for leaving some garment behind. The only other possible place to play was Lindsay's field, which was strictly out of bounds, the only way in being over a five-barred gate with rows and rows of barbed wire on top, and many a lad had his trousers torn, or a hand or leg, requiring a visit to the doctor for stitching, which experience I had, twice. As I have indicated, there were just no sporting facilities at all, but we were all fitba' daft, and it was in these conditions, and from many mining areas that Scotland produced some of her most outstanding players, including the famous Wembley Wizards, who beat the "Auld Enemy" 5–1. Most of these men were part time players, and played happily for a minute amount. I can remember the first large transfer fee for one Bryn Jones in England, the fee being £14,000, which we all regarded as ridiculous – "naebody's worth that" – and the unfortunate Bryn, with this enormous price tag attached to him, found it too heave a burden, and I don't think played a decent game thereafter.

But to return to the rivalry between Bank and Toon schools. I clearly remember our first game of the season, when I was 12. It was a local derby with a huge crowd, and though I was eventually to grow to six feet, I was then the smallest boy in the team, playing as goalkeeper for the Toon school, with, behind my goals, a cordon of big boys armed with bicycle pumps to drive off the Bank schoolboys who would throw a stone at me whenever a shot came in. The crowd was vast, the noise tremendous... but we won 4–0. Great stuff!

On a Saturday, if we had any pocket money left, we watched "the Glens"... the local junior team, Glenafton Athletic, play. If the game was with a neighbouring mining town, there were often fights on the terraces, occasionally "a brek in" when the crowd did not agree with a referee's decision, and many a referee had to run for his life to the pavilion. I used to stand near the door of the Glen's dressing room, hoping to catch a glimpse of one of my heroes when the door opened, never dreaming then that I would frequently be in that dressing room, in the visitor's side, playing in my teens for Maybole Juniors as a centre forward, once, in fact, wearing the blue of my country in a trial match for the international team. I didn't make it!

Returning to my boyhood, I remember actually touching my Glen's hero as he emerged for the field, and I didn't wash that hand for days! As a follow-up to my trial for Scotland, I was denied a cap, rightly, by the brilliance of the Possible's goalkeeper, a teenager called George Niven, who became Glasgow Rangers' goalkeeper for many years. As I have mentioned in another place, however, my four sons all played with distinction at various levels, and when Ian, who was a school teacher, and also played senior for Aberdeen and Kilmarnock, did win a cap, he brought me his number seven jersey and cap, and handed them over with the words: "There, Dad. That's the cap you should have had!' I have seldom in life been more moved. I did keep them for a time, but of course eventually handed them back to their rightful owner. But as an elderly man looking back, it was a gesture that meant much.

We also of course, played games in the streets in those days of few cars – hunting, kick the can, hide and seek, rounders – and on one occasion in the latter I hit the shot of a lifetime. Unfortunately I was the only one who appreciated my lusty blow, for the ball sailed straight through Mrs Stevenson's kitchen window, and one irate lady from that very window, in stentorian tones demanded who had done this – though I thought it pretty obvious, for I was standing, petrified, rooted to the spot, still holding the bat, and not one of my pals was to be seen! That cost my parents five shillings and I lost my pocket money for some time.

While on the theme of discipline, let me nail my colours to the mast and say I believe a "skelp" seldom did anybody any harm. We all had one as boys in our home and also the threat for some heinous crime of "the wee black nippy belt" which was kept hidden and very occasionally used, but the threat was a deterrent as, I believe, emphatically, it was in schools. In my opinion, and that of many teachers to whom I have spoken, it was a bad day for all... teachers, parents and children, when the belt was outlawed by do-gooders who talked in extravagant language of beatings, thrashings and the like. Though we had the odd punishment in our home, the obvious love of our parents countered the discipline, and I believe, sincerely, that both are essential – that discipline is part of loving and training a child – that discipline and love are two sides of the same coin.

Perhaps a mile behind our housing scheme was a farm, where I would work from a very early age amongst the animals, and on my holidays. It was there I gained my love of animals which was to make me a vet, and as I mention elsewhere, I was the proudest lad in Scotland when I was given my first horse to work on my very own – a black mare called Pearl. Ah me... the simple pleasures of youth in a bygone age! The farmer was Mr Hewitson, known affectionately as "Old Puggy", who possessed lungs of astonishing power, and oft, of an evening, we would hear his dulcet tones a mile away as he commanded his collie dogs to "come in ahin"; "lie doon" or "hup roon".

New Cumnock then, was entirely a mining community, with seven or eight pits, low wages, conditions mostly primitive and the work dangerous. The pits, when I was a boy, were all privately owned. There were frequent accidents, regular fatalities, and I recall my grandfather and uncle being terribly injured, severely burned and scarred for life when there was an explosion. They had ventured into an area where there was gas, an area that was supposed to be shut off by a curtain of sacking, which indicated "No Entry", but on this occasion there was no sacking to warn them, and there was an explosion and fire. Next day, before the mines' inspector came, a brand new curtain was erected, the manager maintaining that the Fergusons, father and son, had gone through the door. The inspector commented at the inquest that there seemed to be a lot of strands of new hessian lying about, the curtain was very new, but nothing could be proved, and no compensation was paid, the word of the manager being accepted.

My grandfather was a quiet, upright man, an elder of the church, a foreman, a man who never told a lie in his life, a miner who was respected by all, and moreover – an unusual thing, almost a complete rarity – he had built his own house for his family. Both he and uncle John were a long time in hospital the latter being scarred, like many of the airmen we were to see in a few years in Hitler's war. We always, as children, liked when uncle John visited us, for when he came we, as boys, had to dip into his pockets, and extract the chocolate or sweets he had brought us.

The Union fought to get the two men compensation, but the manager, though undoubtedly perjuring himself, maintained the fault was entirely that of Will Ferguson (my mother's father) and his son, John. The inspector expressed his doubts, but could prove nothing, and as nearly always, the word of the manager prevailed over mere miners, as I have already noted.

My grandfather, peace loving man as he was, though clearly hurt his word had been doubted, accepted the verdict in his usual quiet way, but his son, much more of a firebrand, was embittered and became a rabid socialist with a picture of Aneurin Bevan on the wall to inspire him. Grandpa, as always, found his solace in the word of God and his faith, and refused, though urged on by his whole family and fellow miners, to make a further case of it and carry on the fight for personal justification and compensation. Though but a lad at the time, I recall the hurt and anger of the whole family and understood why the miners, almost 100 percent, felt their only hope of improved conditions and decent wages was the Unions... and though I am a non political animal, I can see and fully understand why New Cumnock voted (as it still does) solidly Labour, for this kind of thing was happening in virtually every pit in Scotland.

Wherever I went that September day, I was reminded in one way or another of the Knockshinnoch disaster and our New Cumnock years. As I cleaned a cow at Meadowhead (removing afterbirth), the farmer, John Smillie, spoke of the disaster as he held the cow's tail, which otherwise the beast would have continually swished onto my face.

"It's a bad business" he said, "they've a gey hard life, thae miners. Mind you, they're a tough lot an' I hivna muckle time for them. You canna trust them, aye on strike, never satisfied. I've a cousin up there at Blackbyres, an' you ken, away back in the General Strike, he had a' his hens pinched by that crowd."

"Not quite all" I chimed in, "they left two and an explanation." John Smillie glared at me and then demanded "Whit kin' o' explanation?"

"Well, they were starving, with no dole money, most of their families were large and they had nothing to feed them. They left two and the note said: 'Not greed, but need; we've left you a cock an' hen to breed!'" I had still been in my pram in 1926, but my mother had often related the story to us. I thought my farmer was going to have a fit. He went very red in the face, glared at me suspiciously and exploded "Dashed cheek! It was still stealing. You canna trust that lot!"

I hastily changed the subject before my farmer really did explode or report me to my boss as a Commy, which I was very far from being.

The next call was at a shepherd's cottage to inoculate his two calves against abortion. He had quite a sizeable garden, all vegetables, and I admired his work.

"These are whopping leeks" I said to him, "and what big onions!"

"Aye, well, they should be, considerin' the dung I put in the grun afore I planted them."

"My father goes in for big onions" I informed him. "He's always feeding them with hen-pen and he and a friend are regularly out with the measuring tape to see whose onions are biggest."

"Aye – you canna beat the dung" he went on, "an' there's nothin' like a bowl o' broth wi' plenty o' leeks in it."

As I drove away on the next case, I recalled a story I had heard of a minister who one morning found a large load of dung had been deposited at the bottom of his large manse garden. Not having ordered any from one of his farmer members in his country parish, he was puzzled as to the donor of the dung – or ding as a genteel lady of our acquaintance called it!... anyway farmyard manure. Eventually he traced the farmer who had left it and thanked him profusely. The farmer patted the minister on the shoulder and said: "Think nothin' o' it, meenister. Yon sermon you preached last Sunday was worth twa load o' dung", leaving the minister wondering which of the two interpretations that can be taken, had been intended by his farmer! (It is maybe a comment on my preaching that no farmer, later on in my life when I had turned my collar round, so rewarded me!)

I also recalled as I drove on how, apropos the leeks, I had delivered thousands as a boy, of young leeks ready for planting, carried on a basket in front of my bike. My father had some sort of arrangement with a nursery to supply the miners with their leeks; they ordered through Dad, the leeks arrived by train in the Spring, and I covered the parish delivering them. Nearly every miner seemed, like my shepherd, to love Scots Broth, the thicker the better – and for this leeks were essential, so every miner with a garden had a bed of leeks. Sometimes I got a tip for my trouble. Once, I recall getting a whole sixpence!

Thinking of bicycle delivery reminded me of another task I had for a time. Near our home was a nursery for flowers; these were made up into bundles, and put in my groaning basket. I didn't know then, one flower from another... but all the bundles were priced at a shilling, and for an evening's work I received... a shilling – which was handed to mother to help with the housekeeping. I periodically thought it was not much fun being the eldest son, with twin brothers six years younger, for I got all the odd jobs to do. Still, I survived, and never did get to like leeks! Ah, me, the days of yesteryear as memory held open the door of our New Cumnock years, as I went on my vet rounds that day.

Up on the Straiton hills where I was treating a cow with Foul in the Foot, or Clit-ill, as the Ayrshire farmers called it, I spied a little green tent beside a burn, and that sent the wheels of memory turning again as I recalled my one and only experience of camping. When we were about eleven, my pal Willie Nisbet and I decided it would be fun to camp, just in our back green, one lovely summer night. We possessed no tent, so slung an old blanket over the clothes rope, holding our "tent" out and down with large stones. We stocked up with plenty of food for a midnight feast – mainly of cakes. We slept on another old blanket each – or rather we intended to sleep the night. It was a great adventure at first, as we laughed, told stories and even sang. By and bye the street lights went out, then one by one the house lights. We tried to convince one another we were having a great adventure, but when an owl hooted, a cat stuck its head in our door, its shining eyes terrifying us in the dark... mysterious shadows fell on our "tent"... noises of night creatures seemed to have a sinister ring about them, we began to have doubts. To keep up our spirits, we consumed our "midnight feast", then decided it would be cosier to sleep together.

"You're shakin', Alec" accused Willie.

"I am nut" I retorted.

A few moments later another tom cat gave a yowl at our door, and we nearly leapt from our skins. As the wind got up and whistled round us, Willie said: "I'm no' feelin' verra weel, Alec. I think I'll away hame an' we can camp anither nicht." I seconded the motion, and two small figures made for the doors of their respective homes, which wise parents had left unlocked. We pretended we'd had a great adventure... but we never repeated it. As I thought of Willie, it dawned on me his father might be involved... might even be one of the trapped miners, and my thoughts went back to these men stuck in a darkness far worse than that of two wee boys in a tent, and apparently, in complete contrast to us, hemmed in with little hope of escape. Theirs' was no midnight adventure, but a disaster of frightening proportions.

I had the evening off and the whole family bundled into the car and headed at speed for New Cumnock. We went first to uncle John Dornan, our favourite uncle, himself a miner who had suffered many injuries over the years, to get news of who was involved in the disaster, and find out how it had happened. To our relief, none of our relatives were involved, but many of the people he mentioned were known to us, especially to my parents. Uncle John is a gentle man, not at all an unfair man, and anything but a firebrand, but he had no hesitation in laying the cause – the blame – on planners and management, rightly so. It appeared the route the men were instructed to dig was getting too near the surface. For several days, odd bits of earth, stones and water had been coming in, had been reported, but the men were instructed to dig on along the same route, getting ever nearer to the surface. And on that dreadful day, with a fearsome rumble and roar, a whole field had come in on top of them... yes a *whole* field. Earth, boulders and worst of all a mixture of peat and water, called sludge had come tumbling down on top of them all like a tidal wave, sweeping everything before it, and before which men fled for their very lives. They were chased all along the main tunnel by that fearful sludge which rapidly filled all the tunnels in that part of the pit. Eventually the men reached an area beyond the bottom of the shaft, and their way to the surface, which was higher than the tunnels they had been working and there they found temporary safety. The shaft to the surface was sixteen feet deep in that horrible sludge, so there was no way out by that route. A head count by the oversman, whose work in the days and nights to follow was beyond praise, revealed a number of men were missing. Andrew Houston, an older man, sought to calm and encourage his men, some of whom were injured, and whilst it was hoped the missing men had found refuge in some side tunnel not invaded by the fearful flood, it was but a slender hope, and their colleagues who had reached temporary safety, as Burns put it... "guessed... and feared".

Having been put in the picture of the background to the disaster, we headed for the scene of it... and gasped, for what we saw was almost beyond belief. Where there had been a field, there was a huge, deep crater two acres wide – so clearly there was no way out for the stricken men that way. Nor did there seem at first *any* hope of rescue by *any* route. It was dreadful as we stood on the edge of that huge hole to realise that beneath us were 129 men... wet, cold, hungry, some injured, and a clutch of fear in every heart, and with every reason to be afraid, for these men knew the score, knew the seeming impossibility of getting out alive. Even if rescuers did, by some mysterious route, get to the entombed men... they might be too late, for swirling around the men was the thing all miners feared – gas – methane that could poison a man's lungs, or cause an explosion. True, it was not yet heavy, of dangerous proportion, but it could only thicken with the passing days and nights... and they had no gas masks.

How was all this known to the folks up top? By the one light in the gloom... the phone to the top was still working, so they could communicate continuously with those seeking desperately a way to reach the stricken men. By means of this lifeline, it was learned that while 129 men had been entombed, a head count had revealed thirteen were unaccounted for. Maybe, just maybe, they had found a place of safety in some side tunnel, but even if they had, with sludge reaching the roof of the main tunnel, how could they be reached? But what a boon was link of the phone... something in life, no matter how seemingly hopeless our plight... the phone of prayer, the link to the One above, that is always open, and many of these trapped men who had scorned prayer before, now, in their darkest hour gave it a try. What a blessing when there is faith in a man's heart for prayer for that man is just a chat with God and handing everything over to him. There were not many of these men, I am sure, with death so near, who did not murmur a prayer.

Looking back down the winding paths of my own life, I can recall numbers of occasions when I could not see the way ahead – I am sure everyone has. Life has all kinds of sludge – illness, especially persistent illness... sorrow... unemployment... marriage difficulties (though I have never known that)... worries about family – and many more things that would pull us down. Like these miners without food, water, medical help, having to wear sodden, filthy clothes day after day, no clean air to breathe, we can feel completely shut in with no way out. Life has its grim times. Then is the time when faith and prayer can make all the difference, and like the sheep in the great Psalm, we can know the quiet mind and sense of security of walking close to their Shepherd.

"Yea, though I walk through the valley of the shadow of death, I will fear no evil FOR THOU ART WITH ME; Thy rod and staff they comfort me"

That was the Psalm my father read to us that night, which he always selected in a crisis, and before we took to the comfort of our blankets, simply, but confidently, he committed to the great Shepherd these men spending the night in a very dark valley. For them, and all who cared for them, it had been a long, long day.

TWO

The Rescuer

A new day dawned, and as the morning mist dispersed, the sun shone on hundreds of miners at the pit head itching to do something – but what, and where? There were also dozens of reporters and photographers from every newspaper in Britain, plus radio reporters. The morning light also revealed a number of wives and mothers who had been there all night. That wonderful practical Christian organisation, the Salvation Army, had also come and dispensed cheerfulness and hope, as well as tea and rolls, and the local ministers brought what comfort they could.

But in the meantime a vital discovery had been made. My mother used to say "there's aye a wye (way)" and a possible way out had been found by the engineers and planners studying the layouts of the various mines. They discovered that an old disused pit, Bank No 6, though two miles from Knockshinnoch, at one point had a tunnel which ran fairly close by. Rescue teams and inspectors had been down and reported that although the roof had fallen in here and there and the tunnel was strewn with rocks, it was a possible way out. It would mean considerable tunnelling to reach the trapped men, but it was the only hope. All the action now moved to the old pit, and again and again appeals went out on the radio for every rescue team in Scotland and the north of England to head for New Cumnock.

But the men who had gone down also reported there was one major snag in bringing the men to safety by the old pit – gas – much, heavy gas, and no one dare venture down without a mask... and as had already been said, these men had no masks. However, ventilation fans were transported down the old pit and men started digging up near the roof, instructing by that lifeline of the phone the trapped men who were fit to start tunnelling from their side. Now there was hope, albeit a very slender hope, and many difficulties to be overcome – the chief problem being now, if the tunnelling was successful, these men were to be brought out through a long, low, narrow tunnel filled with poisonous fumes.

Teams worked non stop beyond the point of exhaustion, their work hampered by the heavy, clumsy masks they had to wear. Regularly the doctor had to withdraw men from the struggle, but slowly the work progressed, the trapped men encouraged at last by the echoes of the digging coming towards them. Eventually, after many hours, the word was flashed to all the waiting throng... "they're through". But how to bring them out alive through the gas... that was the question.

All the proceedings were long and tortuous, and too technical for a non miner to explain in an article like this, but putting it briefly what happened was by the new tunnel they got one man, a stretcher case, out, along the rough, narrow tunnel – all the men wearing clumsy mine masks – but it took two hours and fifteen men! Clearly over 100 men could not come that way. Long before the end the creeping gas would have overcome them. Hopes plummeted! Something else would have to be done – but what?

So often in the long march of history, the hour has produced the man... and so it was here. He was called Dave Park and no better man could have been found in all Scotland. Firstly he was a local man, though now high in the echelons of power of the Coal Board at headquarters, and away from the village. But as a young man he had actually worked in Knockshinnoch. Secondly, he was an expert in rescue work. Thirdly, perhaps more than any other person, he knew about coping with gas. Finally, though this may seem irrelevant, he was a deeply committed Christian, but a very human, bright cheerful man – no long faced believer – and even those with no time for religion respected and trusted him and his presence gave the men a lift. The word was flashed around above ground and below... "Dave's here!"

Though he had been advised against going down, indeed one report says, forbidden to risk his life, down he went, crawling through the narrow escape tunnel. Nor did he arrive alone. He had slung round his neck a sack with chocolate contributed by the miners above for their trapped, hungry – indeed starving mates; little enough, but it helped. But more important, he was wearing something that had never been seen in any mine before – a Salvus breathing mask. It was used by the Navy, was smaller and lighter than the conventional mask, had half an hour's supply of oxygen in it… but the Salvus had never before been tried in a mine. Would it do the job?

But perhaps more important than what he brought was the fact Dave himself had come and the hopes of the trapped men and all those anxiously waiting revived. Dave – if not the top boss in Scotland, was well up the ladder and had come himself as a rescuer. No doubt he had to overcome many doubts and fears, especially from the younger men, little more than boys. The oversman, Andrew Houston, had done a wonderful job in keeping hope alive in his men, but they had all been under great strain – a number were injured, and they had all lived under the shadow of death for a considerable time, so it was natural that some nerves had been stretched to breaking point. I cannot be certain of all that was said and done, but at the time I was told some snapped at Dave… "It's a' very weel for you. You've got yin o' thae masks but whit aboot us, eh? You can get oot when you like, but no' us." "Aye," said another, "whit guid is yin mask for a' us?" Many asked… "Can we be sure it will work?"

But gradually, Dave calmed them, answered their doubts, assured them more masks would be here shortly, enough for all; and most convincing of all, he promised he would be staying till all got out. If they didn't, he wouldn't. Not for nothing was he a leader who could handle men, and gradually the tension eased, the morale rose. He cracked a joke or two, had them singing, ending, my informant told me, with the 23rd Psalm, which even the least godly knew. Despair had been turned to hope, fear to assurance all would yet be well.

The whole massive rescue operation involved many men… it was a great team effort, but without doubt the coming of this one man was the turning point.

Much more could be said, many stories could be told, though most of those who went through this grim experience are now gone. Suffice to say the Salvus masks arrived, and hour by hour men, perhaps six at a time, crawled through that claustrophobic tunnel, and then were helped by waiting volunteers to climb up the long steep hill with a gradient of perhaps 1 in 3; each, as he emerged at the top greeted with a cheer by the waiting onlookers, and with immense relief by relatives. Many a "thank God" was uttered in sincerity before the men were whisked off by a team of waiting ambulances to Ballochmyle Hospital. Dave Park, as he had promised was the last man out, Andrew just in front of him.

Alas there were broken hearts too, for thirteen men did not emerge, and thirteen wives or mothers, comforted by friends, went home to grieve for their men who would not come home.

Such is the price of coal.

The long task of clearing away the sludge was begun and after three months the bodies of eleven men were found, men who had been engulfed by the initial rush of that noisome muck. But they most probably had a quick death, something that was not true of the remaining two miners. It took ten months to find them, in a side tunnel where the sludge had not penetrated. But there was no way of escaping from it, or of contacting their comrades, nor any hope of them being reached, even if their whereabouts had been know, for, as I have indicated, the sludge was sixteen feet deep in places, too deep to wade through, too thick in which to swim. Theirs was indeed a terrible fate. It was thought they had probably survived for eight or ten days, and the manner of these men's deaths haunted me for a long time.

Such indeed is the terrible price of coal!

Twenty-five years later, in the town part of New Cumnock, a memorial in the form of a gas detector safety lamp was erected to remind future generations of the cost of coal – in human suffering and sorrow all down the years in the long history of mining.

Dave Park was awarded the George Medal for bravery, as was Andrew Houston... but many, many others needed courage every day they went down a pit... and many carried, and carry still in their bodies lungs ruined by silicosis, and many other marks and scars of their years below. But they also carry in their minds memories of a real comradeship with the others who shared daily dangers. Now, as with most other places, New Cumnock has no mines, but as I recall the past and think of my roots, I am glad – nay proud – to be a New Cumnockian.

Why have I, a vet and a minister, told this story in my *Dog Collar Diary*? There is nothing about animals or churches in it, you say. Well I have begun this diary with it for three reasons. Firstly, it was part of my early life, and I felt it had to go into this mixture of a diary and biography. Secondly, I wanted to show the other side of miners and the dangerous life they lived, men who seldom have had much praise, and often, by people who don't know better, have been criticised, slated, condemned.

But thirdly, as a minister I see clearly – very clearly – a parable here. Much of Jesus' teaching was in parables and there could hardly be a clearer parable than this. All of us, at times in life, have known the sludge sucking us down, or feel hemmed in by our situation, like these miners. Life can be hard, grim, cruel. But, even if we don't believe in him, God knows us every one and our problems and hurts, and just as Dave Park, a man from the top came as a rescuer, there really is nothing but our own sin and self-will that can cut us off from our Creator; although over the centuries He has had His workers, His teachers, prophets, saints, martyrs, and at one specific moment in time He came in human form to share our lives with their woes and problems.

I can imagine God saying in the courts of Heaven to His own beloved Son: "Now is the time. Go down and be with them. Tell them of me, show them how to live, how I love them... and save them."

That was why He came and so that none could fail to understand, He was given at His birth the name Jesus, meaning Rescuer... Saviour... and following Him, however hard the road... and He never said it would be easy... leads the light... the joy and security of His company all the way... a journey that leads HOME. A hymn puts it well:

O loving wisdom of our God, when all was sin and shame.
A second Adam to the fight, AND TO THE RESCUE CAME.

THREE

The Scotch Vetnary

Clickety click – clickety click – clickety click – click. Hour after hour the beat went on, a noise once familiar to most travellers... but a soothing sort of sound and gradually my head nodded and I drifted into the dreamy state that precedes sleep as the train thundered on, ten coaches pulled by a majestic steam monster. I was used to trains, my father being a railwayman, our holidays all taken by train, and my years of study to become a vet necessitating an 80-mile round trip every day. My folks could not afford the price of "digs" at Glasgow and the only grant I had was £70 for which I had to sit the far from easy Bursary Competition... and £50 of it disappeared my first week at the old Glasgow Vet College, being the fees for the year. True, in my later years, Local Authority Grants were being awarded, and this eased things.

But this train was taking me into the unknown... a foreign land I had only seen once before – England! In my dreamy state I thought back to the last two years when I had been learning my trade as assistant vet to Ian Buchan at Mochrum in my native Ayrshire. I had seen and treated most diseases, made my mistakes of course, but learned a lot. One big drawback was I had done practically no surgery, Ian doing it all, understandably for he, a young progressive vet, was trying to revive an old established Practice which had dwindled to almost nothing.

However, gradually I had been accepted by the very hard headed Ayrshire farmers, mostly dairy farmers with Ayrshire cows. I could look ahead to perhaps spending my life there if I wished, Ian having dropped the odd hint about a partnership in due course. But this was not absolutely certain; Janet and I were to be married in a few months after "goin' thegither" for eight years, most of our courting being walks or cycle runs into the country, money being in short supply. But now, with marriage just months away, I was looking for something better for our future – a partnership now with someone else, partly to improve our finances, but also at the risk of sounding a "holy Joe", a partnership, if possible with a fellow Christian. I felt if I was tying up my life for all the future, it should be with someone who had roughly the same ideals as me, same outlook on life, same beliefs, and good vet though Ian was and who had taught me much (apart from surgery), we were very far from being kindred spirits, and I was certain there would be frequent differences of opinion in many things even if I had become a partner.

As the train rushed onwards towards my destination of Devon... glorious Devon, the memories drifted past like smoke from the engine, of animals I had treated, and case followed case in my mind, I recalled in my first few weeks being called to see a cow at McFarlane of Blackbyre, a cow with a hard quarter in her udder. Easy, I thought as I examined the udder and straightened up and pronounced "Mastitis, Mr McFarlane", my diagnosis delivered with all the confidence of the young and inexperienced. "I'll give her an injection of penicillin and leave you tubes of penicillin to put in that quarter for a week, but I'll look back to see her in a day or two." Mr McFarlane did *not* look please, drew himself up to his full five feet six inches, looked me in the eye and pronounced emphatically: "Mr Cameron! I ken you're a veet an' I'm just a fermer, but I'm tellin' you that's no' Mastitis!" his words emphasised with a glare and a poke in the chest.

"What do you think it is then, Mr McFarlane?" I queried.

"It's a Weed!" he informed me fortissimo.

"We're both right, Mr McFarlane." I countered. "A Weed is the Ayrshire name for Mastitis, but they're the same thing."

"Naw, naw" he put me right again. "There's a Weed an' a Mastitis Weed an' they're different." He took a bit of convincing, but his cow recovered and my stock rose.

It dawned on me then, as I relaxed in the speeding train that if I went to Devon, farmers there also would have a local name for the different diseases, different from the Scots variant and also from the proper name, and I would have not only to learn the Devon dialect, but the Devon disease names. I could foresee I was in for an interesting time... maybe!

But that was still in the future. I was not yet a partner, but hopeful. Out of the blue had come a letter from a Major Davison at a place called Bristacombe inviting me to spend a weekend, expenses paid, with him, see something of his practice, and if we felt mutually suited, he would be happy to offer me a partnership. It seemed too good to be true, and I really felt very fortunate for almost all my contemporaries were still assistants, and here was I, still wet behind the ears, being offered a half share in a young but fast growing practice in one of the beauty spots of England. Ian had not been too keen to give me a weekend off, for it was the height of the lambing and spring calving season... but... well, here I was on my way. If successful in my quest, there were one or two clients I would be glad to leave behind – notably old Mr McNulty, an obnoxious character who spat and swore time about and every time I appeared on his farm, he would snort and say "Huh! The boy again!" But there were many more whom I would miss, like Andrew McWilliam who had a herd of prize winning Aberdeen Angus cattle, who always welcomed me warmly, and latterly asked, when phoning for a vet "Please send Alec".

That kind of thing felt good and boosted one's confidence. So there would be regrets too in leaving, the biggest part being that Janet and I would be 500 miles away from our parents and most of our relatives.

The day drifted on until I was aware of a voice calling "Bristacombe! Bristacombe!" and I woke with a start from my snooze and reached for my overnight bag in case I didn't get out of the train in time, but I need not have worried for the train stopped there. This was the end of the line.

I stepped on to the platform and looked out over a marvellous blue stretch of water – the Bristol Channel – when I felt my hand grasped by a very large man, enquiring: "Mr Cameron? May I call you Alec? I'm Ken Davison and this is Tom Atkins," introducing me to a small young man with him. "Tom's a vet too but is shortly going to Africa as a vet-Missionary. But you must be tired and hungry. Jump in the car. Susan will have a meal waiting."

I felt a bit overwhelmed and suddenly shy with this large man who dwarfed my six feet. Chade Lodge, their abode, was just below the station and I perked up on meeting Susan for she was a Scot, and I also met the brood of three young lads... Peter, Mark and Timothy.

Ken and Tom showed me up to my bedroom, and after enquiries about the journey, to my great surprise, Kenneth said: "You may think this surprising, but, you know, as soon as I saw you on the station platform, I felt sure you were the right man, the man I've been praying for as a partner, for I've been doing the work of two vets for quite a time." We sat down to the sumptuous meal Susan had prepared, and as Kenneth said grace, he asked that both he and I would be guided to the right decision. I was soon to learn that prayer was the life breath of this man and he, in fact, already had a partner in the practice – God – with whom in a very natural way he shared everything, and I felt my shyness depart, and a warmth steal into my heart.

It was a hectic weekend. I had arrived about 7 o'clock and the Major apologised he had to go out again. "I've two calls to make, which won't take long, but I've also two caesars on sheep. Perhaps if you're not too tired with a long journey, you would like to come and see some of our Devon farms?" I was startled.

"Caesars! Do you do caesars on sheep, and why?"

"Oh yes! Not many vets in the West Country are doing them yet, but we get a lot – increasing every year – and mostly done for Ringwomb."

"Oh... er... ah" I stammered. I had never heard of Ringwomb and no caesar had been carried out by us at Mochrum in these early years of the fifties. I felt very inadequate and saw my partnership receding! But I was here now and could only see how things developed.

We did the two farm calls first – a mastitis which I learned a few farmers in Devon called a felon, and a sow with erysipelas. I knew plenty about these two. Then on to the caesars. The first was in a village called Upper Down – queer names these English had, I thought. But then our English friends might have trouble with Aultguish or Tighnabruach.

We arrived at the farm and walked in. I was introduced as a Scots vet the Major hoped would be coming to Bristacombe, the farmer being a Mr Chugg, another name I'd never heard before, but was soon to learn was a common Devon name. We were ushered into the kitchen, and Mr Chugg disappeared, saying before he went: "I'll fetch the sheep; she's been paining' for a fair bit. I only hopes us'll still be in time to save her lambs."

I looked at the Major in amazement.

"Do you operate in the kitchen?"

"We operate in all sorts of places – a barn, a hayshed, the open air or sometimes in luxury, like here."

I was astonished for in Ayrshire I had seldom, in the well-to-do farms there, been allowed in the kitchen – and here was a sheep coming in! Quickly Mr Chugg and his man came, propelling a ewe before them. Again I realised my ignorance, for I didn't know what breed of sheep it was. I recalled in my oral exams at college having to identify various varieties of sheep, of which there were forty different native breeds. I didn't like to show my ignorance here but fortunately at that moment Kenneth said: "This Ringwomb's a bit of a mystery... not least why it's commonest in the Devon Closewool; that's the native breed here."

"Ah yes – Devon Closewool" I murmured knowingly. "We had none of these in Ayrshire."

The memory of our exams, oddly, at that moment brought back the story of one lad in his Materia Medica, pharmacy oral who was asked by the external examiner for what he would use Gossipium. (We had to know all the Latin names for drugs.) The boy had not a clue what Gossipium was, but since there was a wide variety of medicines used in the animal kingdom as laxatives and purges, he dived in hopefully and said, "I'd use it as a purge, sir."

The examiner looked over his spectacles at him and said dryly, "I don't know how you can, unless as a pull-through!"

Gossipium is cotton wool!

The ewe was hoisted on to the kitchen table, a large plain wood, hand made solid bit of furniture, and held down by the assembled males, while Kenneth injected Chloral Hydrate intravenously as an anaesthetic.

"Would you mind assisting, Alec?" asked Kenneth. Clearly I was on trial but since all I had to do was swab, clamp bleeding blood vessels and hand the various instruments to the surgeon, it was not an onerous task. I marvelled at the dexterity of this large man with large hands, the latter contrary to the general opinion that a surgeon must have long, slim and narrow hands. In no time at all he had delivered twins, both alive, but both, like mother, still under the effects of the general anaesthetic.

"They should be alright," he said to the farmer, "but wait until they've come round before you take them back to their shed. It won't take long." Mercifully, he had not asked me to do the stitching, for his speed amazed me and I would have been badly shown up.

"The only problem is that if the ewe or lambs are weakly, they don't come out of the anaesthetic," said Ken thoughtfully. Boldly I chipped in, though totally ignorant of caesars: "Have you ever thought of doing it under local?"

He looked at me in some surprise. "You know, I had never thought of that." One up for me; I felt my stock had risen a little. Fortunately he did not ask me exactly how this could be done (to jump ahead, a year later the practice was doing them all under local, getting on for a hundred a year). We had a quick cup of tea – something I was to find was always provided for the "vetnary" in Devon, and as we, as quickly as possible headed for the door and one more caesar, Mrs Chugg was already scrubbing down the table, form which they would eat their breakfast.

"You'll find the next farm a bit different, Alec" I was informed. "It's a fairly new client – Len Huxley – and I'm anxious to get established there for it's a big farm and Len, though he looks a bit rough and ready, is a good farmer and his word carries a lot of weight in the district." We drove up a long winding road which meandered through a large field, and I was introduced to Mr Huxley.

"This is Mr Cameron from Scotland – I'm hoping he'll come here and join me in Devon" said Kenneth to the farmer, a swarthy, stocky figure in braces and bonnet, which apparently was his normal garb.

"How do you do, Mr Huxley" I said as we shook hands. He stood looking at me solemnly, without a smile, for a long time before he spoke, and then said, "Dang me! Another Scotch vetnary! Us'll soon be taken over by Scotchmen in dear old Debn. Do you speak English or is it that other queer langwidge... garlic or whatever you call it?"

Then his face broke into a grin, he slapped me on the back and said, "Pleased to meet you, Mr Cameron. I like the look o' you an' if you'm half as good as the Major, you'll do. It's high time somebody came to help for he's runned hisself off his feet. And no more o' this Mr... I'm Len to everybody."

The operating theatre at Len's farm was the barn where several bales of straw had been pushed together to form a table and two Tilley oil lamps hung from a beam. Len and his two husky sons held the sheep – the caesar was carried out as before, though I wondered how Kenneth could see to stitch. Another set of twins – a "well done, Major... they be grand lambs" and we were on our way home. It was well after midnight and I could hardly keep awake, but

Kenneth seemed as fresh as at the beginning which was just as well, for he appeared to think... no matter what kind of road, one should never drive at less than 70 mph!

Susan had supper waiting for Kenneth, Tom and me, which was very welcome, then she asked to be excused to go to bed, as did Tom. Kenneth produced the balance sheets for the last three years. I had never seen a balance sheet in my life – I had been hopeless at Maths at school – but despite my ignorance I could see this was a steadily growing practice and at last I too staggered upstairs to bed, after we had talked over the details that mattered in the financial prospects of this growing practice. Just before I dropped off into dreamland, a hard fact hit me: the realisation that I possessed but £100 in all the world, so clearly I would need to talk nicely to some bank manager if I decided to go there. "I'll take you a tour of North Devon tomorrow," Kenneth had said just before I went to bed, "and show you where you would live if you come, which I very much hope, brother, you will."

The next day he showed me the large kennels; I met the kennel maid. Likewise I was shown the surgery, a large and very adequate room, with next door a similarly large waiting room where I was introduced to Mrs Drury, who acted as secretary, receptionist, assistant at ops and general factotum. "I couldn't wish for a better secretary," he said of his efficient and good looking helper. I was taken to the lovely little flat, the upper part of a little farm just on the edge of the town where Janet and I would begin our married life if I accepted the partnership, a beautiful, peaceful place to come home to at the end of the day. Then he took me on a tour on a high plateau from which we could see a panorama of glorious country stretching away out to Exmoor, with far below us, in places a blue, blue sea. As we travelled he named farms and farmers where he was the vet, and gave me a potted description of the practice.

"We're 70 percent farm, 30 percent small animal, plus the biggest private zoo in England. Most of the farms are quite small, family farms which have been in the same families for generations, but there are numbers of very large farms, many of them bought by farmers from other parts of the country, and there are dozens of small-holdings... crofts you would call them in Scotland, most of which depend on the summer visitors and do B&B to make a living, for believe me, in summer we are swamped by holidaymakers.

The more I saw and heard, the more desirable did it seem, and I felt the luckiest young vet in the land to be offered a partnership in this magic country.

Next day I headed north again, saying I would like a day or two to think it over, and discuss it with Janet, but made it clear that the answer was likely to be an enthusiastic yes. I felt duty bound to tell this experienced surgeon that I was a very inexperienced one, but Ken only smiled and said that would be changed in no time, for it was his intention to treat me in every way as an equal partner in our work and share of the profits. I thanked Susan for all her hospitality, wished Tom every blessing on his work in Africa, and said how impressed I was that he was embarking on a work which paid next to nothing. He smiled and said, "Somebody had to go, and when you receive a Call, what can you do, if ever you are to have peace of mind, but say 'yes, Lord'", words that were to come back to me years later. Ken wound it all up with a short prayer… an unusual vet indeed! Then I was off.

There was never any real doubt about what my decision would be, and when I had described the countryside, the practice and not least our snug little flat, Janet could not wait to get to Devon. Ian, my boss at Mochrum, seemed genuinely sorry I was going, and for the first time came out definitely and said I would have had a partnership there. I let Ken know my decision and he wanted me right away, but I felt I really must help Ian through the lambing and calving season… so finally it was decided I would go to Devon in May, two months hence, which I did, living with Kenneth and Susan until August, when the big date of our wedding was to be. My brother Fergus came down to share the long drive north in Kenneth's brand new Triumph car, which this generous man was giving Janet and me for our Highland honeymoon. We enjoyed the journey, Fergus and I, on a road without a single motorway, and infinitely more pleasant and more safe than today.

Janet and I began our married life in a very sparsely furnished home. Indeed it would have been almost completely empty but for the marvellous generosity of family and friends. We did, however, sadly lack chairs, having only one for the sitting room, the other being a tea chest. But what fun and enjoyment we had together adding bit by bit to our home as we could afford it. It was fun and gave us a feeling of achievement. You know, I feel sorry for couples who start their life together with everything the heart could desire, even if they have to get it on the never-never!

After we had inspected every corner of our home, naturally I took Janet to see our surgery premises, and as she was about to go in for the first time she paused and saw outside the shiny new plate on the wall… "Alexander Cameron MRCVS". She squeezed my arm and kissed me and I can remember yet, a lifetime later, the lovely warm glow I felt. I had arrived! The "boy" of McNulty and Co at Mochrum had come of age.

FOUR

The Essential Ingredient

It had been a long, hard day for me, and I was glad to be locking our surgery door that cold autumn evening when I felt someone tugging at my jacket. I looked round and saw three little girls who might have stepped straight out of one of Charles Dickens' pictures of London life in the last century, and the ragged urchins who roamed the streets in the poorer parts of the city. They would be about 9-years old, their faces were liberally coated with dirt, and their clothes were the weirdest mixture imaginable – obviously "hand-me-doons" from older sisters, or even brothers, some far too large, others much too small. I could not help comparing them to my last client, a well dressed, far from poor owner of one of Bristacombe's largest hotels, whose little Yorkshire Terrier had a minor complaint. But this was one of the fascinations of our practice, as Kenneth had said it would be, the varieties of animals – 70 percent farm, 30 percent small animal and the infinite variety at the zoo – but also the varieties of clients, from the very rich to the very poor. Some of the latter could not afford the three and sixpence or five shilling charge in these days of the early fifties. Some got vouchers from the RSPCA… some we just "forgot" to charge. Bristacombe was a holiday resort, and most of its inhabitants depended, in one way or another, on the "season".

My three little urchins were struggling to carry a large cardboard box, and the leader of the deputation, who was still holding my jacket as if to keep me from escaping addressed me.

"Mr Vet, us 'as got a cat here that us fund lying at the side of the road in Oxford Grove. Us thinks it was runned over an' it's hurt bad, maybe dead an' us broght it to you to make it better." Quite a speech from her! Quite a task for me, for though in my third year as partner to Major Kenneth Davison, and I had come up against most diseases and injuries in most types of animals – including a few hair raising moments at the zoo – and though I had, in three years carried out surgery on most domestic animals, having learned much from Kenneth and being, I suppose a passable surgeon, I had not yet raised the dead!

Oxford Grove was one of exceedingly steep streets in 'Combe, with houses on each side opening straight on to the road, and though I was not noted (like most vets) for slow driving, I always came down "The Grove" in first gear. Indeed only recently a large touring bus whose brakes had failed came down a neighbouring, similar street and its progress was only halted when it ran straight into a furniture shop, to the considerable shock of both shoppers and bus passengers. So I thought, before looking in the box, the cat would have been no match for a car speeding down a hill.

I looked at the three girls and their expectant little faces turned up to me, and while my initial, though unworthy instinct was to tell them to come back tomorrow, for I was tired and hungry, I said to the tempting voice "get thee behind me, Satan", and listening to my conscience said "Come on inside, then, and I'll have a look at it". After all, I was meant to try to heal animals, no matter the time of day or night, so, with a sigh ushered them into the consulting room, which was next to our surgery, and helped them lift the box onto the table. I lifted the lid… and gasped. The cat, a large tabby, was breathing, but I wondered how it could be, for apart from sheep savaged by dogs, I had never seen such injuries. I stepped back from the table, my every move watched intently by the trio, and wondered how I could most kindly put it to the girls that their act of compassion was in vain, and nothing could save a cat with such injuries – for they were extensive and absolutely horrific – but the team leader got in before me: "Please mister, say you can make it better! I'm Martha an' them be Jeannie an' Barbara Mary Jane… an' us all loves cats but our Dads says us can't have any for us be right on the street in the Grove, an' us 'ave no back garden."

I looked at the anxiety, and hope on the faces of these poor little urchins, so had another glance in the box, even though one quick look had shown me there was only one thing to do with an animal so mutilated… the only kind thing. Still in its box, I examined it, for though it was a ridiculous thought, I felt it might break in two if I lifted it out. What I could see were two fractured legs; a front and back; the skin of its head was hanging in a flap revealing the bare bone of the skull; it had a damaged eye; there were many cuts all over it, on almost every part of its body, but most horrific of all was its abdomen which had been ripped open and the intestines were hanging out, covered in dirt, and several of them lacerated. I was used to injured animals... after all it was my chosen profession in life to try to treat, and if possible heal them, but I confess I shuddered as I looked at what had once been a big, and I was sure, bonny cat. I felt a bit sick.

I turned to the girls who had been watching my every move and expression on my face, intently, and waiting for my verdict.

"Look, girls," I said as sympathetically as I could, "the cat is very, very badly hurt, and I think the kindest thing would be to take it away from all its pain."

"Do ee mean put it to sleep?" queried Martha, evidently the spokeswoman for the party.

"I'm afraid so. Its best."

"Oh, please try to make it better," she pleased, pawing continually at me in her concern, while Barbara Mary Jane, the whole thing too much for her, burst into tears.

"Look, girls you have done a very kind thing in bringing in the cat... like the Good Samaritan in the Bible. Have you heard of the Good Samaritan?" They all shook their heads. "What I want you to do now is leave the cat with me, and I'll do what I think is best for it, and you try and find out whose cat it is. You be my detectives," and I patted the poor, pathetic little mites on the head. But Martha wasn't finished yet, and pleased again: "But, but, will you PLEASE try to make it better?" she persisted. I yielded and promised "I'll see what I can do," and they trudged sadly out of the door, looking back anxiously at the box and at me.

When they had gone, I took a deep breath, and putting my hands carefully and gently under the seemingly unconscious cat, lifted it on to the table, wondering what other horrors would be revealed. I turned it over delicately and found a few more cuts, but no other apparent fractures, though I have no doubt most of its ribs were broken. It was in the days before we had our own X-Ray, which came about the time Bernard came into the practice, Kenneth having taken up a post in his native Kenya... so I could not confirm about ribs or vertebrae of the spine. I looked at the motionless cat a long time, and as I studied it, three pathetic if somewhat muddy little faces and their pleading looks came back to me. But at last, I decided – the only merciful, kind thing to do would be to put the poor creature out of its misery and away from a world of pain, which pain, even if it survived all the surgery, would go on for weeks. So I filled a syringe with Euthatal, our absolutely painless and instantaneous drug for euthanasia, and as I held it above the cat, about to inject it, with my left hand I gently stroked its bare skull, and its back, and to my astonishment, I heard an unbelievable sound – the cat was purring – loudly. I nearly dropped the syringe in my unbelief. A cat with more damaged parts than whole – and it was purring! I laid the syringe down... I could not go through with it. I seemed as if the patient was talking to me... in my imagination telling me if I would patch it up, it would face up to weeks of suffering and weakness... or maybe it was telling me it still had a few of its nine lives left. Not being an expert in feline language, I couldn't say.

Now whilst I had carried out much surgery on many animals for a wide variety of conditions, I was not a natural surgeon, like my first partner Kenneth who taught me much, and my second partner Bernard: Bernard being quite brilliant and seeming to enjoy it. I did NOT enjoy surgery, carrying out operations, as distinct from treating animals in other ways. But over the years I suppose as I have noted I became a reasonably competent surgeon but had never had to operate on an animal which had literally every bit of its body damaged, for cats are no match for speeding cars. Someone may say "why all the fuss about a cat?" Did the good lord not say not even a sparrow falls to the ground without His Father knowing... and caring about it?

So I went into the waiting room, which in these early years of the practice was also our office, with telephones. The practice was steadily growing, first in Kenneth's time... increasingly with the passing years when Bernard was with me, and not so very long after I started ministering to human beings instead of animals, it grew fairly rapidly with Bernard the senior, five vets, several animal nurses and an animal hospital. But that was yet to come, and on the night I have described I was completely on my own. I sat quietly for a time, planning the various steps to be taken, and the order in which to try to put a broken animal together again, then briefly doing what I always did before surgery – asking God's help.

I remember long ago hearing of the famous Lord Moynihan, an

outstanding surgeon of years back, and also a devout Christian man. He was asked how he could concentrate on an operation with so many others there: anaesthetist, other junior surgeons, nurses, and perhaps students looking down from a balcony. He smiled and said to his questioner: "When I am in Theatre, there are only three people present, the patient and myself." "But that's only two," said his questioner, "who is the third?" The great surgeon said simply, but with utter conviction "God", and somehow I think that many on a theatre table who have no religious beliefs, would probably rather be cut open by a man who knew God was by his side than by an atheist.

I would need a great slice of help from God to save that poor cat! I phoned Janet at our home at Chade Lodge, told her briefly what had happened, and saying it might be anything from three to five hours before I got home, switched the calls coming in to her at home so that I would not be disturbed in the middle of things... and we were off, as with a sigh, I turned to my patient, which would have been no more but for a purr!

It was still lying as I had left it, being totally unable to move, but as soon as I touched it, back came that astonishing purr, as if it was saying, "I know I'm a bit knocked about but I'm sure you will put me right". I felt that the first danger before I started snipping and stitching was shock, so I began with my usual drug, Phenergan. I also gave it a sedative, for on top of its terrible injuries, handling so many damaged intestines would add to the shock. The cat seemed to approve my injections, for it kept purring until the sedatives quietened it. Then an injection to take it totally away from its world of pain and to allow me to get started – an anaesthetic. So the marathon began. I do not want to bore any possible reader with a detailed description of all that was done, so just an outline.

First, most important and most horrific was to clean the intestines, coated with mud; for there was no point in getting every other damaged part repaired perfectly if I could not clean these intestines and repair the damaged ones. So the bowels and whole peritoneal cavity were cleaned: washed with saline solution again and again, handling them as if they were glass, for to leave any dirt or badly damaged intestines would be sure to result in peritonitis and death, no matter how expertly I might repair the rest of the damage. When I had cleaned these horrific naked guts as best I could, I stitched them with a special minute needle for the job, using very fine catgut which would dissolve in time. Then I injected a hefty does of water-based penicillin into the peritoneum and stitched peritoneum, muscles and skin. I felt better when the intestines were out of sight and in the place they belonged. I gave a relieved sigh, had a listen to the cat's heart, and checked, as I had been doing all along, its breathing under the anaesthetic.

Then the eye: filled with Chloromycetin eye ointment and both lids stitched together, as they would remain for ten days. The flap of scalp skin was not quite so extensive as I had thought at first, but with tremendous difficulty it was tacked back. Then, seemingly endless suturing of the many wounds, and the easiest part of all – plastering its front and rear broken legs.

So it was done, and gently I carried the patient to our cattery, situated at the rear of our premises. We were greeted by a chorus of miaows, the other inhabitants clearly puzzled that there was no reply from their new resident who was, of course, still under anaesthetic, but beginning to stir. I laid it on a blanket and covered it with another, while the other cats, some recovering from surgery, others merely being boarded, looked on. Having made the cat as comfortable as I could and given him a sedative injection for the night, I gently patted I am sure the most-stitched animal in Britain, and as I shut his door, I was rewarded with his purr – somewhat weaker than before after all he had been through. No doubt it was my imagination, but somehow it sounded like "Thanks, pal!". So it was done. So was I. Absolutely whacked, my back aching from bending over the surgery table, my eyes tired with so many minute stitches. As I shut the door for the night, three grubby little faces came before my mind's eye... three little girls who like the Good Samaritan had brought in a broken body, when I have no doubt quite a few others had passed by, heedless. I was glad for their sakes I had done it, even though it had cost a small fortune in drugs... but somehow they and I had done what we could, and as I finally locked the outer door at some unearthly hour, I murmured a heartfelt "Thank you, Lord".

Next morning, as I walked in to begin another day's work, the first thing I heard was Martha's voice, questioning our secretary and nurse.

"Did ee put it to sleep?" a puzzled Mrs Drury was asked.

"Did who put what to sleep?". Having just arrived herself, she had not been down to the cats' quarters.

"The vet doctor, and the cat us brought in."

"Who's us?"

"Aw, Jeannie, Barbara Mary Jane and me. I'm Martha and us is good Samitans, but us don't know what that be."

"Should you not be at school?" Mrs Drury queried.

"Aw, school's rotten! Besides, us wanted to know 'bout cat. Does you help vet man with animals? I wish I could do that."

I had been standing in the passage, listening to this discussion and my presence unknown to Martha and Mrs Drury. I now slipped quietly down to the cattery, to be greeted with a chorus of miaows. I looked at my patient, lying on its side and I thought it was dead. I opened the door, stroked it, and at once came that loud purr, which was music to my ears. At least it had survived the night, but it was going to be a very sick cat for some time. I suppose the medical bulletin would be: "Stable, but critical". Just then Martha and Mrs Drury arrived, and at the sight of the cat Mrs Dru', completely imperturbable, gasped: "Mr Cameron… how can that cat possibly be alive." And Martha… well, it was worth all the labour of the night before to see a beatific smile light up her face, at present clean, and a little hand slipped into mine as she said, "You didn't put it to sleep! Oh boys, oh boys!"

"I've never seen so many stitches in an animal before," said Mrs Dru', "How many are there?"

"Didn't count – but we'll need to stock up on catgut and nylon," and proceeded to fill her in on the events of the previous night.

Martha continued to hold my hand and mutter again and again: "You didn't put it to sleep. Oh boy, that's magic!"

Eventually, she reluctantly departed for school, but was back again in the afternoon. Normally I was on a round of farm visits in the afternoons, but this being a Wednesday, operation day for routine ops, I had been in surgery all day. Martha was accompanied by her two side-kicks this time, and of course, they had to see *their* cat. Martha did most of the talking, Jeannie backed her up whatever she said with the comment "that be right, mister vet", whilst Barbara Mary Jane tended to just suck her thumb. Martha informed me "us don't know whose cat it be, so us don't know its name. Us must give it a name, but us don't know if it's a boy or a girl".

"It's a boy, Martha", I informed her.

"Well, if you'll let us, us'll be in every day to see it, but us won't know how to call the cat. Be you married, Mr Cameron" she enquired.

"Now why do you want to know that, Martha?" I queried.

"Well, I just was wondering... be this lady your wife?" indicating Mrs Dru'.

"Now, Martha, just you think... you've heard me calling her Mrs Drury and she calls me Mr Cameron, so she can't be my wife."

"I s'pose not," she paused thoughtfully, then went on. "Just two doors from us is a man called Huxtable and his wife is Mrs Jones – how's that 'en?"

I looked down on Martha with pity: at the age of nine a wee lass facing the problems and heartaches of our licentious age, which with the passing years of the century was to reach the stage when "bidey-ins", as they were called in my native Scotland, were to become almost as common as marriage. I patted Martha on the head and said, "Mrs Drury lives with her husband who is Mr Drury; and my wife, because my name is Mr Cameron is called Mrs Cameron. OK, understand?"

"I s'pose so," she said somewhat doubtfully. Then she went on, "Has you got any boys?"

"Yes, Martha, one."

"How be 'im called?"

"Neil."

"Just one boy – why just one? There be six in our house."

"Oh, maybe there will be more in our house in time" (as indeed there were – Ian, David and Alan).

She smiled, as if everything was settled and said: "Us'll call the cat Neil, then" – not a usual name for a cat, but it pleased wee Martha.

"That will be different from most cats."

Then an odd thought seemed to strike her and she said enthusiastically, "They will be company for each other".

Somehow I didn't think Janet would fancy a big tabby cat, particularly one that looked as if it was being held together with stitches and had two plastered legs, beside our Neil in his cot, but gravely said to the enthusiastic Martha: "That's a very nice idea, Martha, but Neil the cat will have to stay here in his hospital until we try to find out whose cat he really is." Then I felt I should warn her, so put my arm round her neck and said, "Martha, Neil the cat is still very, very sick and might still die."

Her little eyes filled with tears, then she asked "Does you think if us comed to see him every day, it might help?"

"Yes, Martha, come in after school each day, but don't all of you come every time, for you might get in the way of Mrs Drury looking after all the cats."

She never missed a day... the cat got to know her voice, and I am certain that her visits and her voice played a big part in Neil's healing, for he was, for a very long time, a cat hovering on the brink of death. Particularly difficult was how to feed him. There could be no question of giving him solid food – meat or fish – for some considerable time, until those horribly damaged bowels were healed. At first all he had beside him was a saucer of water which he occasional lapped a little. Then of course we tried milk, and also Protein Hydrolysate, a concentrated food in liquid form with a lovely meaty aroma. But he didn't even look at either. In a human being, there would of course be a drip, but we were not equipped for that. Fortunately he had been quite a plump, well-nourished cat to begin with , so I knew he could survive for a time without food. Daily there were injections of penicillin, pain killers and other drugs as required.

On the tenth day, I took out the stitches binding his eyelids together, and Martha held him as I did it (while Mrs Drury hovered nearby), and the wee lass's face, though seldom clean, lit up with ineffable joy – she was helping Mr Vet! The eye was surprisingly good – no permanent damage, no ulcers – just the expected conjunctivitis, but I knew Chloromycetin would soon clear that up. Round One successfully over, and all the multitude of cuts and deep lacerations, dressed daily, also apparently healing. But soon he must at least drink, or he could still die of dehydration. But drink he simply would not do. It was "the Good Samaritan" who solved that for us too.

She arrived one evening after consulting hour carrying a large mug.

"Mr Cameron", she said proudly (it was only since she had helped me with the cat's eye she had taken to calling me by my name instead of Mr Vet, evidently feeling she was a bona fide member of the staff now): "Mr Cameron, I've brought this for Neil to see if us can get him to eat. I made it meself, but us 'as often watched Maw make it. It's called beef tea."

I peered into the bowl, which she had kept well wrapped up in a towel. It looked good, and smelled good, and she had kept it warm.

"Can we see if he'll mebbe eat it?"

"Martha, it looks so good, I could eat it myself. But let's go and try him."

We went to the cattery, and Neil started to purr as soon as he heard Martha's voice. In fact, he had come to recognise her footsteps. Some of Martha's beef tea was poured into a dish... and Neil never even looked at it. Martha was near to tears, but determined not to be beaten. So she dipped her fingers in her mug, and smeared some of her delicacy on the cat's nose and one unplastered front foot. The cat was clearly puzzled at this strange stuff on him, for despite his wounds and increasing weakness, he had continually licked himself clean. So out came a pink tongue and he licked his nose and foot. The procedure was repeated until he had consumed – albeit reluctantly – half the contents of the mug. Martha repeated this every day for a week, when Neil evidently decided that this sticky stuff was good, or it was no use opposing this determined female – and he started to lick it from his dish. We were off... thanks once again to our determined, patient Samitan, who spent hours making him eat. Good for Martha! Wise too of Neil to learn the lesson all males must learn – there's no use opposing or resisting a determined female! I wondered when I dare risk trying some solid food, with the massive damage there had been to the cat's intestines. That too was decided for me by Neil's determined nurse. She arrived one afternoon accompanied by her friends, who had come periodically, and from a bag she produced a lovely piece of tender, white fish.

"Martha!" I queried her, "where did you get the money to buy that lovely fish?"

"Us just went round most folk us knew at the school, and told them it be for somebody very sick, and all he could eat was fish."

I grinned at the ingenuity of Neil's nurse but just to be sure asked: "You didn't say it was for a cat, then?"

"Naw, Mr Cameron, that would just have spoiled everything."

Was there any limit to what this girl would do, I wondered? Martha cut the fish into small pieces... and every scrap was eaten.

Early on in the whole affair, I had informed Mrs Gorman, local secretary of the RSPCA, a lady with a heart as big as her large frame, and it was agreed that when I thought the cat was fit to go to somebody's home, she would advertise it in the local paper. We decided that whilst all the wounds were healed, and the scars beginning to be covered by hair, there was no point in seeking a home until the plaster came off the two fractured legs: a period of about six weeks. She periodically came up from her home and looked at the cat, and on one occasion handed me a generous cheque, much of it I am sure, her own money, but very welcome, and going a good way to covering our very considerable expense.

At last the day came when Mrs Gorman, in her weekly advert in the local paper, along with the "Good homes wanted for Corgi; Collie, Labrador cross; Alsatian" included "beautiful tabby cat". She went further and told the story of the Good Samaritans who had begun it all, their care, concern, daily visits etc... all of which made an interesting piece in the paper for all animal lovers. The regional paper, covering a much wider area, latched onto this, sent a reporter and photographer and a picture appeared of the threesome – cleaner than I had ever seen them, and in what was clearly their best clothes – with Martha holding the cat, Barbara Mary Jane sucking her thumb, and Jeannie with a wide grin which showed the gap in her teeth. They were tremendously excited, and when afterwards I gave them all a box of chocolates, joy was unconfined.

Two days after the regional paper showed the picture and told the story, I had a phone call, a broad Devon voice enquiring: "Be that the veterinary... Mr... eh... Cameron?"

"Yes, Cameron speaking."

"This is Bill Dinnicombe, an' us thinks the cat in the picture be our Tiger. Could us come over, like an' see it?"

"Of course, Mr Dinnicombe, but where are you phoning from?"

"Oi be speakin' from Torrington. Oi works on a farm near here. Tractor man, like, but nine months ago us lived in Bristacombe... in Oxford Grove, you see."

I nearly dropped the phone in astonishment. "Torrington!" I gasped. "That means the cat must have travelled nearly forty miles to get here!"

"Oi knows it doesn't seem very likely, like. Tiger must have wanted back to his old home. Us 'as a little lass of just five who cried her eyes out when Tiger went missing, like, but she's sure from the paper it's Tiger. If it be alright by you, us could come over on Saturday."

So come they did in the presence of my valiant threesome with Martha holding the cat as if she would never let it go. But little miss 5-year old Dinnicombe jumped up and down in excitement, exclaiming over and over again: "It's Tiger... it's Tiger... it be him." She cried with joy, and at the sound of her voice, Neil/Tiger struggled to get free from Martha's arms. She also was crying, and her two mates, at the thought of losing the cat, their weeping only abated when I promised I would drive them to Mr Dinnicombe's farm one Saturday, and see Tiger in his own home.

"Us can't thank thee enough, Mr Cameron, for saving our Tiger, and this lady," shaking hands with Mrs Drury. "You saved him an' we'll try to make sure he doesn't go wandering off again, if us can."

He looked at all the healed scars and said "Oi reckons all your treatment must have cost a pretty penny. Us could pay you a little but mayhap it mightn't be enough."

"That's alright, Mr Dinnicombe, a kind lady in the town, Mrs Gorman, has paid most of it. Besides, neither you nor anybody else could pay for what saved your cat. It was this little lass (laying my hand on Martha's head) and the love she and her friends gave it all this time that made it want to live and saved it. I was just the plumber!"

"Reckon you be right, vet – you can't pay for love. Us goes to a little Wesleyan Chapel, Sundays, in our village an' just last Sunday preacher was talking about love... our love for each other: God's animal creatures an' he called it"... he fumbled in his pockets, "dang it! I writ it down – ah, here it be – he called it 'the essential ingredient'. Master said us should show this to the animals, to other people, and to God, for He said it was this that made Jesus die for us all... on the Cross, like. What do ee think?"

"I think your preacher was dead right, friend. The essential ingredient, eh? I must remember that".

And I have over the years, but somehow I prefer Paul's ringing words – "Love never fails".

FIVE

Veterinary Vignettes

1 The Worm that Wasn't

The big Shorthorn cow was down on her side, deeply unconscious, lying in a loose box on a bed of filth. A glance round the farm buildings in the small farm on the edge of the moor was enough to give me the picture. Some had roofs falling in; gates were falling off their hinges, and no building had seen paint in a lifetime. The little gnome-like figure who came forward to greet me looked as if he did not believe much in razors or even soap. Beyond the fact he was called Woolridge, I knew nothing of him, this being my first visit "to see a bullock wi' worm in t' tail".

As I shook hands with the little man I couldn't but feel sorry for him, for his small farm was one of an increasing number in our area that barely provided a living for the owner: much of his income being derived from government subsidies, without which he could only just survive and make a living, but whose roots, probably for several generations back were in this, now poverty ridden, farm. He mumbled some words to me which, with the combination of a very broad Devonshire accent and no teeth, I simply could not understand. I thought perhaps action was better than words so requested him to bring me a bucket of lukewarm water, soap and a towel.

He ambled off and I got out my bottles: one of calcium, one a mixture of calcium, magnesium and phosphorous, took my flutter valve from its box and laid my tin of needles beside it. One glance at the cow had shown me it had the commonest condition in cattle, Milk Fever or Hypocalcaemia, which normally comes on just after calving and occurs when the blood level of calcium drops below the critical level. The cow becomes unsteady on its feet, then falls, becomes unconscious, with death in a few hours the final result. I had treated animals several times a week in Ayrshire for the condition, though a few farmers there were now treating their beasts themselves. I had been amazed when first coming to Devon in the early fifties to find that very few farmers had seen it, and 80 percent of those who had did not know what it was.

Treatment had varied over the years. At the end of the last century, whisky was supposed to be the cure (as it was for many diseases), but no cow with Milk Fever was ever cured by whisky. But I suppose by the time the cow had been given some, and the vet and farmer probably each rather more, when the poor cow died, they were all past caring! Then, believing it was a germ in the udder, iodine was injected up the teats, and occasionally the cow recovered. Then it was discovered water was just as effective. Finally the udder was pumped up with air, and all old established veterinary practices still had a pump in a drawer as a relic of the past.

In 1936 a Scots vet called Russell Greig took blood samples from 100 cows suffering from the condition, and in every sample, the calcium was low, so now the treatment was simply to inject a large bottle of calcium into the bloodstream in most cases, though if the animal was only mildly affected, an injection under the skin sufficed. How had the water, air, etc worked? Simply by stopping production of milk for 24 hours, and allowing the calcium that was lost in the milk to build up the blood level again. But there were still other weird theories as to cause and treatment, and I recalled my very good friend Arnold Wilson from Yorkshire, with whom I had gone through vet college, telling me he had come across this belief that it was a worm in the tail, and the cure was to cut the worm out. Here I was meeting this theory for the first time, and I could see the gnome had been having a go, cutting the base of the cow's tail, thus revealing the shining white tendon beneath, which they thought was the worm! Mercifully, in this case, the little man hadn't actually cut the tendon.

When he returned with the water, the calcium bottle went in the bucket to bring it up to blood heat, and, as I had done hundreds of times, I injected the contents into the mammary vein by gravity feed through the flutter valve: a bit like a drip in hospital, only much quicker. Then the other bottle was put under the skin as a spare supply. The little old man kept looking at me in a questioning kind of way, and I managed to make out enough of his question as to why I was not taking the "worm" out.

"No need now. My injections will kill the worm and the cow will be on her feet by this afternoon. I'll come back then to make sure she's alright, and I'll explain then what I have done."

I didn't fancy a long-winded explanation to a man who could have been talking Russian! He looked far from happy, but to try to prevent him having another go at the tail with his knife – probably the same one he used for his tobacco – I bound the base of the tail thickly with elastoplast, and emphasised to leave it alone until I came back. When I got back to base, I dictated a simple explanation of Milk Fever to Mrs Drury, and asked her to type it. It was the best I could think of when verbal communication was impossible with little Mr Woolridge, poor little old fellow.

To my relief and the farmer's obvious delight, for the cow had initially been pretty far through when I first saw her, she was now on her feet chewing hay. Crisis over. I handed over my "thesis" on Milk Fever with the bottom line heavily underlined: "On no account look for a worm in the tail or anywhere else, and always call the vet in time". The old boy warmly shook my hand and showed his toothless gums in a wide grin. As it happened he called me back to another cow with Milk Fever a month later, and with great satisfaction I saw he had not been at the tail, and as I got into my car, having treated the cow, another small form emerged from the house and handed me a jar of Devon's famous clotted cream. She had teeth, and I could make out her words when she said: "For Mrs Cameron." Whether the female gnome was wife or sister, I did not know, but it was a lovely warm feeling, not only to have saved the cow, but brought relief and gladness to the little people.

2 Zoo Vet

They looked like two bags of rags on stilts. I had never seen animals so emaciated. Charlie Trevalyan, the zoo owner, had asked me to come up and see them as he thought "they were a bit on the thin side" – a masterpiece of understatement. The goats had their own little paddock which was almost entirely denuded of grass. Charlie had a very fine collection of the animal kingdom from near and far at his zoo on top of the hill, which attracted thousands of visitors each year. They were very well looked after, and the state of the goats was far from typical.

There were lions; bears; various species of monkey, the most mischievous being the Dead End Kids, who featured in a previous book, and caused Charlie to be constantly placating visitors who had got too near their enclosure and would find a hand coming out and removing a pair of spectacles, a ladies' hat or a child's ice lolly. There were chimps; ostrich; kangaroos; puma and many more and he was regularly on children's television with some of his "family". He also had a Pet's Corner, which delighted the children with lambs; rabbits; tortoises; hedgehogs; wallabies; donkeys; a Jersey cow and calf; coypu; ocelot and many more. Often the two goats were in there. In addition – his pride and joy – was probably the finest collection of tropical birds in Britain, and to enter the aviary made one feel that an artist had been let loose to splash the birds with every colour in the world. To enter one of the bird houses was also to experience a tremendous cacophony of sound.

Kenneth and I, and then Bernard, were supposed to be the experts with this wonderful collection, and while it made life interesting, not one of us had heard a single word at college on the treatment of exotic species, nor did there seem to be a single book to guide us. It was also before knock-out darts appeared on the scene – so there was periodically fun and games when we had to confront Charlie's animals in their cages, especially like lions or puma.

While Kenneth and I had our share of fun, Bernard had most, for he was there longest of the three of us, and Charlie had complete confidence in Bernard.

But goats now – as was my remit that day – they were easy and safe: and in fact just looking at them from outside their paddock made the diagnosis of the cause of their slim-line figures easy. I went off with a tin of faeces to study under the microscope. As Charlie and I reached the exit where was situated a pool for the sea lions, Charlie halted and said "Oi be a bit worried about him, Alec," nodding towards the sea lion. Normally there were two, but the female had died some weeks ago and the male looked very forlorn. "He be losin' weight, Alec... doesn't want to eat and is being sick. Can yo do summat?"

This was a different kettle of fish from the goats: sea lions apparently coming into existence after I left college! I would need to consult an expert, of whom there were fewer than half a dozen in

Britain at that time.

So I phoned Oliver Jones at London Zoo, the best known zoo vet in the country, and gave him the symptoms, such as they were. He was on to it in a flash... "Has he recently lost his mate?"

I gaped at the phone: this man was hot stuff!

"As a matter of fact he has, but why do you ask and what do you think it is?"

"Ulcer, for certain – duodenal or peptic. Only cure is another mate. He's pining – stressed!"

I then went into my den downstairs at the surgery, and studied under the microscope samples of the goats' droppings I had collected. Again I gasped. no wonder the poor beasts were thin. They were absolutely riddled with worms, but that would not be difficult to put right. Nor was it. The goats were wormed several times... moved to a different, fresh paddock and their goat sick paddock ploughed up. A further examination of faeces some weeks later showed the problem was no more and the goats were already putting on weight.

I told Charlie about Oliver Jones' diagnosis and the treatment to get a new mate. The likeable Charlie's face fell.

"These sea lions be £300, Alec (a fair sum in the fifties), and I've overspent on other animals. I just can't afford a new wife for Sam. Could you not try summat?"

So I did try, giving the sick at heart animal the standard treatment of the time for ulcers in human beings. It was before the advent of the wonder drug Tagamet, so I used Vitamin B, a lighter fish diet, for he was still eating a little, and the old Bismuth, Calc Carb Kaolin mixture – the white bottle – and in a few weeks Sam was his old self again.

Yes, there was never a dull moment with Charlie's mixed – very mixed – family around!

3 Do it with Dung!

"'Ullo! Be that the vetnary?" roared the voice over the phone.

"Yes, Mr Narracott," I replied, 'you've got the vet."

"Be it the Scotch one or t'other fella, an' how did ee know my name? Has you got a kind o' seein' phone?"

"No, Mr Narracott, I just know your voice. It's... well, it's a bit different from other people's." What I really meant was it was about ten times louder than anybody else's He seemed to think he had to shout at the phone or he would not be heard.

"Aye... but be you the Scotchman or t'other vetnary?"

"The Scotsman."

He roared a groan. "Well, I wants t'other fella."

"Sorry, Mr Narracott, you'll have to put up with me. My partner's on holiday."

"Holiday!" he bellowed about another five decibels louder. I began to fear the roof might come down on us at any moment with the vibration!

"Who needs holidays! Never had one in me life an' look at me!"

I didn't particularly like looking at the Narracott brothers, for as well as having a more or less perpetual scowl on their faces, they did not seem to feel soap a necessity. But evidently he thought he was an example of healthy, handsome manhood. Bill and Bert, two unmarried brothers no longer in the first flush of youth, were two of our most old fashioned clients. They still used horses, almost the only clients in our practice who had work horses. They reared beef cattle, the "Ruby Reds' as they were known locally, and their animals were of a very high standard, and fetched good prices. Their farm was Barton Mill, out Mortecombe way. They seldom called a vet, and they had never really forgiven me for innocently undervaluing for insurance purposes a bullock that had been electrocuted. I had put it right, apologised, but they had not forgotten.

"What's your trouble, Mr Narracott?" I asked.

"Trouble? Who said I had trouble? Ain't nothin' wrong wi' me!"

"I meant why do you want a vet. What animal is ill?"

"Us 'as a lame hoss. Not proper trouble... only lame."

This phone call was becoming a marathon and my head was singing with Bill, or Bert, I couldn't be sure, having all the stops out in his vocal organ.

"How long has it been lame?" I queried.

"'Bout ten days... mebbe a bit longer."

Now it was my turn to roar. "Ten days! You should have had it seen to before this."

"Us 'as been treatin' it ourselves, but some ways it hasn't worked this time. I suppose us'll need to put up with you, then."

"Oh, Mr Narracott, I wouldn't want you to have a vet you don't like. You better phone for one of the Barnstaple vets. Good day to you."

"Hey, wait a bit", he said hurriedly before I could put the phone down. "Barnstaple be further away than Bristacombe, an' they cost more."

I'd had about enough. "Look, Mr Narracott, do you want me or not? I've other beasts to see too, and folks who, unlike you, will be glad to see me. Make up your mind NOW!"

"Alright, Mr Scotchman, when can you come?"

"I'll be out within an hour," and put the phone down. I had to take two aspirins for my head was "dingin'" with the battering my ear drums had taken.

Bill and Bert were both standing in the yard consulting their pocket watches when I arrived, attired in their usual garb of flapping old army jackets with the elbows sticking out; trousers tucked up and tied at the knees with string in the old fashioned way; the lining of Bill's bonnet was hanging out; and their pipes of thick black tobacco drawing nicely.

"It be 45 minutes since I phoned, Vetnary, an' this is a good hoss."

"Mr Narracott, I said I would be out within an hour and I am, and if you have let your horse suffer for more than ten days, I hardly think you can complain about another 45 minutes. Besides, I had two other visits to make to people who had phoned before you."

Bert sneered "I reckon it'd be to see somebody's pet poodle. They pay better."

"Mr Narracott, it is no business of yours what animals I was treating. It wasn't a poodle, but if you don't mind me telling my next visit I was at your farm to see a horse you had neglected, then I'll tell you where I was."

I had never spoken to a client like that before – nor indeed afterwards, but my anger showed, and Bert hastily said: "Nay, you can't do that. I reckon you'm in the right."

"Well, I'm here now, so show me your horse. Where is it?"

"In its stall in the stable."

So we headed for the stable which was dark, dingy, dirty, festooned with cobwebs. There were two horses: big handsome Shires, though most of my work previously had been with Clydesdales. I didn't need to ask which was my patient, for one was standing on three legs, just gently resting its near front foot on the ground, like standing on tip toe. I walked up beside it, stroking its back and talking quietly to it, until I got to the leg and saw it had the corner of a sack with something in it over its foot. What I didn't like was the swelling going up its leg, a temperature raised 5 degrees and a racing pulse. The big horse was standing with drooping head, clearly in considerable pain... a very sick animal indeed. The stall was dark, narrow and they had no electricity. I knew before I touched the leg that the minute I got to the foot, the seat of infection, he would rear with the pain and there was no room in that stall to avoid being kicked.

"Put a halter on him, Mr Narracott, and let's have him outside."

"Nay, Vetnary," said Bill "us manages to dress his foot in t' stall."

"How often do you dress it?"

"'Bout every third day" said Bill. "This be my hoss, t'other's Bert's."

"What's on his foot?"

"A poultice."

"Well, a poultice is alright, but every third day is useless. It should be at least twice a day. Let's have him outside where I can get a proper look at that foot."

"Look ee here, Mr Vetnary, us was workin wi' and treatin' sick hosses before you was borned. If us can treat that hoss in his stall, so can you. Get on wi' it", emphasising his words with pokes on my chest.

"So you refuse to bring him out? Is that final?"

"Aye."

I had been keeping my temper with difficulty, but now it snapped, so I left them in the stable, took my black waterproof coat off as I headed for the car, and got in. I was about to drive away when the two brothers came running out of the stable, shouting.

"Hey! Where be you goin'?"

"To my next case where I know the farmer will do as I ask!"

"B-b-but what about my hoss?" stuttered Bill.

"Get another vet or go on treating it yourselves. It hasn't just got a lame foot. It's got an abscess on the foot. You can see by his leg the poison has spread and he now has septicaemia or blood poisoning. He might live another four days in agony, and I have every intention of reporting you to the RSPCA for cruelty and neglect. I am NOT refusing to treat your horse, but I cannot treat him in your small, dark stall. As soon as I touch that foot, he'll rear and come down on me. I have no intention of making my wife a widow just yet.""

They muttered to each other, gave me dirty looks, but eventually did as I asked. When we got him outside, as soon as I laid my hand on his swollen leg he fidgeted and pranced about.

"We'll need a twitch", I said, and reached into the car boot. I was in no mood to be gentle with these two rough characters, and I cannot stand people who misuse the dumb animals God made, any more than the human beings He created. The twitch is a short pole with a short rope on the end which is put on the horse's nose and twisted tight, causing discomfort, or even pain to the hose, the idea being he will not notice so much what is being done to him elsewhere, a very old means of restraint. Then I cut the string round the sack containing the poultice, and pulled the thing off. The horse neighed and reared high, just missing my head with his iron shod hoof as he came down. In the stall he most certainly would have killed or badly injured me. But I didn't wonder he had reared when I saw the mess on his foot. The stench nearly knocked me down.

"What on earth is in this poultice?" I snapped.

"Dung."

"Dung!" I said in disbelief.

"Our faither and grandfaither always swore by dung poultices for making heat. There be nought to beat a dung poultice."

The smell was dreadful and what I could see of the foot pretty grim. I got a hose and washed away from the poor animal's hoof the so-called poultice. The horse reared and kicked and was clearly in agony. It swung the two brothers around, one holding the halter, one the twitch, and though it was maybe not very Christian, I confess I was glad to see fear on the faces of these two characters. But I was more concerned about the horse and gave it a fairly hefty shot of Pethidine to take away much of its pain.

"Your horse has the worst poisoned foot I have ever seen. It would start with a nail prick... maybe one of its shoe nails that missed the hard horn. Then your filthy dung made things worse, so that now the poison is all over his system, complete blood poisoning. It's a toss up whether we should save him from any more pain and shoot him now or try to save him. There's no guarantee we will. What do you want?"

"He be a right good un" murmured a somewhat pale face Bill. It was the first time for a very long while that these tough nuts had known – and shown – fear.

"Dost think you can save ee, Mr Vetnary?" asked a contrite Bill.

I looked at these two hard cases, and the very ill, sweating horse and said: "Right, we'll have a go. I can only hope my injection will keep him from getting Lockjaw, for nothing can save him if he gets that. The germ that causes Lockjaw is in earth or dung and you've wasted a lot of time getting help. Dung poultices… if they were ever any good, went out of fashion many years ago."

They were now somewhat subdued and much more biddable. The foot was so tender, I knew I would need to chloroform the horse before a blacksmith could remove the shoe, which simply HAD to come off. We had been shown at college how to shoe, and how to remove a shoe, but I had never done it and had no farrier's tools. Besides a blacksmith knew his job far better than a vet. I gave the horse a massive dose of penicillin, as well as the anti-tetanus jab and promised I would try to get a blacksmith and come back after tea with him. I told them to hose out and thoroughly disinfect the stall before the horse went back in, and departed for my next call, leaving two very subdued, somewhat shaken brothers.

Well, I got a blacksmith whom I knew, and in the early evening he and I arrived at Barton Mill. I could not be certain, but it looked to me the brothers had washed their faces for our visit! They took the horse out to a lean, level patch of grass, and I fixed the chloroform mask on the horse's head – with difficulty – for he pranced and kicked continually. I didn't really like using chloroform for most vets had lost a horse under the anaesthetic. We had been fortunate so far. I recognised the tremendous advance Simpson had made when he discovered this, the first general anaesthetic, displaced in man and small animals by more recent and much safer drugs… but chloroform was still the anaesthetic of choice for the horse. I got the brothers to walk the horse quietly round in a circle, and every now and then added some more chloroform to the sponge in the mask until he eventually became wobbly on his feet, and finally, gently, went down.

Only then did I see the full extent of the abscessed, poisoned foot, as did the farrier. It seemed that he, like me, had never seen anything like it, and he gave the elderly brothers a mouthful of broad Devonshire, liberally sprinkled with oaths. It was an impressive performance! While he took the shoe off, I was watching the anaesthetic carefully, and the animal's breathing. Normally Bernard and I went out together to a task requiring this particular anaesthetic, but Bernard was enjoying a hard and well-earned rest somewhere. Once the shoe was off, I got busy with the hoof knife and pared down through the normally hard horn, but in this foot it was softish – a bad sign – until the dam burst and pus came pouring out.

"Good for you, Alec!" said the farrier; "he'll feel better now."

When the flow of filthy pus had slackened I applied my poultice, composed of a mixture of bread and epsom salts, which had been heating slightly in the house. This was tipped into the corner of another sack, and I instructed the heavenly twins to apply a fresh one every day. I had found this old fashioned dressing very effective for "drawing" out an abscess, in my opinion as good or better than Kaolin. Then, as quickly as I could, I whipped off the mask, and in a few minutes the big horse heaved himself to his feet and in due course was led back to a clean stall. My attitude towards the brothers had been pretty dictatorial... but it had paid off, and with poultice for a few days being applied by the brothers, and a daily injection of penicillin from me, the big Shire, in time, recovered. I thought the brothers would be in grave danger of collapsing when they got my bill, and the blacksmith's, but it was considerably less than the price of another horse.

On my last visit, Bill actually shook hands with me. I nearly collapsed, but he had a reason, and hesitantly said "About that cruelty job – you won't report us, will ee?"

I smiled, clapped him on the back and said "No! We'll let it go, but you know, you did cause your horse a lot of pain... and I wouldn't use dung poultices again. They really do more harm than good, even if father and grandfather swore by them."

"Aye, Bert and me sees that... an' thank ee. He be a middlin' good hoss, you knows."

I felt that in this sentence, the Scotch Vetnary had gained some prestige – but probably only till the account arrived!

SIX

"Change Course!"

It was Kenneth who started it. He was much in demand as a Lay Preacher, and though Church of England himself, he cared not where he preached, whether Methodist, Congregational, Baptist, Free Independent... wherever he was invited, he went, and invariably he would be asked back, for he was an impressive preacher. The Methodists in particular, had many Charges in their circuits and a minister might find himself in charge of as many as eight separate places of worship, so the poor man or his office bearers had to find possibly seven preachers each week, and Kenneth was out nearly every Sunday, for the practice was normally quiet that day. He had a pleasant, easy manner, clear voice, and though educated in a public school, was at home with the farming and country folk of north Devon, understood them, spoke their language, and furthermore he had a message to proclaim. So he was much sought after in the various chapels, as everything non-Anglican was termed, Anglican being Church.

I just caught the tail end of the conversation as I walked one day into our waiting room, which was also the secretary's abode, and naturally where the telephones dwelt.

Kenneth was saying "Sorry. I'm already booked for that Sunday but I'm sure my partner would willingly come."

I stood rooted to the spot in horror and then stammered "You... you... you weren't saying I would take a service somewhere?"

He gave his disarming smile and said, "Yes, you're taking a Harvest Thanksgiving service on such and such a day, and such and such a Methodist chapel."

As the full impact of this dreadful thing went home, I exploded. "Not me! I've never preached in my life – I can't preach – I don't want to preach; I'm a vet, not a preacher, and I'm not going. So there!"

But such was his charm, persuasiveness and disarming manner, he just smiled and said "You'll manage fine. You've spoken at our Covenanters" (a youth organisation), and to conclude this tale of torture, such was his influence and power of persuasion, Joe Soap – after several miserable weeks – went. Not for nothing was he a major!

I remember arriving early at the little country chapel to be greeted by an office bearer, and with him viewing the marvellous, very beautiful display there always is at Harvest in the country. But I also viewed nervously the masses of missiles – eggs, tomatoes, plums, potatoes, cabbage – and I wondered if I would be pelted with anything ere I had got through this simply awful ordeal. The office bearer left me, I spotted a box for gifts, and put in half a crown. I thought if I bribed the Almighty, he might see me through!

Well... somehow I did, unscathed, and shaking hands with the worshippers at the door, which apparently was the done thing, one or two actually said they had enjoyed the service – which I had not! One said he liked to hear my funny language, and he'd had fun when I was preaching trying to guess what I meant: "Just like a crossword", he said. Huh! Funny indeed! The guid Scots tongue! Two men had waited behind when all else had departed. One was the office bearer who had first met me, and he came up to me with a big smile on his face.

"It is our custom", he said, "to give the preacher what is in our gift box. Usually there is nothing, but I'm glad to say there is half a crown today. Here it is with our thanks."

What does the Old Book say? "Give, and it shall be given unto you."

The other little man was waiting to ask me to take the Harvest in their chapel in two weeks. I stalled like mad and said I would need to consult my partner, and find out what he was doing that day. Actually this didn't matter two hoots, but put off the hour of making a decision! I arrived home as pale as a ghost, Janet said, which was at least better than being red from a tomato or slimy from an egg!

The little man who had invited me to his chapel phoned me every night for four consecutive nights until, after consulting Kenneth, who said "Go, brother, go!", just to get the little man off my back I said I would be delighted to come. What a barefaced lie. Then the awful truth struck me. If they went round each other's special services, half the next congregation would already have heard my one and only sermon, so I would have to write another. Oh, michty me… what had I let myself in for if this continued. For in labouring over my first ever sermon, I had discovered the truth every preacher knows: namely that a sermon is 10 percent inspiration and 90 percent perspiration.

But it seemed as if the Almighty was taking pity on me, for I had the rare experience of having, for my second sermon, complete inspiration… and in a most unusual place. I had been up at Whitehill Farm to inject a cow with sodium iodide for Actinobacillosis… better known as Wooden Tongue, an easy enough task. But we did not particularly like going there, especially on a wet day, for in an age when there were few cattle grids, there were *six* gates to open and shut both going and coming. It was an odd place to be thinking of a sermon, as I got out and in the car, but on the way out, the "heads" of an address came to me clearly, and having closed the last gate, I wrote down the important points of the sermon before I forgot them – and it was that bit of paper I duly took into the pulpit with me a few days later, something so sketchy I would never have done when a fully fledged minister. Pure inspiration, but alas a rare experience.

From then on, I had regular invitations, folks wanting to hear the Scotch Vetnary who, apparently, was something of a novelty! But the practice was growing all the time, and we got to the stage when we could not risk both being away on a Sunday. That, I felt, was a godsend for me, and I volunteered to cover for Kenneth in the period of his Sunday when he was away. It is perhaps a measure of my feelings about preaching in these early months that I would rather "clean a cow" (remove placenta), an unsavoury task, than climb pulpit stairs. If you have not by now gained the impression that preaching held little appeal for me in these early days, then I have been sorely remiss in my narrative.

Then, after three years, Kenneth went and spoiled it all by going back to a practice in his native Kenya. I missed him much of course, for I was still a comparative youngster, and raw in some areas, but missed also his friendship. I ran the practice for a few months on my own, but I quickly realised this was just not on. I was out from morn till night, and often through the night... I was seeing nothing of my wife, and by now, two wee laddies, Neil and Ian, and every night I simply collapsed into bed. It couldn't be done by one any more. Who could I get? I knew who I wanted, but would he want me and Bristacombe? He was Bernard Paterson, who had seen practice with us several times, and but recently qualified as a fully fledged vet. Furthermore, on top of his ability, about which I had no doubt, he belonged to that select band known as "the salt of the earth". He was quiet, unassuming, gentle... and furthermore, a sincere Christian with a deep, strong faith, but unassuming in that too as in everything else. So the Christian character of the practice would be maintained. He came enthusiastically, for a very short time as an assistant, but quickly becoming a partner. There are some people in life with whom one just clicks as a close friend, and Bernard's friendship had been (and still is, though somewhat long in the tooth now – the few we've got left) a very special thing for me.

Bernard was also a Lay Preacher... probably more experienced than me, but until he became known by the chapels around, it seemed as if all the places Kenneth had gone asked me, like the mantle of the old prophet Elija falling on the young Elisha, though I was far from being an Elisha. I was also asked to take over as secretary of the North Devon Crusades – one of Kenneth's many tasks. About four times every winter, the committee of these Crusades filled the biggest hall in Barnstaple, the market town of North Devon, 1,000 people coming to hear a notable minister or evangelist. I was being drawn in more and more – though in no way did I seek it – to various Christian efforts. But I was still a vet first and foremost, and that I intended to remain, for my love of animals – all animals – was, and is a very deep thing, part of my whole being.

Then two things happened about much the same time. Bernard was asked to take a few services, which he did, and the word soon spread of this – yet another vet – who was a fine preacher, a winsomeness in his conduct of worship that warmed the heart and educated the mind, so he was much in demand. Four of us, all young married men with young families, members of Brookfield Free Church, the liveliest in the area, formed a quartet to conduct services, all having a part in the service and – wait for it – actually singing. And though any time we sang I expected there to be a bolt from Heaven, or the congregation rush the platform... we became known over a wide area, and much in demand. Three of that quartet eventually were to become ministers with the fourth very gifted with children and teenagers. One of the three to turn to the ministry was, of course me, though never was there a more reluctant minister.

When Bernard joined me, I had no thought whatever of the ministry. We worked well together, were happy in our work, and as I've said, close friends. The practice continued to grow steadily, but with all my involvement in church work, being, in addition to what I have mentioned, a Sunday School teacher and church deacon, I was slowly but steadily having to face up to the question of changing from working with four legged animals to two, and of becoming in some way full time in the church. On the face of it, the very idea was daft. Here I had work which gave me great satisfaction. I had gone through a difficult 5-year course to be a vet followed by two years as a poorly paid assistant. I had now experience of almost every disease of animals; I was head of a steadily growing practice which promised a future for my wife and family where they would lack for nothing. Further more we lived in a truly beautiful part of Britain, living and working amongst kindly folks whose rich, rolling tongue was music to the ear. Many of our clients had become real friends, and one seldom left a farm without a cup of tea, and often a jar of the famous clotted cream. The church was full of young people, young couples, a cheerful, joyful church which gave the lie to the long faced image of Christians. To think of leaving all this was indeed daft. I was "maze as a brish" as the Devonians put it – not sane!

Why then had I any thoughts, any feelings, any pull towards the ministry? That is easily answered. From the priceless heritage of growing up in a very humble but Christian home, throughout my teens increasingly Christ became real to me… not a figure who lived in a church, but a friend on my side. I had no Damascus Road experience of sudden conversion, but gradually I came to believe and experience that a living faith in Jesus was life's greatest treasure, affecting and enriching every part of one's life: in home, in relationships, in work and in sport, and providing an anchor for the voyage of life.

What Samuel Rutherford, that little man who was minister of Anwoth (Gatehouse of Fleet) called "the loveliness of Christ" had become very real to me… had laid its spell on me, and if this seems a weak, wishy washy kind of thing… well, is love weak? This loveliness Rutherford knew despite the terrible times in which he ministered, the Covenanting period, when to follow Christ was often to lead to a scaffold. Furthermore, in his family life, he knew much sorrow, in himself he knew much illness and weakness, imprisonment, constant persecution... yet he talks of "the loveliness of Christ" and to see him, or hear him preach was to know the reality of this to him, no matter his circumstances. I have no doubt he had his down periods, but he had a faith that lifted him, a friend who never deserted him so that in prison in Aberdeen he could cry triumphantly: "Jesus Christ came into my cell last night and every stone flashed like a ruby".

So gradually month by month I became aware of this niggle within me, which Janet also felt, that if a true Christian faith in a living Lord was life's greatest blessing, maybe I should be trying to pass it on to others. In other words it was a "call". Now one can have a call to almost anything in life. But this call to the ministry, in many ways to my deep dismay, for Janet and I could not have been happier with our lot in life, went on and on and grew until it became as Masefield put it: "A wild call... a clear call... that may not be denied".

To leave my beloved animals would make me miserable, but to ignore this call, as I believed, from God, would mean I felt, I would never know peace of mind and heart again. It was an increasing struggle for three years. I longed for a dove to wing its way down from Heaven with a message in its beak as to what I should do – but doves must have been in short supply in the Heavenly dovecote, or were all moulting, for none came.

But the Almighty speaks in many ways – in one's conscience, in one's reason, through other people and mot of all in His word, the Bible. I would not have considered this drastic change if Janet had not been one with me in it, for I believe it is *essential* for a couple to be one in such a step. I cannot praise her enough for as a vet's wife life would have been much easier and comfortable for her, but whenever anyone talked about the sacrifices she would have to make, she always said she didn't marry a vet or a minister but Alec Cameron, the man... bless her. So finally I bowed the head and said "You win, Lord - but under protest, mind!"

I remember very vividly, as I look back over a lifetime the night when the battle was fought and the decision was taken. I was sitting in the surgery after evening consulting hour, my head in my hands, wondering what to do, and feeling for some reason, I must say *that night* to Janet: "I'll have to make enquiries about how one becomes a minister in the Kirk of Scotland. It's not likely they would take anybody like me. Who ever heard of a vet becoming a minister?"

I got home and almost as soon as I went in the door, before I could say a word, Janet said "I think, my dear, you must take steps for the ministry".

I was speechless! I gaped at her. On the very night I was going to broach the subject finally, my wife did it first. What was this? Some kind of telepathy? Many will have differing explanations. To me it was the signal to go ahead. The long battle was over, and I was duly accepted by the Church of Scotland, its first vet!

The next three years at Trinity College were not to prove easy, though a picnic compared to the vet course all those years before. I had to pass an entrance exam on the Bible and New Testament Greek, about which I knew nary a word, but took a crash correspondence course while still practising my trade with the animal kingdom. Then my father, while I was still in Bristacombe, unexpectedly took ill and died in his fifties. As a young man, he had wanted to be a minister, and a fine one he would have been, but with no financial support in his day, it was just not on. I have always regretted he did not see his dream fulfilled in his eldest son, but he knew of my decision and acceptance and I like to think he was happy at his desire being fulfilled, a generation on. But this posed a big problem. As a station master's wife at Dunlop, mother was in that cursed thing, a tied house, with virtually no money, and ineligible for a council house. So, much of my share of the practice which we had earmarked to see us through, now with a family of three (and in time four) had to go to buy a little bungalow for mother. When we moved north to begin my studies, we lived with her for a time. This helped her through her time of grief, but could only be temporary, for it was just not big enough for mother, five of us, and my unmarried brother Fergus.

Now there is a verse in the Bible which says: "God shall supply all your need according to His riches in Glory by Christ Jesus." Many times we have seen that promise fulfilled, our needs met by what many would call luck, a fluke, fate, etc. To us over the years, it was just God fulfilling His promise.

In my very first week as a student, I was asked to take the services at the Laigh Kirk, Kilmarton, a largish church of 900, the next town to Dunlop. My performance must have pleased the office bearers, for they asked me to do the next month, for all of which I was paid.

So it went on from month to month, for the powers that be were trying to unite the Laigh Kirk, where the minister, Andrew Hastie had died. He had been a fine man, greatly loved, and I must have been anathema after him. The proposed union was with the Cairns Church, which had also had a fine minister, Dr Wright, who had retired, but as so often happens, the vacancies dragged on, neither kirk wanting a union. (In fact they fought it out for more than two years.) After a few months, when it was becoming clear we really could not live much longer crammed into Mother's bungalow, unexpectedly a team from Laigh Kirk Session approached me. I thought: "This is it. They want to change their preacher"... but no, it was to ask if we would care to move into their huge manse of twenty rooms, and if I could, in addition to services, take Bible Class and Youth Fellowship; when possible, visit sick and elderly; and also when I could take funerals. If I could see my way to do this, they would pay me virtually a minister's stipend. Wow! Needs met! "God shall supply..." It really was like a manna from Heaven. Mind you, it taxed me to the limit, for in addition to preparing sermons and talks each week, I had my studies at Trinity. But somehow the good Lord enabled me to get through.

We also had a bonus in making friends with the Congregational minister, Bill McPherson, who appears again towards the end of these memoirs. Bill and Sheena, like us, also had four wee laddies. Bill, in time came into the Church of Scotland, and apart from Jimmy Duncan, a fellow student, Bill for the thirty years of my ministry, was my closest ministerial friend. We had inherited a magnificent garden at Laigh manse, and a large lawn, with trees all around and the children of Bill and Sheena almost every day played a wide variety of games in our "estate".

It was here, as I mentioned in a previous book that we almost lost David, not quite three. We had recently added to our fold with baby Alan, and Janet was up in our bedroom attending to the baby when she happened to glance out of the window to where a lovely gean tree grew. She nearly had a fit! The game had clearly been cowboys and indians, and whether David was a goodie or a baddie, Janet did not enquire. The others had a rope tied round David's midriff and he was being hauled off the ground by the rest of the gang, his face as red as a tomato, trying hard not to cry. Janet did the crying... a yell that must have disturbed any passers-by. But the lynch mob got the message their victim's mother did not quite agree with their actions, so let go the rope and David fell to the ground with a thud.

Sadly Bill and Sheena did not escape a like tragedy, for their youngest lad, as mentioned elsewhere, attempting to climb the wall at their back door, caught his little jersey on a protruding nail, it was pulled up round his neck, and he died in a so simple accident.

On the whole, I enjoyed my three years at Trinity, and with my very busy life, the time flew past. I had one big disappointment. There were two courses in my time – the BD which could only be taken by someone with a prior degree, and the Modified Course, geared for those usually older men, who had no prior qualifications.

In my time, about half the students were coming, like me, later in life to do the Divinity Course. Those taking BD, normally had a prior MA. I started on the BD course, not that letters after one's name meant much to me, but I had no desire to be unique: the only minister in Britain whose previous qualification was MRCVS (Member of the Royal College of Veterinary Surgeons), the normal vet qualification. I thought a minister with only MRCVS would seem a queer fish – or animal! A minister who was a vet? "Strange, 'tis passing strange!". But the university authorities did not know what to do with me, and also a doctor at the same time. So they came out with the statement that a vet, doctor or dentist could not acquire a BD, since their existing degrees were not equivalent to an MA. This caused a bit of "stooshy" and the Dean of our Faculty at the time, Professor Gregor Smith, fought hard for the doctor and the vet… to no avail. Certainly I could understand that someone with a 3-year Arts course had covered a wider area than our medical courses, but their argument fell flat on its face when they admitted people with BSc in Pure Science, Agriculture, Forestry etc: every bit as "narrow" as doctor and vet, and two years shorter. But what did it matter? I was allowed to take the BD course, with the understanding there would be no BD awarded at the end. So I did the BD, with one exception. I dropped Hebrew after a year, but carried on with Greek, in which the New Testament was written.

In the final year all BD students had to specialise in Old Testament, New Testament, Systematic Theology or Church History. Most did Theology, reckoned the easiest, but I chose Church History, in which I had long been interested. One of my closest friends, Ronnie Blakey, now in a very important position at 121 (Church Headquarters) also did E.H. (Church History). Ronnie and I generally sat together for college lunch. He has a brain about twice the size of mine – maybe more! – had sailed through the BD course, is a brilliant musician whose father all his life had been organist in Renfield Street, Glasgow, and Ronnie played for our college choir. I count it a privilege to have him as a friend, and I have no doubt he is worthy of being Moderator one day. To his astonishment and mine, I beat him in Church History and gained the prize: my one claim to fame. I have never let him forget it!

Some people spend many years collecting letters after their names. I do not think these things matter one iota. It is the person who matters. Some of our ministers, male or female, with no degree whatever, and no knowledge of Hebrew or Greek (no longer considered essential) have proved themselves better parish ministers and pastors than some who have spent their lives gathering degrees, though in no way do I despise the quest for knowledge. I enjoyed my Trinity years, but looking back over the years, I believe I have learned more in the subject of Life and Living, often from old folk, than in many obscurantist doctrines that seem all important to many whose first task surely, is to preach the Gospel of Redeeming Love, preached by One who was a Carpenter to trade and had not a degree to His name.

SEVEN

True Greatness

In my younger days there were three giants in the Methodist church – Weatherhead, Sangster and Soper – very different men, but close friends. It was said Weatherhead loved the people, Sangster loved the Lord and Soper loved an argument! He still does, and as I write this the indomitable Lord Soper, at the age of 90, is still taking on all comers in Hyde Park.

In my own Church of Scotland or Presbyterian, the death of Lord McLeod of Fuinary set me thinking of my choice of greatest in my own Church. George McLeod was surely the greatest orator of his day, with also the most wonderful, beautiful, all embracing prayers. For the finest preachers I have to select two... Dr James Stewart and Rev Tom Allan. Both were fascinating to hear, both were evangelical, having Christ at the centre but without the hardness, narrowness, judgemental style of preaching sometimes associated with the term evangelical. Both used apt, interesting illustrations and they could hold a congregation of 1,000 spellbound and silent lest they miss a word. But the greatest teacher, as distinct from preacher, was undoubtedly Dr William Barclay; and while I have heard all the others preach or read their books, I was singularly privileged in having Barclay as my New Testament teacher and in knowing him well. He was the one teacher in my time at Glasgow Trinity who could both instruct and explain the most difficult passage, and at every lecture fire you with the joy and thrill of being a Christian.

Furthermore Dr Barclay was able to get this across to millions on radio or television, and indeed his TV ratings rivalled *Top of the Pops*, and most of his listeners were folks who were never near a church.

He was a superb Greek scholar and one of a very small band who had gained a first class Honours in Classics at Glasgow University. Constantly in his talks he referred to the deep or subtle meaning of a Bible word, making its meaning leap to life and show vividly what Jesus had meant when he used a particular expression. The Bible came alive. He was renowned across the world as scholar and theologian, author of more than fifty books, translator of the entire New Testament with each verse or passage explained clearly for today's world so that the man in the street could understand; the scholar could be satisfied and sermon helps given to countless preachers! Yet this unique man of immense ability and phenomenal output took time to get to know all his students by their Christian names, and at coffee break would often sit down at a table beside a student while the other professors stayed in their own little huddle, and he would chat with the student on any topic from Greek to goal-keepers and how his beloved Motherwell were faring in the league. He watched them often and generally stood on the terracings instead of sitting in the stand, so that he could be near ordinary people. He was world famous in the scholastic realm, but what is perhaps not known by so many is what a great human he was... a man of deep compassions for his brother man, be they high or lowly, with a special interest in, and concern for all his former students.

He never sought greatness or fame, rank or position of power – as some do – people who just love to be on an important committee (preferably as convenor), set their sights on fashionable churches and hope one day to be Moderator of the General Assembly. Poor souls! I pity them. Now the Church needs committees and courts and people to run them, but not for Barclay the courts of the Church, however important. Of course there have been many fine Moderators who were also humble men... but Dr Barclay felt his rôle was to teach, which he did superbly, and when offered the highest position in the Church, politely declined (as I mentioned elsewhere), feeling he owed it to his students enrolled for the next year, including many who were coming from America specifically to be in his class. As I have already indicated, in my view Willie Barclay was the best and clearest communicator of the New Testament in my lifetime, and he could make it all understood by duke or dustman, and was probably happiest about the latter understanding the wonders of the faith.

I recall one afternoon standing all alone in Trinity Common

Room studying the notice board – not the details of the latest German book of theology at a fearsome price – but something much more important: the college football team of which I was a member (though something of a veteran), for the annual match with New College, Edinburgh, our deadly rivals, when I heard a voice hail me "Alec! Could I have a word with you?"

It was W.B., as his students called him, who had come in unnoticed. We sat down and he asked "Do you happen to have heard this radio series I'm doing leading up to Easter?"

"Yes, sir, I've heard each one and think they have all been superb."

He gave a wry smile and said "I'm glad you think so for a lot of people seem to think very differently, and I've had some hard letters."

"Surely not!"

"Oh, yes, one Free Kirk minister went on at length, pointing out my many errors and called me a heretic." He paused a moment and said "There were many similar, but the hardest was one who wrote 'now I know why the Lord took away your daughter. It was to save her being corrupted by your teaching'". Willie's eyes filled with tears, then he added "There was no signature; he just put at the bottom: 'yours in Christ'".

My blood boiled that anyone dared to think himself a Christian after such a dreadful accusation, for Willie's daughter Barbara had been the light of his life until she and her fiancé had been drowned in a boating accident. We sat on in silence for a time, myself wondering why he was telling me all this, and he went on: 'Now on Sunday next I'm proposing to say..." and he proceeded to give me the outline of his address, and particularly one or two points which clearly worried him, then to my utter astonishment he asked "Now, Alec, what do you think of it... honestly, mind?"

I gasped in amazement. "Dr Barclay... you, the most respected and loved New Testament scholar today are asking me... a very ordinary student what *I* think of it?"

"Yes, Alec, for you see I've known you for more than two years, and I think you and I are about on the same wavelength theologically... both open evangelicals trying to show the love and joy of the Lord, though sadly, an increasing number on the far right think they are the only ones who are evangelical. It's tragic, really, and it's dividing the Kirk."

"Well, sir, for what my opinion is worth, your address is first class, completely sound to the Scriptures, explains your theme clearly, and furthermore is inspiring. It lifts you... and I wouldn't bother my head about what any of your narrow minded listeners think."

Willie gave a big grin, said "Thanks, Alec" and toddled off, leaving behind one bemused student. Here, I thought, is true greatness, that a man of his knowledge and stature should seek the opinion of someone as ordinary as me.

On my way home as I drove on the quiet back road to Kilmarton where I was still acting as Student Pastor in the Laigh Kirk, I thought of the remarkable man who was William Barclay, and of his seeking my humble opinion... and I really could not have been more ordinary. Then I suddenly remembered that Jesus had done something vaguely similar. As his disciples squabbled with one another about who was the greatest among them, fired with ambition for the important places in the coming Kingdom, Jesus taught them a lesson they were never to forget. He took a little child, set him in the middle, and said: "There's your pattern, your model. Whoever among you would be great in the Kingdom of Heaven must become as that little child". I was no child, but compared to a man of the stature of William Barclay, I was just as little.

I am never more relaxed than when driving a car on country roads, for I had ten years of practice while a vet in Ayrshire and Devon, and often my mind wanders off in some direction or other, while remaining in complete control of the car. So it was that day. I recalled another occasion when Willie had taken me into his confidence.

A former student, then a minister in the central belt, had become involved with an ultra Protestant organisation and been appointed leader. Some time later a large sum of money had disappeared, thousands... a lot of money still, but in the early sixties a vast amount. The finger pointed at the minister, though I believe a very long time later his name was cleared. But that was not known then... the minister took what was described as a nervous breakdown and was sent to the Crichton Mental Hospital in Dumfries for treatment. After a time Willie had a phone call from the consultant psychiatrist who asked Willie if he could possibly visit the patient, who was asking for him. He reported: "His problem is not mental, but spiritual, in the realm of faith. In fact I doubt if he has ever had a faith".

It was at the time the New English Bible was coming out, and

Willie was an adviser in its translation, necessitating trips from Glasgow to England. He still had his college lectures to prepare and deliver, and many other demands on his time. But… simply because a former student was in need, Willie visited him on several occasions to try to save his sanity, and implant in him a faith. Furthermore, he told me in confidence one day that he was trying to pay off the debt of embezzled money so that the minister would not go to prison with all the attendant scandal to his family and the Church – for it was believed at that time that the minister was most surely guilty.

There was to be a sad, and indeed cruel ending, for my beloved teacher sat down beside me one day and said: "Well, Alec, he's gone… fled to Canada without paying back a penny, but that doesn't matter. But, you know, he never even said 'Thank you'."

He was deeply hurt and my heart went out to this gentle, trusting, caring man… and some called this compassionate Christian a heretic!

As I proceeded homeward that afternoon my thoughts switched back to our chat of that day… this was the man whom numbers of lesser mortals slated, and accused of being liable to corrupt his daughter's beliefs!

I remembered Barbara's death well. It was high summer and Willie was occupying the pulpit of a large Edinburgh church. On the Sunday following her death, with her body still not recovered, he still went into the pulpit and in a letter written to a friend afterwards said: "If we who are the messengers of the Gospel of eternal life cannot go on, who can?". He also thanked her for a poem she had given him some time before, and said what a comfort it had been to him and his wife – a poem of victory and triumph.

Shall I wear mourning for my soldier dead,
I – a believer? Give me red,
Or give me royal purple for the King
At whose high court my love is visiting.
Dress me in green for growth… for life made new,
For skies his dear feet march, dress me in blue,
In white for his white soul; robe me in gold
For all the pride that his new rank shall hold.
In earth's dim gardens blooms no hue too bright
To dress me for my love who walks in light!

That poem shows clearly the faith of W.B. in the life to come. Indeed he had the faith of a little child. God was his Father, Christ was his

Saviour and he was content to leave life here and hereafter to his Lord.

For relaxation – so called – Willie, for over 20 years conducted the Trinity Choir. We practised every Friday afternoon, and in the spring term put on several concerts in different churches, as well as the big, final one with wives and "old boys" present, in Trinity. We sang all kinds of songs... high brow, popular, sacred and secular. Each year seemed to turn up a master pianist, solo singers, instrumentalists and comedians. Over thirty years later as I write this, I can picture from my place hidden in the back row, the different emotions flitting across our beloved conductor's face as we sang – smiles, mischief, joy, pride, and in the moving pieces the hint of tears – and all this in a man who was stone deaf and had to wear an enormous hearing aid. One day when he was in the middle of a TV series, he received a letter from a Jewish lady in which she said: "Dr Barclay... I observe you wearing a hearing aid which seems to give you trouble. My late husband, just before he died, purchased one for over £100. I am prepared to let you have it for half price." Willie read that letter out to his New Testament class who, with Willie, were dissolved in mirth! Although he was a man of many anecdotes and stories, at the beginning of each concert season, he always picked two; and at the start of each performance he told them to the audience while we in the choir dutifully laughed.

One final memory came to me as I neared Kilmarton in the car, a story he used to tell against himself with many a chuckle. When he was at the height of his fame and his face know to almost every TV viewer, he was sitting one day in the foyer of a hotel where he had stayed the previous night. A lady came up to him and said how much she enjoyed his lectures. At that time W.B. held the Chair of New Testament in Glasgow University and was a world-renowned personality. But the lady was clearly puzzled by one thing. She asked: "Where exactly is your church?" Willie replied that at present he did not have a church. She was clearly concerned, so patted him on the shoulder sympathetically and said: "Never mind. I'm sure you'll soon get one!"

Well, he serves a higher Church now, and among those with him in Glory there are many who are there because of the faith they found through him. I am sure it is a gladsome company, and perhaps the old Trinity Choir is adding its little bit to the Heavenly Chorus.

EIGHT

"Go to the Country"

"Your congregation will know what time you get out of bed in the morning when they see your chimneys smoking. They will also know pretty well everything there is to know about you... but don't make the mistake of thinking this is nosiness. It's genuine interest, for in the country, folks truly care about one another. Nobody is lonely unless they make it clear they want to be left alone. Furthermore in the country you are surrounded by the beauties of nature, you have peace to pray, to think, to meditate, and your life will not be so rushed and busy as in the cities. Go to the country for your first Charge anyway."

So said the after dinner speaker at Trinity that day. Since most students came from towns and cities and hoped to return to similar places, I think it was felt someone should put in a good word for the rural Charge. So far as Janet and I were concerned, he was talking to the converted, for with our background – growing up in the country, having been a country vet – I had every intention, if somebody would let me, of going to the country. I felt I would be more use to the Lord, and more at home, with farmers than ship-builders; foresters than lawyers; shepherds than shop-keepers.

Our speaker went on: "Mind you, always you will be given great respect and not treated as incomers, as most people from the towns who have moved to the country are until they get involved in the life of the village. It is true that you might have to initiate more things yourselves than a city minister who might well have more natural leaders for different departments than his brother in a scattered rural area. But if you show you are genuinely interested in the lives of your people, and get involved in at least some community activities, you'll get as much assistance as you need. It all depends on yourself.

"When I first went to a country Charge thirty years ago, about two years into my Charge I attended my first General Assembly and bumped into a former student with whom I had been friendly, and who had also gone to the country. He told me he was hating it, so I enquired why.

"'No help whatever! I have to do everything myself. Let me tell you a wee story, Bill. You know I'm single, live alone and look after myself. A story got round the village that I was never to be found in the manse any day between two and three, and some of the elders asked me to account for my absence each day. So I invited the whole Kirk Session to come together one day, took them through a wood, across a few fields, until we came to a railway embankment where I sat down and said: "She'll be along in a few minutes". They looked at each other. I could read their thoughts: "Ah-ha... so there was a lady involved". By and by a goods train came puffing up the line. I watched it from the moment it hove into sight until it disappeared, got up, and said: We can go home now. They looked at each other, mystified, till the Session Clerk said: "Do you mean to tell us, you come here every day to watch a train?"

"'Yes,' I said, 'I come to see something that moves in this parish without me pushing it.'

"I think my friend thought I would be full of sympathy at his lone struggle, but I chuckled, then said seriously: 'You shouldn't have to be alone in the work of your church, Tom, but let me ask you a question. How many folks have you on the Kirk roll?'

"'Just over 200, Bill, but what has that to do with it?'

"'How many times have you been in their homes in two years?'

"'None, Bill, except anybody who's seriously ill. If they want me they know where to find me.'

"'Except between two and three' I chuckled. 'Come on, Tom, you're a friendly fellow... you used to play football, table tennis, and I remember you organising a super concert in your probationary year. Try getting to know your folks, you old mutt, and you'll see a difference. Show them you really care for them, and you'll soon get volunteers and helpers for any scheme you have.'"

The speaker, a man approaching 60, looked round us all deliberately and concluded his address. "I've gone back again to the country for my last Charge, and there's no lack of helpers. I have no lawyers, bankers, folks with masses of Degrees, but I guarantee my farmers, shepherds, foresters can match any Kirk Session in the land in their enthusiasm and willingness. There's an old shepherd of 65 who herds 600 sheep. They all look the same to me, but he knows them every one. I advise starting your ministry in the country; but whether in town or country, know your flock and they will support you to the hilt in anything you try. On a Sunday you will be thrilled, as they look up to the pulpit, by the warmth in their faces as the hungry sheep look up to the shepherd, and know their herd will feed them with the diet they need – that we all need – the food another Shepherd said would satisfy the heart. What's that? What but the Word of God, garnished with love, so that your flock go home week by week cheered, comforted, maybe challenged, and feeling you *do* care for them, and more than you, the good Shepherd Himself is always with them, especially when they get coupit on their back as we all do whiles. That's the gospel I know, and the recipe I've found *does* work. Give the country a try first, gentlemen. After all, that's where the Lord Himself began."

The vacancy at Kilmarton was brought to an end when the two churches eventually agreed to unite, some three months before the end of my Divinity course. I was paid a great compliment when a group of elders visited me and asked if I would be willing to stay on as minister of the Union. So I consulted Rev Andrew Eastham, who had been Interim Moderator, or minister in charge during the vacancy, and a wise man. He listened to my report, then said: "Well, Alec, it's a great tribute to you and what they think of you but you mustn't consider it. For two-and-a-half years you have been the blue-eyed boy, and as a student allowances have been made for you, but it's vastly different being the minister. You are in charge of everything and a church of 1,200, especially after the bitterness of union discussions, is far too big for your first Charge."

I knew he was right, but it was a sore temptation to stay on in the very gracious manse with the glorious garden, and clearly I was well thought of by the elders at least. So the Charge was filled, and we moved out into a little cottage that Andrew had found for us to rent until my course finished. It had a grand Scottish name, if somewhat lacking in beauty: Tattie Ha', which means Potato Hall!

My days at Trinity came to an end and about thirty of us were set loose on an unsuspecting public, looking for a church like so many ships seeking a harbour.

To keep the wolf from the door, and feed and clead (clothe) four rapidly sprouting sons, I got a job not too far away from Tattie Ha', there being a shortage of teachers at the time.

It seems unbelievable with 3 million unemployed as I write this to remember that there actually was a period in my lifetime when employers in virtually every trade and profession were almost begging for employees, even those – like me – with no qualifications for the post. So here was I – a vet, a minister – now trying my prentice hand at teaching and being received with open arms by the headmaster, such was the desperation. I taught – well I was supposed to teach – English and Geography, but it is better if a veil is drawn over my efforts for three months whilst I waited for a church to take me: but at least the family could still be fed and get new shoes!

The commonest method for a church to get a minister was to advertise in the *Glasgow Herald*, *Scotsman* and *Life and Work*, the church magazine. Verily wonderful were some of the adverts, which held out so many attractions that only somebody requiring his head examined could ignore them. The manses all appeared to be in first class condition and much to be desired. No mention was made of a wee bit of dry rot, the twenty rooms with no central heating, nor the garden of half an acre untouched by human hands for thirty years. Yes, I do mean twenty rooms, and many of the gardens reminiscent of the wilderness in which the poor Jews wandered for forty years. You see, there were plenty of ministers available then and even more vacant churches.

I had a silly kind of bias about applying for a church. I suppose I had a lingering feeling that if God had *really* meant me to be a minister, and it wasn't a ghastly mistake I had made, He should finish the job and plank me down in a church of His choosing, and all I had to do was sit back and wait for Him to get busy. How naive can you get! But just in case He wasn't going to work that way, I applied for a vacancy in an Ayrshire village. I knew the fish were nibbling a bit for on three successive Sunday evenings when I was preaching for a minister on holiday, there were four men eyeing me pretty closely from the back row – a Vacancy Committee for sure. On the third evening there was also another large contingent watching my every move, the two groups staring, maybe glaring would be nearer the truth, at one another. I must confess to being highly amused. On the way out at the door, team 1 whispered I was on their short leet of two, and they would decide on Tuesday week. I made my way to the vestry to find a deputation waiting for me: members of Team 2. They introduced themselves.

"We're from Moorton. We just formed our committee this morning. We have had more than fifty applicants, but were hoping for one from you. Are you no' interested?"

"Oh, certainly I'm interested if Moorton are interested in me."

"Well, just to keep everything richt and in order, could you apply?"

So I sent off brief note, for I was sure they would already know everything that mattered about me, since Moorton was the neighbouring parish to Kilmarton, where I had preached, and done much else for 2½ years, and had in fact, preached twice in Moorton when their minister, Rev Bruce Young, had exchanged pulpits with me. I had two thoughts on my drive back to Tattie Ha'. The first was it felt good to be wanted, and the other that God does indeed move in mysterious ways. Ah, well, wait and see.

I might have been doubtful a little if I had known then what I discovered many years later when I was minister of Aldermouth, my second Charge. I was one of a team of three appointed by Presbytery to be present at a meeting of a Vacancy Committee and Kirk Session of a large church in the north. It was obligatory for every Vacancy Committee to invite this small committee known as Advisers to help out if they wanted advice on their deliberations. Advisers! What a joke! Our presence was ignored and we were not asked to speak the whole evening, which was maybe just as well for my temper was a boiling point by the end of their meeting.

They had a team of all those who had heard four men preach and met the candidate, and each team reported on their man... fair enough, you might think. A lady reported initially for candidate number one. He simply would not do, for he hadn't a wife, and a wife was imperative for the Guild. A nice man, an excellent preacher, the right age – but no wife. Out!

For team two, the trouble was the minister's wife. They had travelled some distance, and wondered at the manse if they might freshen up. Now neither minister nor wife had known a Vacancy Committee was coming that day, for normally such scouts for the vacant church do not announce their coming, but prefer, as secretly as possible, just to arrive so that the minister doesn't get a chance to preach "a fast horse" as a favourite sermon is described. Now not only did that manse wife treat them well: made a nice cup of tea, almost another breakfast, then excused herself, but she told them to feel at home until time for worship while she got the children, three under five, dressed for church. But well, the manse didn't seem very tidy... clean, oh yes, but toys lying about everywhere and children a bit difficult. Now I know the difficulty my wife had every Sunday morning to get our four into their kilts, and spruced up in time for church without entertaining critical visitors. The wife's hair was a bit untidy too – no, she wasn't quite the standard they expected for their church.

Report number three was delivered by a vast, tweedy woman who announced that she knew as soon as he came in by the way he went up the pulpit stairs he would not do. (How *should* one go up the pulpit stairs, I wondered.) There were a few other things. He got mixed up in two of the intimations (very likely pushed into his hand as he came out the vestry door!).

The last of the four possibles simply would *not* do... he read his prayers. Shame!

My two fellow Advisers were muttering to themselves while I tried to control my soaring temper and blood pressure. We were given no opportunity to make any comments. That meeting went on and on and so-called Christians dissected their four best candidates. Oh yes... the bachelor got the job!

If I had known away back at the beginning that discussions of Vacancy Committees were like that, down to the children's toys and the wife's hair, I might have been less sanguine about being chosen by one of my two Ayrshire Charges! However, it had not been like that, for seventeen men and women, the entire Vacancy Committee of Moorton turned up the following Sunday evening at Mochrum, where I had begun as a young vet.

When I got back to Tattie Ha', two elders and a minister, Rev George Michie, standing in for Andrew Eastham who was on holiday, were waiting for me. Janet was glad to see me for she had been trying to entertain her visitors who gave her no clue for their visit, though she had a good idea, having introduced themselves as being from Moorton. They had reached Tattie Ha' some time before me for I had called in to see my mother in her home at Prestwick. When I arrived, she merely said: "This is Rev George Michie and Mr Aitken and Mr Wilson who would like a word with you," and departed to leave the men to their deliberations.

Rev George said: "We're from Moorton and I'm sure you must know why we are here tonight."

"Well, beyond thinking it is something to do with the vacancy, I can't say."

There was quite a bit of "kidology" passing to and fro, so Rev George cut the thread of polite chit-chat and said, simply: "The Vacancy Committee would like you to be Moorton's minister. It was a unanimous decision."

I was being canny so asked "Was it really unanimous or did you agree to make it so?"

"No! A bona fide 'yes' from each of the seventeen."

Then he went on: "We would like your decision by Tuesday".

At this point I asked that Janet join us in our discussions, for from the beginning my entry to the Church was a united decision, a oneness that went into my whole ministry, a wonderful union that encouraged me in everything I tried to do, and which saved me from many mistakes. When she came into the room, I told her of the purpose of the visit, but made two observations, one real and sincere, the other mischievous! "Gentlemen, I'm highly honoured and thrilled by this invitation, but you told me just a week ago you had received over fifty applications. Since you've only been in existence for a week, I feel you've been less than fair to all your other candidates for the post, probably a number of them fellow students and friends of mine from Trinity. You can't have seen or heard many of the others."

Mr Aitken and Mr Wilson, whom I discovered were known as Jimmy and Maxy and who were to become good friends to me, hastened to explain. "Well, you see Mr Cameron, we advertised Moorton long before we were given permission to call a minister by Presbytery, but Presbytery takes ages to do a thing and whit do they ken aboot the kin' o' minister we want? So for weeks we've been goin' through all the applications. We wanted somebody in his thirties, married, and who'd had to work for his livin'. (Naughty, Jimmy and Maxy! Ministers have often to work gey hard.) This mornin' we went in teams of three to hear all the ones that we thought were suitable, and we were scattered like the Children o' Israel the length o' Scotland – and weel, we heard you twice an' a wheen o' us heard you when you were at Kilmarton – an' you bein' a vet an' everything, we a' felt you were the yin." They paused, looked at me anxiously and said, "We a' hope you'll say aye or there will be a wheen o' disappointed folk in Moorton."

I replied – sincerely: "Well, I'm highly honoured but there's a wee snag. You see I applied some time ago for another church in Ayrshire, and they have indicated I'm on their short leet. We'll have to take a few days to consider it. You've said you would like my reply by Tuesday. That doesn't give us much time to weigh things up, see the church and manse and have a look round the village and parish. It only gives us tomorrow to see everything, and also feel sure this is the place for us. But we'll be thinking and talking about it and most of all, praying for God's guidance for your sakes as well as our. Why the hurry, may I ask?"

The two elders looked down, shuffled their feet and flushed a bit. Finally they said "Well, we feel the sooner the better."

I saw Rev George give a quick smile. Clearly the Tuesday deadline was because the news had got round about the rival kirk reaching their decision on the Tuesday. Clearly too more things than the price of blackface ewes and the poor pig subsidies were talked about at the market, for since the two Charges were not too far apart, the farmers of both would know one another, and the pedigrees of their kirk candidates had got around.

When our visitors had gone, Janet and I danced a jig round Tattie Ha'. Somebody wanted us – maybe two. One was certain, the other yet to be decided. So on the face of it, the choice was easy. But if we accepted Moorton's invitation, we wanted first to see what kind of place it was... the church, manse, village and a bit of surrounding parish. So we deferred our decision for another day, praying the good Lord would guide us.

We spent the next day conducted by Duncan, the treasurer, exploring. We met at the manse; an old, solid building with walls two feet thick. There were coal fires in every downstairs room, a spiral stone staircase leading to the bedrooms... but no modern comforts like central heating of any kind or double glazing to warm the ten rooms... in short a typical manse of the period, the seventeenth century. Duncan informed us we would need to pick some wallpaper for some rooms were to be done up, but "we hope you dinna pick the dearest paper for money's a bit ticht". (I wonder how many ministers have heard their treasurer say that!)

The very large garden around the manse was in three parts. Running the full length of the lawn on one side was a wood of about fifty trees, and I could picture our brood giving their parents many heart-stopping moments, as they imitated Tarzan in their very own jungle. Then there was the large lawn which was not quite, but nearly, a hayfield and I was informed Duncan could get me a rotary mower cheap. Then there was the walled vegetable garden, with some rhubarb in one corner being the only vegetable to be seen. The rest of the garden had about thirty years' growth on it of every weed known to man – and maybe some that were not! Grass among the weeds was head high, and I hesitated about wandering in, just in case I came across the skeleton of some long-deceased cleric!

There had been a time early in the century, our very good friend Nan Archibald told us, when the walled garden was immaculate, in beds with boxwood hedges. A place she knew well, for her grandfather had been minister there most of his life, and the garden was his pride and joy.

As our faces grew longer and longer, thinking we would be taking a leaf out of the Children of Israel's book, for they knew a bit about wandering in deserts, Duncan assured us if we came it would all be tidied up for our coming – grass cut short, wilderness ploughed up by two farming elders, Jim Garven and Jim Shanks – and potatoes planted. "Nothin' like tatties for cleanin the grund" Duncan assured us. Duncan added "we ken you're keen on gardenin an' we want you to be happy here and stiy for a while."

I marvelled as we moved around just how much the folks of Moorton already knew about us. What had the after dinner speaker said at Trinity? "There's no strangers in the country."

From the manse we crossed the road to the beautiful little church, built in 1643... cross-shaped, whitewashed, surrounded by its ancient graveyard. It looked as if it had been there from the beginning of time; there was a great peace about it and I fell in love with it right away.

My attraction to the church increased when we went inside. There were no stained glass windows, statues, paintings on the walls or any special features, but the little church was very beautiful in its simplicity of construction. The pulpit was in the middle with three separate groups of pews, in front and on either side of the pulpit, with above each area a separate gallery: one still reached by an outside stone staircase. The galleries in a bygone age would have been "Laird's Lofts" and the arrangement of seating would make the congregation seem a large family gathered round their minister – the sheep in the flock looking up to the shepherd.

But what set off its beauty was the fine woodwork of pulpit and pews, all the wood shining with years of polishing. An elderly man was busy even as we entered, with his duster. Duncan introduced him; "This is Andra who keeps our wee kirk shining. He's been beadle for about forty years and loves his kirk. Sometimes we say to visitors we'll gie them £5 if they can find a speck of dust or cobweb, but with Andra here nearly every day, we ken oor money's safe."

Andrew shook hands with us and said: "We're a' lookin' forward to you comin'."

"Hold on" I said, "we haven't decided that yet and besides maybe the congregation would vote against me."

"Tuts man!" he replied, "nae fear o' that! I've heard a wheen o' ministers in my time an' I've heard you twice an' I think I ken a gude minister when I hear yin. We heard aboot that ither kirk being efter you but everybody in Moorton is hopin' you an' Mrs Cameron will come here."

"Well, that's a real compliment and I'm grateful. I sincerely believe the beadle is the minister's right hand man, and I'm certain if we do come here you and me will get on just grand."

I then climbed the pulpit stair and viewed the whole church and realised what a panoramic view the preacher had, being able to see everybody in the church clearly, right to the back of the galleries. It would truly be a large family gathered in this ancient building... voices lifted in praise, heads bowed in prayer or an attentive throng listening to their minister read the Scriptures or in his sermon. On the side of the pulpit was the famous sand glass, like a large egg timer which I recalled from my two previous visits was turned with great dignity by Andrew at the start of the sermon.

"How long does it run?" I queried.

"Forty minutes," Duncan informed me. "But we hope you don't preach it dry ower often. Long ago the length of the sermon was two-and-a-half glasses. But the folk got a rest half way to go outside and stretch their legs. Generally the Lairds went hame at half time."

"We're right proud of our wee kirk," said Andrew.

"And you've every reason to be," I replied sincerely.

"You ken, there used to be three kirks in Moorton" Duncan informed us, and I was to find he was no mean local historian.

"One o' them had a beadle who was too fond o' the bottle," said Andrew. "The minister was aye on to him aboot it, but it made nae difference. One Saturday nicht the beadle was gey fu' an' takin' the breadth o' the road. The next morning before kirk the minister got on to him. 'That was a terrible state you were in last night, Angus. You bring shame to the church.'"

"I wisna drunk," Angus retorted.

"Come now, I saw you with my own eyes" said his minister.

"Look, minister," said Angus. "I'll prove to you I wisna drunk. Hoo mony moons did you see last nicht?"

"One, of course."

"Weel, you were mair drunk than me... for I only saw half a yin!"

Andrew summed up his story with a chuckle. "Moorton was a gey rough place at one time, long ago, but it's a lovely quiet wee place noo – a grand place to stay an' bring up a family with the bonniest kirk in Ayrshire."

We had a quick walk round the churchyard, saw the jougs and outside bell rope and the many famous Covenanting graves. At the two gates was a stone built sentry box and I asked their purpose.

Duncan enlightened me. "Long ago after a burial elders would stand guard through the night for a few weeks to protect the graves from body snatchers."

Andrew joined in: "Aye, the doctors used to come doon from Glesca to rob the graves for specimens for their students. The elders still stand there on Sunday mornings – but a' they have to guard is the collection which is taken at the gate in a special kin' o' table."

Duncan joined in again – "There's an old woman in the village who said the doctors wanted the bodies to study the internals."

We all laughed at the quaint description.

We bade the two men goodbye, had a quick drive through the neat, clean little village with many really old houses, and the beginnings of a large estate on the edge of the village. As we drove back to Tattie Ha' we felt certain this was the place for us – provided the congregation voted me in. That evening I phoned the Interim Moderator with our decision, and also the Interim Moderator of the other church. I found that hard to do for it transpired he was all but certain they would have chosen me.

Somehow that night I felt abundantly rich. The next chapter of our lives was about to commence and we felt we could scarcely have found a more pleasant place to begin. The vet would soon be the minister. We thanked the Lord – and started choosing wallpaper – not too dear!

NINE

"A Correspondence Fix'd wi' Heaven" (Burns)

"Go to the country," the minister had said to us as our divinity course neared its end at Trinity – and we had gone, being duly voted in by the congregation of Moorton, a church of some 600 members. I had an unusual beginning and looking back on it now, I feel the good Lord was saying with a smile: "This lad found it a fair old wrench giving up caring for his beloved animals – I'll break him in gently". For you see my first service at Moorton was in a cowshed!

Jim Garven, one of our farming elders, in his quiet, shy way had come to me a few days before my first Sunday as Moorton's minister and asked, "I was wondering if you could possibly take a service at Dalmusternock (his farm) for a troop of Scouts from Glasgow who are camped with us. They aye have a service on Sunday mornings at camp, what they ca' a 'Scout's own' and they've asked me to ask you if you could come this Sunday. They haud it ootside usually, but if it's wet, they'll go into the byre. You see, they ken about you being a vet and think you might be a bit different from some ministers they ca' stiff and starchy."

I clapped Jim on the shoulder and said "Delighted! I think this is maybe God's way of breaking me in to my new job."

Since the Moorton church service was not until 12 o'clock there was time for worship with the Scouts. It was wet, so the cowshed it was, and as I went in, memories chased one another through my mind of calvings, Milk Fevers, Wooden Tongue, Clit-ill, Mastitis and a host of other ills I had treated in my four legged animals in byres. Now it was the two legged ones. The lads and their officers looked at me curiously when I arrived. I don't know whether they expected I would have horns and a tail or somehow look different from other ministers. We had a grand time, and my ministry had begun where my previous work had ended.

We found Moorton a delightful place, the people warm hearted and welcoming, and of course, being Ayrshire folks ourselves in an Ayrshire church, we almost at once felt at home. We also found to our delight that the lovely little church was also a lively little church, really the centre of almost every activity in the parish. Nearly everything, except the Rural, revolved round the kirk. Much was there when we went. We started in time one or two new things and the little church buzzed with life. For the women there was a strong Women's Guild and a Mother's Circle for the younger women. There was a Men's Fellowship; Girl Guides and Brownies; Scouts and Cubs, all well led. The Cubs in particular involved almost every boy in the village, whether Protestant or Catholic, largely because of the enthusiasm of the leaders Joe Wilson and Ian Black who in addition to all activities associated with Scouting, started a Cub football team, which attracted a large crowd of vociferous supporters every game. There were also Sunday School, Bible Class and Youth Fellowship teams and there were very few youngsters and teenagers not involved in some organisation. They were supported by willing parents who ferried them to away games.

Call the football bribery if you like but I felt it was good whatever way one looked at it. It provided healthy exercise for youngsters, it welded them together, it had spiritual value for nobody could be considered for their team if they were not regular in their organisation, and many of these young people went on to become confirmed as church members.

The old folks were well cared for too, the Church Guild of Friendship providing a knife and fork meal in our church hall monthly throughout the autumn and winter, the meal followed by a concert: some of the concerts being put on by well-rehearsed Sunday School youngsters. In the summer there was a car outing for the senior citizens when over twenty laden cars took them on an outing. I was speedily put in my place in this one, for after leading the convoy on its mystery tour, I was relegated to the middle "for you go ower quick!" Most important, however, for the old folks was a regular visit by younger women to all living alone, whether church members or not.

We had a Bible Study group, and all in all, it was a church very much alive, and giving a lie to the frequent accusation by many – though not in Moorton – that the kirk was a dull place and out of touch with young people.

Moorton kirk was involved with youngsters from five to 95! It was a privilege to be their minister, be welcome in every home in the whole parish and *feel* the enthusiasm for God's house and the things of God throughout the village and surrounding parish. It seemed to me we were one big family and every Sunday, in what was usually a well filled kirk, to feel I was surrounded by a large family at prayer – and enjoying it.

But if there was a truly live church in the present, there was also a noble past. 1643 when the church was built was at the time of the Covenanting struggle which went on for fifty long, cruel years, and Moorton had more martyrs than any other parish in Scotland, and the immaculately kept old graveyard round the church bore testimony to the struggle, suffering and sacrifice for Christ's cause.

I soon found that many people visited our little church and the graveyard. The church was kept open from dawn till dusk and in our time there suffered no vandalism whatever. A considerable time was spent by many of the visitors going round the Covenanting graves with their moving epitaphs, and also many other graves of the people of the parish going back more than 300 years. Sometimes bus loads came and I had to conduct the visitors round and give a brief account of the years of struggle. Frequently church groups booked in advance for their visit, and the women of our church, with typical country generosity had tea laid on for the visitors after I had given them an outline of Moorton's part in the fight for freedom, and shown them the Moorton flag which specified the reasons for the struggle in the words "For God freedom and Covenanted work of Reformations".

There are not many church members today who realise what the kirk in Scotland owes to these forebears of 300 years ago. What was it all about? Basically two things – freedom to worship as they had done since the Reformation in 1560, and most important to have their Lord as king and head of His Church.

You see, the Stewart kings believed in "the divine right of kings". They claimed they ruled the land by the will of God, and saw it as part of their divine right to rule the Scottish Kirk in every detail, as they chose. They introduced Bishops, who evicted the Presbyterian ministers from their charges, replaced them by curates and priests, who in turn introduced Laud's Liturgy and prayer book which laid down how everybody should workshop, and the very words they should say in their prayers, something very foreign to our ancestors here in Scotland and still too recent after the Reformation, so to Scotsmen it smacked of Popery. All this seemed bad enough, but the real crux of the whole struggle, something not always understood in Scotland even today, was the monarch's claim to be head and lord of the Church. Not so, said our forefathers... "we are loyal subjects of your majesty but we have but the one King and Head of the Church, and that no earthly monarch. The Lord of Glory, Jesus Christ, is the king and head in His Church." But the Stewart kings, some of them not over endowed with wisdom, insisted the Scottish Kirk must obey their edicts, and in time those who did not were put out of their churches – half the ministers and congregations leaving – or being forced to leave their kirks, and if caught worshipping in some lonely farmhouse or a barren moor, the principal areas of suffering being in south-west Scotland – Lanarkshire, Ayrshire, Galloway, Dumfries-shire, they were tried, invariably found guilty, imprisoned, sent from their beloved homeland across the sea to the new world across the Atlantic, packed like herring in a box, and finally with James II, the most vicious of the Stewarts in what was known as "the killing times", usually executed, often without a trial.

They were, for the most part, ordinary men and women who showed tremendous courage, but of course eventually many took up arms to defend themselves and resist the king and his laws. It was, as I have said, fifty long and very terrible years living rough on moors and in hills and caves, but in the end they succeeded in their struggle and to this day the Kirk of Scotland is dis-established. There is still but one head, and the monarch of the day, while respected and venerated, is but a member, like any other in the Church of our little land.

But very terrible was the cost – and little Moorton paid a high price. For example four men met for prayer at Midland farm, a mile from the village. They knew the Dragoons were in the area and made plans to flee lest the farmer and his family suffer. But one of their number, an old man named Fergushill took ill and could not go, and the others refused to leave him despite his urging them to do so.

They were all caught – and executed – for praying! The most frequently photographed gravestone was to James White, who likewise was shot while seeking refuge at Little Blackwood farm. To compound their killing, they cut off his head, took it to their camp at Newmilns and played football with it. His epitaph reads:

> This martyr was by Peter Inglis shot;
> By birth a tyger rather than a Scot;
> Who that his monstrous extract might be seen,
> Cut off his head and kicked it o'er the green.
> Thus was that head which was to wear a crown,
> A football made by a profane dragoun.

Most of the Covenanters, as I have said were ordinary men and women, not high born or well to do, though many of the Lairds of the south supported and shielded him. Very few of them had experience of fighting, and indeed it was only after many years that some took up arms, having seen the death of many of their number... and very often a very brutal death.

One who did know the art of war was Captain John Paton, farmer at Meadowhead in Moorton parish, elder of the kirk, but also having seen battle on the continent where he had fought for Gustavus Adolphus, the great Swede, fighting alongside one Dalziel, a professional soldier, and the two men became close friends. But in the Covenanting struggles, Dalziel, by then a General had to fight on the king's side. Late in life Paton was captured and General Dalziel visited Paton in Kilmarnock jail. It was a poignant meeting for the two men had been very close and Dalziel was deeply moved to see his old friend in such a state... and with execution, despite his age, awaiting him. Dalziel however, said to him: "John, if I had met you before you came hither, I should have set you at liberty, but be not afraid, I will write His Majesty for your life."

This he did, a pardon was indeed granted and sent to the Bishop of Edinburgh where Paton was by then being held. But the Bishop kept back the pardon, and only released it after Paton's execution with the statement it had arrived too late, for he was determined such a prize as Paton should die. Despite his advanced years, he was hanged in Edinburgh's Grassmarket, his last act being to hand his Bible to his wife from the scaffold. Strangely, but rather wonderfully, the last few chapters are missing so the last verse is "And they overcame him by the blood of the Lamb, and by the word of their testimony, and they loved not their lives unto death".

There could hardly be a more appropriate description of the faith that kept these men going year after year, constantly seeing many of their companions, men and women, departing by the road of execution, yet refusing to yield and in the end gaining the freedom to worship they sought, and their Lord the crowned King of His Church. It is a long time ago, and I freely acknowledge there were fanatics amongst their number and men who would have fought with their shadow... but they were greatly in the minority. Perhaps we should cherish the freedom they won far, far more than we do. They had, as Burns so aptly put it a century later in his *Epistle to a Young Friend*: "A correspondence fix'd wi' Heaven"... or in Jesus' picture, the house of their lives was built on a rock – the Rock of Ages – the Lord Himself.

There were many, many others in Moorton who paid the price. Often I wandered through the graveyard at dusk and mused on these men and what drove them on. I imagined it would be a gloomy place, perhaps even spooky... but no, there was a peace about it as if those buried there "after life's fitful fever slept well".

There are only two recorded examples of "supernatural" happenings. One was in the night perhaps a century ago when suddenly the kirk bell started ringing. The villagers trembled in their homes... "It must be a warning of some kind." Eventually one brave spark crept to the kirk gate and saw a white figure with horns and a tail pulling the outside bell rope. He fled for his life and spread the news which, if possible, made the villagers even more fearful. It could only be the Devil himself, they reasoned. Only with the morning light did they head for the church in a body to find... a white cow tied to the rope. Some joker had enjoyed the night of his life!

The other instance was in the 1960s. On Guy Fawkes night our boys always had a large bonfire in the manse grounds. They let off fireworks, enjoyed the goodies mum had prepared, they and their friends sizzled sausages, roasted potatoes, had a sing-song and thoroughly enjoyed themselves. But never would they depart till dad had told a ghost story. On one such night my brother Fergus was present, and carrying with him a large white sheet, kept well out of sight. As the children prepared to depart for their homes, he crept into the old graveyard, draped the sheet over him, his intention being to appear over the church wall when the children reached his chosen spot. But no ghost was ever seen. Eventually, with all the children safely away, he came limping out the gate carrying his sheet. Unable to see properly through his ghostly attire he had walked into one of the old horizontal gravestones, supported about two feet off the ground by six legs, and he had given his shin an almighty whack. No doubt a limping "ghost" would have been an innovation, but all ghostly nonsense had been driven out of him, and all he wanted was somehow to bathe or otherwise soothe a badly bruised shin.

But to leave such "happenings" and nonsense behind and return to more worthy matters, and to the seventeenth century, I used to wonder why Moorton should have so many martyrs, and I believe the answer is not hard to seek. The answer lies, I am certain, in Moorton's first minister, William Guthrie. He was not a soldier – he abhorred fighting and killing – a man of peace. But such was the power of his preaching, people walked as far as twenty miles... yes twenty miles, to hear him preach. It was said of him that whether fishing for little brown trout in the burn that flowed past his manse or fishing for black sinners in his parish, Jesus seemed always by his side. Men and women stood in an unheated building, with an earthen floor and no seats, for up to three hours – and they went away with a glow upon them as though they had met with God Himself.

To put it more theologically, he was a man filled with the Holy Spirit, and he carried out his ministry despite almost constant ill health. I have been amazed in reading the lives of many of the saints how many of them struggled with illness or suffered sometimes daily pain; yet they carried out the tasks God had given them. Contrary to what so many people believe is their due, Jesus never promised His followers an easy passage in life – but He did promise He would be with them always to share the load and give needed strength for His tasks.

Guthrie put the fire in the hearts of so many – not a fire for battle, but the strength to hold on till a better day would surely dawn. He had a ministry of almost twenty years in Moorton: unusual considering his Covenanting principles, but he was, in a measure, protected by several of the Lairds of Ayrshire, notably Rowallan, and the king had no wish to antagonise these men in high position.

But he was finally expelled from his pulpit on the orders of the Bishop by the Curate of Calder near Edinburgh, for no Episcopalian nearer would risk carrying out the task on so popular and saintly a man. The Curate received £5 for carrying out his task and was accompanied by twelve Dragoons. Guthrie knew they were coming and preached his final sermon to a vast crowd at six in the morning. When the Judas and his troop arrived, Guthrie gave them a meal then prayed, as his Master had done on the Cross, for their forgiveness. Despite his bodily weakness, Guthrie had pointed hundreds on the pilgrim way. He died not long after his eviction.

With my love of history, I felt singly honoured to preach where such a man had preached and minister in a parish, many of whose inhabitants were direct descendants of Moorton's Covenanters. Ordinary they were, many unable to read or write, but these ancestors had endured unspeakable things because their kingdom, as Jesus put it, was not of this world – but they were sure and steadfast over fifty long years, guided by their "correspondence fix'd wi' Heaven".

In the last year or so of my Moorton ministry, I found myself thrust into a limelight I did not seek. One thing followed another.

First of all Duncan, my treasurer and as I have said a considerable historian, came to me deeply concerned that all the Covenanting relics were about to be sold to an American for £2,000, no mean sum in the sixties. We both felt they should remain in the parish and discussed plans to accomplish this. Since I have spoken of this in detail in my first book, *Vet in the Vestry*, sufficient to say we formed a Trust, with a direct descendant of Captain Paton who lived outwith the parish but enthusiastically joined our little Trust. Lord Rowallan, former Chief Scout and one time Governor of Tasmania agreed to be chairman. So with four of us, the Lochgoin Trust came into being: Lochgoin being a farm right up on the moor, a place of refuge for many a hunted Covenanter, and farmed as tenant farmers for hundreds of years by the Howie family, and they held and claimed the relics as their own.

We raised the money and on a Sunday I will never forget we had first a memorial service in church, followed in the afternoon by a Conventicle, or blanket preaching at Lochgoin on a glorious July afternoon, with 600 people present. At this service beside the large Covenanters' monument, Lord Rowallan handed over the title deeds of the farm, which he owned, to the Trust with the proviso that one room in the farmhouse be kept as a memorial room and museum to house all the relics – articles like Captain Paton's Bible and sword, the Moorton Covenanting banner and many others, where they will permanently reside, and where they are visited each year by hundreds.

The Cameronians were present at both services, which could not begin until the Captain in charge of the detachment marched up to me and said in a loud, clear voice: "Reverend Sir, the pickets are posted, there is no enemy in sight. The service may proceed."

At Lochgoin they marched around the boundaries to "protect" us as they had done at many a Conventicle in the Covenanting struggles. The Cameronians were, of course, the only regiment founded by and named after a religious leader, Richard Cameron, the young "lion of the Covenant" and all down the years in many a battle, they were the only regiment where every man carried a Bible in his kit-bag. This Conventicle and Lord Rowallan's generous gift of a large moorland farm to the Trust gained a great deal of publicity and was followed by me being asked to write an article on Moorton, the Trust and the Covenanters in *Life and Work*, the Church of Scotland magazine.

I was then asked by BBC television to give five half-hour talks on the Covenanters and Cameronians, all the talks to be recorded on the same afternoon without autocue, the moving screen used by most speakers on "the box". This was accomplished in much fear and trembling and I chiefly remember the terrific heat from the lights in the little studio and the father and mother of all headaches I had when I staggered out, for to memorise 2½ hours of lecture taxed me to the limit.

There was also a broadcast radio service, the first ever from Moorton, and in those days when services went out live, I can picture as I write this, the sea of faces in a full church, all along with me watching intently the light fixed to the pulpit, for when it turned red, we were on the air. A broadcast service takes much more preparation than one might imagine. The sermon has to be submitted in advance to the BBC, to make sure the minister is not preaching heresy or party politics. Everything has to be timed to perfection, so the minister's prayers, even the Lord's Prayer timed, the readings, the organist's closing voluntary. There is just no way of correcting a mistake, so all in all, it is something of an ordeal for all taking part. Then for a week or two come the letters from listeners praising, criticising, correcting something that had been said, someone seeking help or who has been helped... so all in all it is quite a marathon, but it put little Moorton on the map once more.

STV asked me to do a week of 5-minute *Reflections* and what I chiefly recall was the autocue, with my script on it, breaking down in the middle of my very first talk leaving me stammering and gulping like a stranded goldfish!

Now while I was glad of the publicity all this gave to Moorton, pleased to be able to say something of our "roots" in Scotland's Kirk, largely unknown by church members, I was really happy most of all being able to "say a good word for Jesus Christ" as a well known minister was advised by his grandmother as he began his ministry. Naturally I was delighted at the formation of the Lochgoin Trust, ably led in recent years by Col Bill Munro, all the other originals except myself being long gone, but I was emphatically *not* glad about an undesired spin off. What was this? Simply that Vacancy Committees, all from large city Churches, regularly turned up at Moorton services and asked me to consider becoming their minister, each group seemingly exceeding the previous one in pointing out the desirability of their church... wonderful choirs, larger stipends, modern manses etc. To all I said a polite but emphatic "Thank you, I'm honoured, but sorry, no." I had applied for no other church, nor had any desire to do so, being very happy, as were my wife and family, with our dear wee Moorton. But it had an unsettling effect on the congregation who treated their visitors to some hearty scowls! It also unsettled us.

But among these approaches was one from a place called Aldermouth in the north of Scotland, a very large church of 1,200 members and 500 adherents. I had only once driven through the place, had never seen church or manse, the stipend was very little more than little Moorton – but for some reason this one would not go from my mind. Again, this has all been detailed in a previous book. Months went by and I did nothing, but one evening a long time after the first approach, I felt a tremendous compulsion that I must phone and find out if the vacancy was filled. In retrospect, I believe it can only have been the working of the Holy Spirit, for I learned later that at the very time I phoned the Interim Moderator, the Aldermouth Vacancy Committee was with him to inform him they were completely divided on the three men who were their short leet. Sufficient to say I was promptly invited to come north in a fortnight and preach in a neighbouring town before their whole committee. I did so with the proviso that even if they found me acceptable, I might decline, for the truth was we were all so happy in Moorton, we had no real wish to move... but there was that wretched niggling in my mind which would not give me peace. However, I did preach, was quickly asked to be the sole nominee, and unanimously voted as their minister (when I preached twice, morning and evening) by the good folks of Aldermouth Old. Even then it took me ten days of struggle, doubts and uncertainty before finally saying "yes" to that inner voice which had given me no rest until the decision to move had been taken. It was not doubt about Aldermouth's people, those I had met being warm and welcoming. It was love... the love many ministers have for their first Charge and its people. It was also a measure of doubt that I was the right man, fitted and gifted enough for what was the biggest Charge in the Highland Region.

However, the upshot of all this was that we did move to another most beautiful church, seeming like a miniature cathedral to me after little Moorton, equally beautiful but in different ways. There were magnificent stained glass windows, particularly the one of the Last Supper, just behind the Communion Table, so that I felt every Communion I took thereafter that the Lord was at the Table. The woodwork was equally as polished as Moorton's by the beadle John, who was to become a very close friend, with never a difference between us in twelve years. The manse was built in the grand manner to match the church and dubbed Culzean Castle by Janet's brother, Alec... not a bad comparison. My sons, very reluctant to move and leave all their football behind, were somewhat placated when they found they had their very own field with goalposts, a field belonging to the manse at the foot of the garden. Truly, as you must have gathered, never was there a minister more reluctant to obey a Call, but soon the welcome as I got round the homes, the challenge and the sheer busy-ness of an enormous church for which for quite a number of years I had no assistance of any kind kept me from pining for past things. I had been launched on what were to prove the most hectic years of my life, busy, but happy, among kind folk.

I was comforted in the decision I had made by a little poem which really summed up my move.

> I heard His voice... "Come, follow"... that was all;
> Earth's joys grew dim, my soul went after Him.
> Will you not answer if you hear His Call?

I never ceased to be amazed that such a large church should call someone so ordinary as me – a vet, would you believe! Queer the kind of folk God calls to do His work. But then, Jesus had chosen very ordinary men too – fishermen, tax collectors – folk like that. He Himself had been a carpenter, with no university Degree or high position. Amos in the Old Testament had been a herdsman, and as loathe as me to go where God wanted him. The greatest king of Israel, held to this day in higher esteem than anyone else by the Jews, had been a shepherd boy, with a very mottled career in his private life.

So maybe it wasn't so very different for whoever was called in our day, whatever the congregation or whatever task He wanted them to carry out... for all, high born and humble, rich or poor, black or white need the same gospel of Redeeming Love. I had simply been entrusted to preach it to my new "family" at Aldermouth, and large though the family was, I, in time felt we *were* one large family with, in addition to the 1,700 on the Roll, 300 young people in Sunday Schools, Bible Class, Youth Fellowship, plus the uniformed organisations; in time a Playgroup and Mother and Toddlers Group – in fact twenty-two different departments in the church. As the years passed, I felt we all grew closer and the sense of belonging together increased, and it was a tremendous thrill to me every Sunday to climb the pulpit stairs in fear and trembling and look out at a vast crowd... but a family, His family, ably led and guided by the real strength of the Church, a kirk session of 70 elders.

Yes – hard years for me – but privileged years, for not every minister gets the support I received and sees the hand of God at work in many lives. Thank you, Aldermouth. It was and is my prayer that somehow in my efforts folks would find "a correspondence fix'd wi' Heaven".

TEN

The Real Person

It is surprising just how many things one can see from a pulpit. For instance, at the start of the sermon, I have often seen the Pan Drops being passed along the pew. I don't mind in the least except that I am not included! What I do object to a mite is when a paper poke containing caramels, each one having to be unwrapped with a rustle is used instead of a pan drop or boiling. I have seen many a wee lad or lass getting a skelp from mother to encourage good behaviour while the minister is speaking. Many a time I have seen a young fellow cast adoring eyes at a lass in a neighbouring pew, or noticed one of the choir members pondering deeply who the new man in the congregation can be... and wonder whether he's married!

Once, when but a lad in Bank Church, New Cumnock, where I grew up, and which church we all attended from an early age, I was startled... and delighted to hear the minister explode and say, "Would the young man tickling the young lady in the back pew kindly leave her alone and turn to me instead!"

These were the days when worship was a very solemn business, there was never a laugh, and many of the congregation seemed to feel that a church face was a very solemn one. I got a poke whenever I crossed my legs, so that momentous day when I exploded in laughter, and the whole congregation seemed to have stopped breathing, I earned a good slap, and lecture when we got home. I suppose it all comes under the general heading of eye contact which was deemed all important in our training at Divinity College. They used to teach us "when preaching, maintain eye contact with your congregation. You will be wise to have your notes at the pulpit, but look at your congregation as much as possible".

Sometimes you look out at blank or bored faces. Frequently you see somebody having a peep at his watch (you only really worry when he starts to shake it!). Sometimes there are frowns from folk who obviously don't agree with you. But always in every church where I have been minister, I have found someone smiling encouragement and registering joy – and what a lift this is to any speaker. As well as my wife, who prayed me through every service I took – what a boon! – there has been at least one other of the audience who has spurred me on with a smile. In my first Charge at Moorton, a lady called Mrs Mack, right in the middle of the congregation, always had a cheerful smile.

I am sure nearly everybody, in Scotland at least, knows Mrs Mack. She was the old minister's housekeeper in the very long running and highly entertaining serial of STV *Take the High Road.* She plays the part of a sour faced individual – nosey, gossipy, critical, self-righteous with a great selection of ridiculous hats – and has been throughout the years without doubt the most disliked individual in Glendarroch.

Yet that is the woman who cheered me, for in real life she is Gwyneth Guthrie and the complete opposite of Mrs Mack. She was always in her place in church, always with that delightful, encouraging smile on her face – a smile that came from deep down, for Gwyneth's faith was a very real and joyful thing to her. Furthermore, she was our next door neighbour and sometimes would pop in for a chat. She was a wife and mother, and her family and ours were young together. She was, and I am sure still is, a real livewire, full of the joy of living, bright, mischievous, a tomboyish lass ready to tackle anything. I remember one day driving home to find Gwyneth at the top of a ladder trying to open one of our upstairs bedroom windows, wile my wife Janet steadied the long ladder at the bottom. I got out of the car and stared, wondering what was going on. I was informed I had gone off with the key of the manse, and the women were trying to get in the only window which was slightly open. The whole scenario ended with a blushing minister and girls hilarious at the bottom.

That is the real Mrs Mack, and for Gwyneth to play the part of someone the complete opposite of herself is a piece of superb acting year after year, in all sorts of situations. You can never be sure that what you see, particularly first impressions, is the real person. There may be a lot more to them than you think.

Also at Moorton half way though my stay there, we engaged a young lad of about sixteen to play our Hammond organ. He was called John Bell, a very fine organist. But he was a child of the sixties, a bit of a rebel with long hair and the like after the fashion of the teenagers of the time. I was, when he arrived, putting on a concert with the children, a very popular annual affair, and I had been playing the piano for them and trying to put together the show. I was glad to let John take over at the piano, for I am sure my piano playing curled his hair, as I felt my sermons also did. From the beginning it was evident that John was a young man of considerable talent, and in time he took a degree in music, but followed this up with a Divinity course, feeling a real call to the ministry, much of the seed being sown, I am sure by Colin Bell, at that time in a Kilmarnock Charge. John was a natural leader, and eventually won the election to be Rector of Glasgow University, normally a post held by some notable from the world of politics or entertainment, and I believe John was the first student to be elected.

By then we had moved on to Aldermouth, and out of the blue arrived a letter enclosing two tickets for his installation as Rector, and a long letter which I deeply cherished, for in it he said I would never know how much my preaching had meant to him, and the effect it had been on his life... and I had been thinking the very opposite. We were not able to attend his installation, but over the years he has come to see us and I am proud to number him among my friends.

On becoming a minister, John was given a very run down church in Glasgow – and by the power of the Holy Spirit and his own natural rapport with the teenagers few ministers can reach, he breathed new life into it. He had become a member of the Iona Community, and there his love of music blossomed. He founded *The Wild Goose Worship* group – not like modern groups one sees – but a group which depended not on flashing lights, every musical instrument one can imagine, and an abundance of noise... but men and women, usually unaccompanied by any instrument, singing in perfect harmony and great beauty, on television, and the tapes they made. John does not in any way disparage the use of any instrument in the praise of God (like the Psalmist long before him) and he is, as I have indicated, a quite brilliant organist.

The Church of Scotland began to sit up and take notice of this young man, and the Panel on Worship, after they had got over the shock of his appearance (for to his long hair he has added a beard and wears a large cross round his neck which rather shook the traditional minister in black and who favoured (like me) the short back and sides hairstyle), and he became in great demand to speak and demonstrate all types of music to a dozen, or a large audience on television. He is, in fact a workaholic in the Lord's service and has paid a price, having a coronary in his thirties. In due course the Church of Scotland Panel on Worship commissioned him to create a song book of sacred music to supplement the normal hymnary, a book for our age, but which does not eschew the Victorian hymns, and so *Songs of God's People* was born, and is being widely used to speak to today's generation, many of the contents having been written by John himself, for hundreds of new hymns have flowed from his pen, many of the words, sometimes the tunes written by others, or folk songs from round the world providing the music. John is very much a Church of Scotland minister, but is completely ecumenical, his book in his own words being "a tribute to the diversity of the Church", and as I write this, before me is a recent letter in which he casually mentions he is shortly off to Australia to a fortnight's conference of Roman Catholics. John Bell is the leading exponent of sacred music in our land today, is an organist extraordinaire, and behind the outer man which startles the traditionalists is a man of deep faith and joy in his faith in Christ. Throughout his rise to now worldwide fame, he has remained a very ordinary man who still speaks with his broad Ayrshire accent, and is a man of deep humility whom God is using for the good of the worldwide Church, whatever denomination, for in the end of the day titles won't matter a lot to God, who has given John his gifts, as to each of His children.

The real person, as I have tried to show, may be very different from the outward appearance. It has been ever so. The folk of Blantyre a century ago saw a very ordinary lad working at a mill... but the Lord saw one who could become a doctor, minister, and fierce combatant of slavery in the dark continent of Africa, and David Livingstone became His man. People saw in a young Pharisee away back in the first century a man who kept the letter of the Jewish law and was a fanatic in his hatred of these pestilential Christians – a man to be feared but Jesus saw one who, if converted, turned around, could spread the gospel of redeeming love to all mankind, so Saul of Tarsus became Paul, the greatest missionary ever who exclaimed with deep conviction "for me to live is Christ". A few years earlier, when the human Jesus walked the earth he saw a man called Andrew, an ordinary, perhaps dull kind of man, as ordinary as anybody can be, a fisherman to trade, yet Jesus made him his first disciple and he is the only one who is the patron saint of three countries.

I said Jesus saw people's potential. It should be *sees*... for He knows you and me, the real us, whatever we may think of ourselves or others see in us, and calls us to be lights in this dark world, like Gwyneth Guthrie, and not folk – sometimes in the name of religion, who put out the light – like Mrs Mack. In fact He gave us all the same commission – "Let your light shine before men that they may see your good works and glorify your Father which is in Heaven."

ELEVEN

A Chat with a Friend

It was half time in the match at our local football ground, and it being one of the few Saturdays I didn't have a wedding, I had gone to see how our local team, the County, would fare against the champions, Caley. I had another interest too, for one of our sons, aged 16, was playing for the County, something two of his brothers subsequently were to do, sometimes having also played for the school team in the morning. In short, I was a proud father. Near me were two men, obviously friends, and I couldn't help but hear their conversation. It appeared one of them had been almost involved in a car accident, and he recounted to his pal... "You ken, Willie, it was sic a near thing, I gey nearly prayed!" His companion was clearly surprised and enquired, "Do you believe in prayer, Andy?" Andy thought for a bit, then said "I'm no richt sure but I'll tell you somebody who did, and it seemed to help him, and it was to him jist like ordinary talking... nae special words an' a' that kind o' thing." Willie enquired who this "natural" prayer was and was told "Eric".

This made me prick up my ears, and made me feel both sad and proud, for Eric, as well as being a friend, was one of my elders. When I first approached this humble man to accept the eldership, I remembered how he had declined, not feeling good enough. But to my delight, two years later he had agreed to be ordained as an elder. Eric was one of many fine men I was fortunate to have in my Kirk Session composed of 70 elders. He was one of the best known men in the town, and it was but recently I had buried him at the age of 53. Already I was missing his support, his laugh, his down to earth suggestions for the church he loved and his wholehearted involvement in everything from our church concerts when every organisation took part, to his unashamed talk on "My faith and Sport" at one of our weekend conferences for all the elders when we talked, worked, played and prayed together. Our loss as a church was great... but not to be compared with the sorrow his wife May and son Brian were knowing. Their home had always been a sheer delight to enter, the welcome warm and sincere – and the comments of the two men at the football match were more evidence, if any were needed, of the witness to his faith in his Master which clearly shone out to others. Yes, Eric would be a tremendous loss to our church... and indeed to the whole town where he served as superintendent of the graveyard, and always his compassion and concern for the mourners, while not showy, was very real, deep and sincere.

Will Shakespeare wrote: "The evil that men do lives after them, the good is oft interred with their bones", but for once the bard of Avon is not wholly right. The good often *does* live on, in a variety of ways, not least in lives touched, influenced and sometimes completely changed by the example and encouragement of a good man or woman.

Our church of Aldermouth Old is huge, but also very beautiful. On only a few occasions did I see it full to its 1,000 capacity; but one of them was Eric's funeral, for everyone in Aldermouth knew him, and all involved in north soccer were represented. The papers paid their tribute: "He was one of north soccer's true gentlemen"; "He never had a harsh word to say for anyone... even a referee who had given a doubtful penalty against his team in the last minute!"; "He always seemed to find good somewhere in everyone".

The referee supervisor said to me after the funeral, "When Eric is there, we know there will be a welcome, everything will be prepared, and rarely will there be trouble on or off the field."

He served Aldermouth County all his life as player, captain, trainer, committee man and coach and in his twenty years in the latter capacity he gave a start to many a young player in Scotland's national game. Many, in time, would leave for a bigger team and bigger wage, but they could not leave behind the influence of this good man, who for twenty years produced team after team whom he taught (another old fashioned phrase) "to play the game". If any player was a bad influence on the team, or a player was responsible for dirty play or dirty language, Eric would try might and main to change them, without waving a big stick, but if he felt a man was a continued wrong un, even if the star of the team, Eric with great reluctance would release him.

Wherein lay his secret, that held him firm in winning or losing, and in the last cruel months of disease, when he never lost his smile or concern for others? The answer is simple. He had his rule book, the word of God... he had a wonderfully happy home and he had a Companion with whom he would have a chat regularly, his great Friend and Captain. I thought as I made my way home to the manse, my spirits high, that Eric would have been proud of his team that day, for they had beaten the mighty Caley with a goal in the last minute. I was proud too, for my laddie had scored it – a dream finish.

As I sat in the study in the evening, mulling over my sermons for the next day, I found my mind wandering off to the conversation I had heard between the two men on prayer and my mind dwelt on the subject for a time. I thought of a recent census which, while showing church membership continued to fall, the vast majority of Scots not only believed in God, but believed in prayer. Of course for most of us prayer is reserved for the times we are up against it and need help... and there came to mind a story Andrew and Nan Archibald, our close friends, had told us of a certain crofter called, of course, Angus.

Normally Angus was a cheery soul, but one day in his west highland village when the minister met him, Angus was anything but a ray of sunshine. The minister enquired what was wrong and Angus replied, "Och, minister... 'tis the factor. He says I haf to be out of my croft in a fortnight – chust two weeks! Och, 'tis terrible awful, for my father and grandfather farmed that croft all their lives and I haf nowhere to go. Ach, yes, 'tis just the ferry worst thing that could have happened, and me up to date with the rent."

The minister tried to console his downcast member and suggested Angus should try prayer. Angus mournfully said, "I suppose it has come to that... yes indeed, minister."

A week later the men happened to meet again – a very different Angus this time, face wreathed in smiles. He just bubbled over before the minister could say a word. "Och minister, that prayer iss a wonderful thing, yes indeed. The Lord's the poy, the factor's deid!"

Somehow I don't think that was God's way of answering prayer!

But of course it is only natural in a time of stress or worry to tell

God about it, and even if we hardly ever pray at other times, we have Jesus' assurance that no prayer goes unheard by our great Father, though the answer is not always what we expect or desire. Joseph Scriven was an Irishman who emigrated to Canada and on the night before his wedding, his fiancé was tragically killed. Scriven, naturally, was desolate with sorrow, but in time wrote a hymn which has comforted many, so far as we know the only one he ever wrote:

> What a friend we have in Jesus; all our sins and griefs to bear;
> What a privilege to carry, everything to God in prayer!
> Are we weak and heavy laden, cumbered with a load of care?
> Jesus only is our refuge, take it to the Lord in prayer.

I know very well, after a lifetime as a minister, praying with and for people, that often the answer is different from what we want, and indeed sometimes as a parent to a child, the answer may be "No" or "Not now". There are great depths in prayer, and often we will not know why we did not get what we wanted, until we meet God face to face... and really if we have chosen to live our lives, and make our decisions all along the way ourselves, is it not a bit presumptuous to expect God to give us the answer we want *when* we want? But often, because His name is love, He does.

Hugh Redwood, a preacher and writer of many years ago tells a true story of a wee boy called Alfie who lived with his widowed mother in a poor London house. The day came when Alfie's only pair of boots were done beyond repair and his mother, too ashamed to send him to school in his bare feet, was worried sick about what to do. Seeing this, wee Alfie said "Don't worry, Ma, I'll tell Jesus about it". So, saying his prayers as he went to bed, the wee lad asked please for a pair of boots of a certain size, and went to bed, confident his needs would be met. Now believe it or not, or call it coincidence, later that evening a neighbour knocked at the door, handed in a parcel and said "I don't know what took me tonight, but I felt I must clean out a cupboard and I came on these boots. They're too small for my Billy and he scarcely wore them. Maybe you could use them?"

Well, couldn't she just! She took them, thanked her neighbour and laid the boots at the foot of Alfie's bed. In the morning, there was a great shout, just like on Christmas day: "Ma, they've come. They fit, and there isn't even a hole in the roof!"

Piffle! Rubbish! Some of you might say. I can only repeat, it happened – and such things have happened in many lives. The story of the Muller children's homes in Bristol has many instances when they were down to their last bag of flour… and one came. Of course these "miracles" happen through other people, but that is usually the way God works His miracles and Jesus made it quite clear that we were no Christians if we did not care for others as ourselves.

But if our prayers stay on the level of just asking God for something for ourselves, we miss much of the richness of true prayer. For a start it is a two way thing, and just as a couple grow closer together in a happy marriage, as it is meant to be, until the partners often know what the other is thinking without words being spoken, so with real prayer. It is a chat with a friend, and as the years go by, we grow ever closer, so that often no words are needed.

I remember Tom Allan, who worked himself to death for his congregation in The Tron, Glasgow and also for the waifs and wanderers round the all night coffee bars, almost inevitably taking a heart attack while still in his forties. He was probably the best known minister in Scotland at the time, with a large column in the *Evening Citizen* every Saturday. After his recovery he was interviewed and asked: "Mr Allan. We all know you nearly died. Could you tell us what you felt at that time?"

Tom thought a bit, smiled, and said to the newsman: "John, I was too weak to pick up my Bible… I felt too weak even to pray, but truly I have never felt Jesus nearer to me, and I was able to chat to Him without actually forming a word. Strange as it may seem, my feeling was one of deep joy."

I understand… I can vouch for Tom's experience. For in several visits to Intensive Care and Cardiac Care units as a patient, where, despite the magnificent care of these units, I was experiencing severe pain and utter weakness, I could feel the presence of Jesus in a very deep and real way, without any spoken words of prayer. As the hymn puts it: "Be still, for the presence of the Lord is moving in this place".

But the illustration of His nearness I like best concerns a wee Glasgow laddie, who in the hungry thirties worked in a shipyard. Every day in their half hour lunch break, he would eat the "piece" his mother had prepared, then disappear. His mates followed him one day out of curiosity – to a church – where Jimmy sat down in the quietness then said, "Jesus, it's Jimmy." That was all. He had a hard time of it afterwards, was called a "Holy Willie" and much more. But still he went.

One day there was an accident in the shipyard and the Chaplain was informed one of the men was badly hurt and in a certain hospital. He hurried there and found – as you have no doubt guessed – it was wee Jimmy. The boy was unconscious and clearly had not long to live, so the Chaplain took his hand, and silently in prayer, sat beside Jimmy. That Chaplain said afterwards, with absolute certainty and not a shadow of a doubt, that just as Jimmy died he heard a voice say, with all the tenderness of the world in it, "Jimmy! – It's Jesus".

A sob story, you think? Imagination… unreal? Not so, for in nearly a lifetime's ministry, while not having experienced exactly that, I have seen and heard similar things.

Prayer – yes it's for real, and a tremendous gift to all who trust and know the mighty God who is also the suffering Saviour, and one day will be the reigning King. Yes, a generous gift that wherever we are or how hard our lot, we can, ALWAYS have a chat with our Friend.

TWELVE

One of These Days

It began with a scurrilous anonymous letter (oh, yes, ministers get them) which I read through three times, examined my conscience carefully, then quite certain that all the accusations were false, put it where it belonged – in the bin. Then Jocky staggered in.

Jocky was an alcoholic and we had succeeded, through virtually daily, long visits to the manse, in keeping him "dry" for three months, but evidently he had been drinking again most of the night, was at the weeping, sorry for himself stage and remorseful, pleading with me to take him to the mental hospital where he had been many times before. I took him, handed him over, then on the way home the exhaust fell off my car, and then... but you don't want to hear any more of me. I am sure everybody knows what I mean – we all get days like that.

In the evening I sat back in my study chair and reviewed the day, wondering when last so many things had fallen unexpectedly out of a cloudless sky.

I must have dozed a bit, for I realised I was smiling at some events in my vet years at Bristacombe which I could laugh at now, but at the time had seemed an unmitigated disaster. It was my early years at Bristacombe with Kenneth as my senior partner; it was August and he, Susan and the three boys had gone off on holiday and I was holding the fort alone. The practice, which fairly rapidly was to give a good living to five vets, was still at the growing, early stage with just the two of us. There was also at that time Mrs Drury, our secretary, receptionist, bookkeeper, anaesthetist and general factotum who was worth her weight in gold. Normally she worked until 5.30 when my wife took over the phone calls at our home, but that day she was to be away until 7.30, and Mrs Drury had offered to stay on till then and give me a hand with evening consulting hour. The practice, even then, was far too much for one vet, but since August was usually a quiet month on the farms, one man working flat out could get by for a fortnight.

I remember I came into the office whistling, for it had been a satisfying day: all my patients were improving, we had gained another large new client who seemed well satisfied. Veterinary practice was then, as now, private, so one had always to be on one's toes, not only and primarily for the animals' sakes, but also to keep the owners happy. That day had also been one of blue skies, when the narrow, winding Devon lanes were a delight to drive along. In short, I was at peace with the world, totally unaware that the sky was about to fall in on me!

I noticed the waiting room as I passed it, was full of people with all kinds of animals, said "First please" as I put on my white coat, and went into the surgery where, to my surprise I found a parrot in its cage sitting on our bench.

"That's Sam," said Mrs Dru, "his nails need cutting and his owner is collecting him later."

The first customer was a middle aged lady bearing a cat basket. She introduced herself as Miss Fotheringham and put the basket on the table. "It's my Siamese cat" she said, as I opened the lid and immediately something flew over my shoulder and landed on the bench beside the parrot.

"Have a banana" invited Sam, being a perfect gentleman.

Now I don't know if you are acquainted with Siamese cats, but some of them are a bit highly strung and indeed pretty wild, and this certainly proved to be wild with a capital "W". It appeared as if it had been a circus performer, for it leapt for our highest shelf and ran along it, cascading bottles and boxes in every direction. Both Mrs Drury and I jumped for it, but it dodged us and started on the next shelf, and hundreds of mixed up pills went rolling over the floor. Mrs Fotheringham retreated into a corner, wringing her hands and repeating a kind of litany which when something like this: "Oh darling puss, Mummy's here! Oh dear, dearie, dearie me. Isn't it a mischief! Do be gentle with it. I'm sure it's that dreadful bird that's frightening it. Poor, poor darling. Oh, please be more gentle with the poor little thing…" over and over again as Mrs Dru and I stalked the little darling round the room.

Then the lady gave a scream "Oh, you're frightening it!" which seemed to be the signal for the cat to start its demolition work on the next shelf. In the midst of this bedlam the parrot's cage was knocked over and Sam flew round and round the room, and Mrs Dru and I vainly tried to capture the now two escapees.

Just then the door opened and the head of Mr Gomes, the minister, appeared round the door. "Could I have a word with you, Alec?" but as he spoke his hat was whisked from his head by a zooming parrot. The minister peered at the chaos, then calling, "I see you're busy... I'll give you a ring" he made a rapid escape and the chase went on.

Sam was obviously impressed by the cat's demolition ability, perched on the curtain rails and said, "Cor swab the decks" followed by a bout of high pitched, hilarious laughter, while Miss Fotheringham besought us to be gentle with her little darling. I couldn't see how we could ever catch that acrobatic feline, but saw a slight chance with Sam, reached to the curtain rails, was soundly pecked but hung on to him and got him back in his cage.

Just then Mrs Drury's voice said "I've got two legs!"

I thought it an odd time to talk about her anatomy, but said "Yes, I've noticed and very nice they are."

"No, I mean the cat's legs," she corrected me, so I hastened to her aid, and though not recommended in the best books, I grabbed the cat by the scruff, and between us we bundled it back into its basket and firmly closed the lid. Phew!

Mrs Drury and I stood gasping for a few minutes for we'd had a hectic time. Miss Fotheringham came out of her corner, still wringing her hands and obviously far from pleased with us, while I looked at the massive ruin of our stocks of drugs, scattered, crushed, mixed up all over the floor. Sam was also shaken and clearly impressed with the cat's ability to create chaos and kept saying "Cor! Shiver me timbers! Swab the decks!"

Finally I turned to the lady and asked, "What exactly is wrong with your cat?"

She enlightened me "Oh, I've just got it and I wanted to know if it is a boy or a girl. You see, I'm getting another next week for company, and I wanted to get a suitable companion."

So all that earthquake had been to sex a cat! I was not amused, but carefully had a peep in the basket and said "Female", and put the lid on – tight!

"How much is your fee?" asked the lady.

It should have been at least fifty pounds, but I wearily pronounced "Seven and sixpence".

"Really. I am surprised!"

Looking again at the debris, so was I.

"No, I'm sorry, I made a mistake... ten and sixpence."

I received a most un-ladylike glare, but she paid up, reluctantly, apparently quite oblivious to the ruins of our practice, the scratch on my cheek and on Mrs Drury's hand, and the feathers floating everywhere.

"When can I bring the other?" asked the lady.

I thought quickly, "Next Thursday evening. That's our sexing day!"

It was also my half day and Ken would be back. I thought I should not deprive him of some fun! When the maiden lady and her "gentle" companion departed, I looked at our pretty secretary and said, quite innocently, "I didn't know sex could be such a problem!"

She blushed, looked down and said demurely "Not in our house".

I was saved by the bell... the telephone ringing in the waiting room where Mrs Drury's desk was situated. I went to answer it, and noticed to my surprise that all our other waiting customers had disappeared. Clearly the apparent methods of this vet which include crashes, thuds and screeches from the patients had driven them off in a body! The phone call was from Skinner, our roughest farmer, twenty miles away on Exmoor... a calving case. I did not normally like going there, but when I thought of the mess and confusion next door, I felt better towards Mr Skinner.

"Er... Mrs Dru... I'm afraid I have to go out... an urgent calving case. I'm sorry to have to leave you with this mess; can you manage?" (If I had known about Commercial Union then who don't make a drama out of a crisis, I would have been on to them!) But our gallant helper was her unflappable self again.

"Of course I'll manage, Mr Cameron... but perhaps you could wash your face before you go out, and take the feathers from your hair!"

I was halfway out the door when I remembered Sam. It would only take a few minutes to clip his claws, so to the accompaniment of screeches and expressions no man should use before a lady, for our parrot obviously did not appreciate chiropody, the job was done, when, presumably to show there were no ill feelings, he said "Have a nut!"

My trip to Exmoor was in a perfect summer evening and I eventually managed to shut out of my mind the slapstick farce I had been in, and think ahead to the calving. Skinner rarely sent for us, then only when he was stuck and usually too late. It would not be an easy calving, something, when reasonable, I normally enjoyed. Sure enough I found the cow had been in labour for hours. There was a bucket of cold water in a corner, and something hard in it, which proved to be the soap, which must have been in the family a very long time. So, after putting on my calving coat, I put plenty of antiseptic in the water and smeared my arms with obstetric cream, for the soap was lather-less. An examination of the cow revealed a tail and the rear end of the calf... a breech presentation with legs down.

"Why didn't you send for us earlier?" I demanded. "It's a breech, and after all this time the calf is almost certainly dead." (You had to deliver a breech presentation quickly for the calf gets suffocated in the uterine fluids.) Skinner just grunted, which could have meant anything, but after getting the hind legs of the calf into position, my calving chains put on, between us we pulled the calf out, while the poor cow bellowed and Skinner swore. It was a big day for animal noises of all kinds! Sure enough, it seemed the calf was dead. I tried artificial respiration, mouth to mouth resuscitation, to no avail. So I used an old method of reviving an apparently dead calf – I went out into the yard and swung the little animal round and round my head, but my arms were slippery and it flew out of them, skidding on its side up the yard, and when I got to it, it was breathing! It seemed in keeping with the slapstick of the evening that the little calf was saved in this way... and I probably broke the "hurling the calf" record!

Finally I reached home very late and had a dinner which Janet had been keeping in the oven for hours... but it tasted just grand, and I ate it, punctuated by chuckles and gulps as I thought of my activities from teatime onward. Janet wondered what it was all about but I thought she would never believe the madness of the last few hours, not at all what the vet books recommended.

"You've got a big scratch on your cheek" she suddenly noticed.

"Mrs Drury's got one too" I replied.

"How did they happen?" she queried.

"Sex... just sex" I said with a twinkle.

"Wh...what? Tell me."

"I'm too tired to explain tonight, lass" I yawned.

She stared at me, then spotted the twinkle in my eyes, and knowing that things then and all our lives have been absolutely true and straight between us, she laughed and said "Oh you!", but still threw a dishcloth at me as I headed for stairs and bed.

Yes. One of these days!

THIRTEEN

The Right Kind of Medicine

I visited my old friend Henry Dow today in the nursing home which will probably be his final earthly abode, for Henry is very frail in body, and particularly mind. His wife Nanna and daughter Anne were there as they are most days, and sometimes his grandchildren also come to see him. He seemed too tired and weary to even bother to listen and often he would fall asleep in the middle of a conversation. Sometimes he gets very down in spirits, and who can blame him after years of progressive illness. This is the unlovely side of advancing old age, and Henry is nearer 90 than 80.

Over the years we have had good times together on the golf course and many a Sunday evening, I would visit Henry and Nanna, for my sake as well as theirs. For, at the end of a heavy Sunday, many a minister is down and drained, and in their company and conversation I would have my batteries recharged, and before I left their bungalow home, we always had a wee prayer.

Those of you who have read this book so far or any of my other writings will know the importance of prayer to me... its power and the peace it can bring. But sometimes there is better medicine for the body, mind and spirit. I know, for I have been so to speak, on the receiving end.

I recall one particular stay in hospital. I was fairly ill and had just come out of the intensive care unit, and felt as weak as a new born kitten. I'd had three ministerial colleagues visit me in quick succession that particular day, who wisely, seeing how weak I was, stayed but a short time, and left me with a smile and a blessing. Then came pastor number four, a colleague very new to the ministry. Clearly he felt by the look of me I hadn't long for this world (which was not so) and clearly he also felt he should give me the whole works!

He began by drawing the screens around me (although I was in a single room). "Gosh." I thought, "I must be gey bad".

Then he said "We will have a passage from the Word of God" and we did. It probably wasn't Psalm 119 which has 176 verses in it, but it must have been a close rival, and long before the end I was mentally gasping for air! Then he said "We will pray"... and he did, rivalling the reading for length and praying that "Thy servant will be restored, or if it is not Thy will, grant him a peaceful passing."

Now there is nothing wrong with the theory of all this, but a great deal wrong in the practice. The result of a ministerial visit, like the visit of a good, human and humble doctor, should be to leave the patient happier and uplifted. In the instance I have just related purely as an example, I was infinitely worse than when, with no doubt the best intentions, that pastor had come.

My visitor had not long gone when I heard the voice of another minister speaking to a nurse as he came along the corridor... so I pretended to be asleep... and escaped!

So there was no prayer today, but in the circumstances, a better medicine. Henry appeared to be sleeping but at the word "Stilboestrol" which Anne, for some reason said, Henry's eyes opened, life came into his face and he was on our wavelength. You see, Stilboestrol is the name of a medicine used by doctors and vets – and Henry had been a pharmacist and optician, and no doubt prescribed that drug many times.

It brought back to me a story (which I just briefly mentioned in a previous book) and I thought the story might cheer Henry up, so told him of this incident from my vet days at Bristacombe.

One evening, just as I was finishing my consulting hour, a man called Bert Richardson walked in with his beautiful English Setter on the leash. The dog was in fact the only English Setter in the town, highly pedigreed, good natured, and the "family" of Bert and his wife for they had no children, and doted on their really lovely bitch all the more. Bert was a very likeable man, but unfortunately had the worst stammer I have ever known. Bert that night was in a fair old state and I wondered what had happened to make him seem to me to be in danger of taking a fit, particularly as Sheila, his bitch, seemed at a glance to be alright.

"I've c...c...c...come from a t...t...t..."

"Your tea?" I suggested.

"No a t...t...t...taxi."

"You've come from a taxi, Bert, but what's wrong with Sheila?"

"I've b...b...b...been t...t...to ex...ex..."

"Exercise her?" I queried, trying to be helpful, for a conversation with Bert could be a pretty lengthy affair.

"No. You see, I want her t...t...t...to have p...p...p."

"Pills?" I suggested.

Impatiently Bert shook his head. "Pu...pu...pu...pups."

"Ah, you want to breed from her. Of course, for she's a beauty, but there's no English Setter dog in Bristacombe"

"No, but there is in...". Here he stuck completely.

I could see us being there all night so suggested "Barnstaple".

Bert shook his head, and I was getting anxious, for I had never seen him as bad as this. His face was purple. So I tried "Braunton?" Impatiently the poor man shook his head. I suggested "Bideford" but that only produced another impatient shake.

"You don't mean Exeter surely!" Exeter was 60 miles way, but eagerly Bert nodded his head. "Bert. Did you take Sheila all the way to Exeter in a taxi?"

He nodded miserably. "Th...th... there's a Crufts' prizewinner there – a real smasher. J...j...j...just r...r...right for Sheila."

"Good for you, Bert, but that would cost you a pretty penny for a taxi and mating fee."

Here he really did froth at the mouth, so I made him sit down, while the lady of the hour curled up at his feet. After a pause he went on, "Sh...Sh...Sh...Sheila w...w...w...wouldn't mate."

"You mean you've been all the way to Exeter to a dog, waited for hours while the meter was going, and Sheila wouldn't take the dog?"

He nodded miserably, then continued with a woebegone look on his face. "B...b...b...b...but that's n...n...n...not all."

"There's more to come, is there?" Again there was a miserable nod.

"When I was p...p...p..." He stuck completely and took out his wallet. I cottoned on.

"Oh! Paying... what, the dog's owner?" He shook his head. "The taxi driver, then?" Bert nodded. "What happened when you were paying the taxi driver?"

"I let go of Sheila's lead j...j...just for a minute and when I t...t...t...turned".

Here I was really afraid he was going to have a convulsion for his face got so red, and he ruffled his hair.

"When you what?" I probed.

"Turned round and she was being mated by Jasper…"

It came out in a rush, understandably, for Jasper was the scaliest, roughest mongrel in town, with so many different strands in his mongrel heritage, it was not possible to say what kind of dog he was – except most certainly not an appropriate "husband" for a gorgeous English Setter. Whenever a bitch was in season, you could be sure Jasper would be paying a call, and despite his rough appearance and wandering habits there was a likeable bit about him and like many mongrels, was highly intelligent, and never far away when there was a "desirable" lady!

As I listened to this disastrous story from Bert, I almost choked myself not to burst out laughing. One hundred and twenty miles round trip to a dog high in the aristocratic world, Sheila had turned up her nose at him and in a flash mated with the roughest dog in town. Bert was looking very woebegone as if the world had come to an end, and I wished there had been a bottle of brandy in the surgery, but there was not. So he had to make do with a glass of water as he sat slumped in the chair.

I clapped him on the shoulder and said to the poor man: "Don't worry, Bert, there's no harm done. I'll give her an injection of Stilboestrol and there will be no Heinz pups, no miniature Jaspers going about."

His face cleared, but he was clearly not sure and asked "C…c…can you g…g…g…guarantee the stuff will work?"

"One hundred percent certain, Bert. And no damage done to her, so next time she comes into heat in six months or so, you can try again. From what you've told me, Bertie my lad, you'll need that time anyway to save up for another trip to another dog. Don't worry… away and have your tea. So he departed, mopping his brow, as I mopped mine too, but knew that the Stilboestrol injection would do its job.

At the end of the story, Henry's face relaxed, there was a smile as he pictured the scene of the two dogs – and then he laughed – and I hadn't seen Henry laugh for many months, and for a time he was transported to a different world to that around him.

Good, clean, wholesome laughter is worth much… indeed a gift from God, and you know, I kind of think the good Lord prefers a smile in His house than a deadpan, glum face. In fact, I feel that a real funny man like Tommy Cooper or Norman Wisdom in their day, and these three worthies on the TV in *Last of the Summer Wine* do more good at times for "down" persons buffeted by life's storms than those of us who wear dog collars.

Nobody in the Bible had more disasters, and knew just about every calamity he could have, but Job ups and says: "God has filled my soul with laughing."

There is a time for prayer – and a time for laughter – and both are good, effective medicine.

FOURTEEN

Persistent Lawbreaker

For many years I have regularly broken the law... and I'm not in the least repentant.

Oh, I'm not talking about the parking tickets I have had, or the occasion I was booked for speeding, though that one took a bit of time to live down. We were living at Kilmarton at the time where I was acting as student pastor in the Laigh Kirk and each day motored to Trinity College in Glasgow. That morning I had been late getting away for two of the children were poorly and I'd had to take them to the doctor. I was anxious to be at Trinity in time for it was the last day of term when we had communion, and being very hard up, seemingly, for candidates, I had been voted president of the Divinity Students' Council (the DSC) so I was certainly expected to be there. So I put my foot down to try to make it, but on the outskirts of Glasgow two large men in blue stepped out from some secret lair, held up their hands... and that was it. Copped! By the time they had finished with me, I knew it was impossible to make communion in time but decided to go on to college just the same where on arrival I was surrounded by my pals demanding to know where I had been.

"I was tight for communion," I explained, and it was only when there were roars of laughter I realised what I had said. What I had intended to say was "I was tight for time".

But the law I have persistently broken is a law of the church. There are two forms of baptism... infant baptism or adult (believers') baptism, the latter being where the person is being baptised as a sign of his or her faith. Adult baptism is practised by Baptist Church, Pentecostal, Plymouth Brethren and others while infant baptism, or christening, is the form of Roman Catholic, Church of England, Church of Scotland, Congregational, Methodist and others. My daughter-in-law Shirley is a Baptist, I have many Baptist friends and respect their views, but take issue with them strongly, that this is the only valid form, or the only one supported by Scripture.

When Dr Billy Graham, who had been a Baptist minister prior to becoming the world famous evangelist he is, first visited Scotland, he spoke to a group of ministers of all denominations. One bold Presbyterian spark challenged him on his Baptist beliefs and practice. "If the water is up to the candidates knees, is that enough?" he was asked.

"No" said Dr Graham.

"Well, up to the waist?"

"Afraid not" said Billy.

"Chin?"

Again the answer was "No".

"Well, what about when the top of the head is covered?" persisted the questioner.

"That's it, you've got it," said the evangelist.

"So it's the top of the head that matters. Well, that's exactly what we cover," said the Church of Scotland man to roars of laughter, in which Billy Graham joined, and was big enough man to tell that story against himself to others.

When I was first a minister, each request for baptism (usually of a baby, but sometimes of an adult, for it is not generally known the C of S also practises adult baptism), was a matter for each individual minister to decide. However a good few years ago now, the Church decreed that baptism could only be administered if at least one of the parents was a member of that Church. The law was well intentioned, for it was felt many people were just using, or abusing, the good offices of the Church and after their child was christened, they were never near the place till another baby came along. But I... and many others, thought it a bad law, a self defeating measure, for one of two things would happen. Either one of the parents (probably the mother) would join the Church "just to have the bairn done" or the couple would say: "If that's you attitude, to pot with you" and you have lost that couple, probably for ever. I felt it was better to at least "have a foot in the door" and maintain some kind of contact with the family.

So I continued to baptise all comers from my own parish. I have never knowingly baptised a child who was in another minister's parish, apart from one group of exceptions, which I will mention in a moment. It was never automatic, or taken lightly, and I always visited every couple, even if it was their sixth child, went over the service with them, especially the vows, which are searching vows, urged them to consider Church membership, and in my Aldermouth days, ran a short course on Church membership for adults, and wrote to all who had been for baptism inviting them to come, and emphasising there would be no pressure at the end of the course to become Church members. Twenty-eight, mainly couples, came to my first classes, and twenty-six were confirmed, and many became regular worshippers. Many, of course, continued to request baptism who had no intention at the time of Church membership, and I normally baptised their child, even though I was quite knowingly breaking the law.

Whilst I regard baptism, of course, as a solemn sacrament it is also a joyful family occasion, and very frequently I have baptised a child or children of a couple I had married, who had then moved away from my parish, and were attached to some other church anywhere in the British Isles, but who very much wanted, especially their first child, to be baptised in the church where they had been married, and if possible by the minister who had married them. Since the mother's parents were in all probability still in the original parish and home church, it seemed wholly natural to me that they would all want this family occasion to be where it had all started, and these were amongst the happiest baptismal occasions I had... but strictly speaking, breaking the law.

Baptism is supposed to be in the face of a congregation who have their part to play, but I have carried out the service in a house so that granny, who was incapacitated, could be there, and I recall on one occasion, with an ordinary bowl for the water, doing a family of six, from a newborn babe to a girl of twenty-three, herself married. But again, not good, said the law. I have baptised many children privately in church, when for a variety of reasons, the couple felt they could not stand in front of a whole congregation, and I always invited them to bring their friends with them, making their own congregation.

I remember one occasion at Moorton when the phone rang and a voice asked "We wis wonderin' if you would christen the wean?" I recognised it as the voice of John Brown, who farmed right up on the moor, was regular in church, his wife almost never.

"Sure, John", I said "I'll come up and see you and go over the service."

"Aye, but you see, minister" said John, "there's a wee snag. I ken you're supposed to have it done in front o' a' the folk, an' neither me nor the wife could dae that."

I smiled, picturing John clutching his phone anxiously and wondering if the minister would oblige. This was a special baby to the Browns for they had two teenage daughters, and then out of the blue had come a son... John's pride and joy, and a lad to succeed him on the farm. In due course I visited the Brown family farm, and went over the vows with the couple, as I always did, while mostly they sat silent, and too shy to query some point... but not John.

I asked "Do you promise to bring him up in the nurture and admonition of the Lord?"

John snorted "Haud on meenister, jist haud on; that's an awfu moothfu'; whit's nurture and ad... whatever it wis?"

I answered "I see you've started lambing, John, Any twin trouble or pet lambs?"

John looked at me as if I was daft. What was the man raving about? However, he decided to humour me. "Aye, we've yin pet lamb an' a richt nuisance it is, feedin' it every fower hours wi' the bottle!"

Now it was my turn, "Now you haud on, John; feeding... that's nurture. It will be the same with your wee laddie. He gets fed regularly... he has to be... but he needs spiritual and moral nurture too... regularly."

The penny dropped. We explained admonition likewise, with sundry references to training collie dugs, and breaking in "cowts and fillies". John soon grasped the parallel that admonition and discipline are blood brothers.

Meantime John's wife was scandalised, her mother "black affronted".

"Whit a man you are, John Broon, askin' the minister a' thae questions. You've aye tae ken the oots an' ins o' everything – speirin this an speirin' that."

But I was delighted and said "Well done, John. If there were more seekers like you there would be more finders. After all. Himsel', the great Laird o' Heaven an' earth, as a young man in the Temple did quite a bit of speirin tae."

But to revert to my allusion to house baptisms, that too is law-breaking. I care not! Indeed one of the happiest baptisms I had was my last, at Hutton, on a farm with masses of friends and relations present, and carried out on the lawn on a glorious June Sunday. I will long remember the joy of that day… but yes, breaking the law.

Then what about the tinkers or travelling people who have no parish, and a small number desire christening? Then there is the case of the newborn child who is not expected to live long. Long ago the Church of the day taught that unbaptised children did not go to Heaven, and were even buried in unconsecrated ground. Very early in my ministry I was asked late one night to go to a hospital to baptise a newly born babe not expected to live many hours. The mother was not from my parish, unknown to me. I found her very distressed, and trying to console her, said something like this: "Lassie, lassie, do you think your Father who loves you and your baby would shut him out of Heaven because a wee pickle of water had not been sprinkled on him? Of course not, but for your peace of mind I'll baptise him, the wee mite."

I did, with no vows taken, and though some might say I was perpetuating a superstition, I felt I was doing the compassionate, Christ-like thing and the relief afterwards on the mother's face told its own story. Happily the baby lived, and happily the Church laws on baptism do not exclude this compassionate act.

As I have said it is not always realised that the Church of Scotland also baptises adults… indeed a person cannot be confirmed as a Church member without prior baptism. Naturally the minister does not struggle to take the adult in his arms, and the person being baptised takes the vows of allegiance to Jesus Christ, of the parents as in infant baptism. One evening at Aldermouth I baptised a twenty-one year old lass who came, absolutely on her own, and took her vows in exactly the same manner as in the Baptist church, except that in the latter, as I have said, there is total immersion. I had previously instructed this girl, as I always did, and also as was my custom, asked an elder to be present to represent the Church. On this occasion the elder was Bobby Sim, who had retired to Aldermouth from Glasgow, had lost his transference certificate from his Glasgow church, and been admitted to our church by resolution of the session. He was a fine man, bright, perky, mischievous, very kind, an excellent baritone singer and choir member… and great fun. In short, he was a pillar of the kirk and his faith to him a thing of joy, so it was natural that we should in time ordain him an elder. After I had baptised the girl that night I commended her for her dedication and courage in coming all on her own to take her vows at baptism.

About a fortnight later, Bobby came bursting in to my vestry hour one Thursday evening, for although folks could see me at the manse any evening I happened to be home, they could be certain to get me on a Thursday. Bobby immediately exclaimed in great agitation, the words tumbling out, "Mr Cameron, I hivna been able to sleep for a fortnicht. You mind that lassie you baptised, and praised her courage? Mr Cameron, I've never been baptised."

I think he expected me to be shocked, but I sat back and laughed. "Bobby, we've broken all the laws of the Kirk. You should not have been admitted to your Glasgow kirk without baptism... we naturally assumed you had, and we don't expect to have to ask new members if they are baptised, but I don't think with the faith that just shines out of you, you'll be kept out of Heaven for want of some water on your head."

But Bobby wasn't having it. "Ah, but you see, Mr Cameron. I want to be baptised and take my stand."

So with his wife and a friend present, in due course I baptised him, then a man in his seventies, and taking his vows with great sincerity. I cannot remember a much happier occasion. Dear Bobby... he's been with the Lord for a good many years now, and you know, I think he and the Lord will have had a chuckle about breaking the rules committees make.

So let the bairns – of all ages – come, even if I'm excommunicated for making my law-breaking public. Did not the Lord say "Let the children come, and forbid them not, for such is the Kingdom of Heaven"? I know full well, let me say, before my Baptist friends rush to write to me, that these words were not spoken by Jesus specifically about baptism, but I think the spirit's the same for "the promise is to you AND YOUR CHILDREN and to as many as the Lord shall call, even if they are afar off".

Do you think this unrepentant law breaker might get bail?

FIFTEEN
The Dream

My mother used periodically to tell the story of how once in the early days of their marriage, my father suddenly, in the middle of the night, leapt right over her in the high, built-in box bed, to the wall at the back. If he had jumped the other way, he would probably have broken his neck!

"Hugh! Hugh!" she gasped "what in all the world are you doing?"

"Oh!" said my sweating father, "that was a near thing. There was a bull chasing me, and I just got over the dyke in time!"

Clearly, of course, a nightmare – a trait I seem to have inherited from my father. Not about bulls, for although I have treated many sizes and breeds, and put many rings in noses and was certainly careful with them, I don't remember ever being afraid. No, my fear is for heights, and just to stand on a chair to replace a light bulb turns my legs to jelly, and when our family were young, I regularly saw one of them falling over a cliff, for some reason most often Neil, the eldest, and me trying to grab him.

Often as a minister I dreamt I was in the vestry at Aldermouth with ten minutes to go to the service, maybe 500 people in the church, and Jim, our marvellous blind organist asking for the Praise List, and John, our beadle, asking for Scripture Readings for the reading board… and I hadn't a clue what my sermon was about! No doubt psychiatrists would have some big word – besides crazy – to describe my state!

Of course, I suppose I could have done what my friend and fellow minister tells of one notable divine. Willie was a pupil at Mochrum Academy, long before me, but he was the pride of the staff, for he was a fine scholar, and regularly was held up to us following on as an example of what dedication could achieve, despite poverty.

In Willie's story, the minister had got through praise and prayer and come to the sermon. He leaned over the pulpit and asked his congregation: "Do you know what I am preaching about today?"

Of course they all said "No", and he replied "Neither do I" and went home, followed by his bemused congregation.

The next week was similar but at his question some said "yes" and some "no", so he advised all who knew to tell it to those who did not, and again departed for home! Well, I suppose it might be worth a try. It would certainly be different and none could complain about the length of the sermon!

Nightmares – unpleasant things.

Sometimes, however, the dreams are more pleasant, when something good is happening to me, or I have just put the world to right, but sadly I can never remember them when I awake.

Many people have dreams in their sleep, dreams which fade with the dawning... but there are also the dreams we have when awake – day dreams – which most people have at different stages of life.

When but a lad, I dreamt of being a farmer... oh, a proper organised dream with so many dairy cattle (Ayrshires, of course), sheep, pigs, hens, and all the rest, and as I mentioned earlier in these memoirs, most of my spare time was spent on farms. Alas, my parents did not have the wherewithal to start me on a farm, so I became a vet instead. Again, as mentioned before, there was my football – the civilised kind that is played with a round ball – and I had approaches from several senior teams to become a full time player, but working with animals was far more important to me, so the senior teams were politely refused.

But that did not stop me from playing for my country in my dreams, the high point being when, as a centre forward (striker nowadays), I scored the winning goal for Scotland against England at Wembley – the goal of course coming dramatically in the last minute. (Sorry, my many English friends, you're not a bad lot!)

All parents, of course, have dreams for their children, and the dreams I'd had for myself were transferred to our four sons. Whilst all attained good degrees at university or college – far more important than in a sports field, they all had their moments there.

I recall over the years Neil, our eldest, in a Highland League cup final scoring the winner with a rocket shot from forty yards. His brother David in the same game, on his eighteenth birthday, and almost his debut, playing a brilliant game in defence. Alan, the baby of the family, when only eleven, captained the Highland Region team in the primary schools competition, whilst Ian, as mentioned elsewhere, did combine soccer with teaching, playing for Aberdeen, Kilmarnock and his country.

Apologies to readers for this catalogue of family affairs. Put it down to an old man remembering with pride his own dreams being fulfilled in his sons!

The Bible has a lot to say about dreams, which were taken seriously. For example, Joseph being warned by God in a dream to flee into Egypt with the Mary and the infant Jesus.

The prophet Joel says: "Your young men shall see visions and your old men shall dream dreams" – and he is right.

The visions of youth and the dreams of age are more than passing fancies. Have you ever thought what the world owes to its dreamers? We tend to think the great changes, advances, discoveries, have been brought about by dashing men (and women) of action, and while this is true to some extent, behind them have been the dreamers.

Just one or two examples to illustrate my point.

For example, Britain stopped her ghastly traffic in slaves when Parliament passed an Act... but in Parliament one lone figure, a hunchback with rather an ugly face, William Wilberforce, pleaded and fought to bring it about, his crusade taking twenty-five years. Ugly he may have been, but it was said when pleading the cause of men and women who were bought and sold like animals, his face shone like an angel's, and his attractive, resonant voice stirred the conscience of the British people.

Seeing the many homeless, unwanted, illegitimate children sleeping in dustbins, under bridges – any possible shelter – Dr Barnardo dreamt of proper homes, and chances in life for these pathetic waifs and strays, and this man of deep compassion and Christian commitment followed his dream of a proper home and chance of life for these unwanted children. Maybe our land today needs another Dr Barnardo?

Sickened by the vice in London – the gin parlours, crime, cruelty, ignorance, William Booth dreamt of an army whose only instruments would be love and practical caring, following one of like mind in Galilee. And despite reviling, stoning, mocking, even killing, his Salvation Army goes marching on, and thousands of lives have been changed by their message.

One of the greatest dreamers of our day was Dr Martin Luther King who had his dream of a day when the black people of America would be treated equally with the white. "I have been to the mountain top; I have seen the promised land" he told a vast crowd the day before an assassin's bullet silenced his word... but not the dream, which others have taken up and carried forward to that day when all men will be brothers, regardless of the colour of their skin.

In our own little land, Robert Burns, Scotland's great ploughboy poet centuries ago had that same dream of equality for all, the day "when man to man the world o'er shall brithers be, for a' that."

Dreamers! Dreams! The world needs them still in every corner.

"Follow your dreams" said President Bush to the Polish Solidarity movement when it looked as if it would be swamped, and what astonishing almost unbelievable changes we have seen in eastern Europe in just a few years, after more than forty years of the Cold War, with always the threat of the bomb hanging over our world.

Yes... much has been changed for the better by men and women following their dreams.

Yet much remains to be done, and it is here we turn to Jesus. For soaring above all the dreamers of the centuries and often inspiring and spurring them on stands this lone figure... preaching, teaching, crossing all dividing lines. He hands the torch to us, to pray and work for the coming of a Kingdom where evil will be banished, good will reign, as He teaches us to pray "Thy Kingdom come. Thy will be done in earth, as even now it is done in Heaven." His is the supreme dream and promise of its fulfilment.

Those who know and believe the promises of the Bible know that Kingdom will not be till the one who was born in a stable, died in unbelievable agony on a cross, rose triumphant over death and reigns as King of the heart of all who believe in Him, reigns as King of this world. This is not a popular doctrine... yet one verse in every thirteen in the Bible speaks of this second coming – and I believe His word. Tell me, friend, what other hope can you see for the world?

I said we had to *work*, as Christians, to make the dream come true. I am not a social gospeller, as they have been called, but if a person's faith does not issue in action, it is an incomplete and indeed selfish faith.

Dag Hammarskjold, former secretary general of the United

Nations wrote in his book *Markings*: "In our age the road to holiness necessarily passes through the world of action."

It will indeed be a bad day when the Church accepts the invitation, and indeed command by many governments, to abandon the world, for its function is not to abandon the world, but change the world. That can only be done when changed men and women accept the obligation of working for a changed society in every way open to them. If we believe that God was sufficiently concerned with humanity, to take humanity upon Himself, then we must also believe that God is concerned that men and women should have decent conditions to live in; the millions of hungry across the world be fed; all have a right to the best possible health care; antiquated prisons be torn down and human conditions provided; and the refugee, the homeless, the underprivileged peoples of the world be treated as we would wish ourselves to be treated. For too long now those who name the name of Christ in all sincerity as their Saviour, Lord, Guide and Commander in Chief in the endless fight with evil, have been playing a gentle little religion that gets nothing done!

No one put this better than Studdert Kennedy, the famous "Woodbine Willie" of the Great War, who spoke out against those whose religion consisted in taking communion, in long prayers and so on. It was, in fact, therein that he saw the failure of the Church.

"We have been calling men to services" he said, "when what they wanted was the call to service. Nobody worries about Christ as long as He can be kept shut up in churches. He is quite safe there. But there is always trouble if you try to let Him out!" I have seen this, oh so often, and in so many people whose religion is so correct and so genteel – and so powerless.

For example, for ten years, when in my last Charge in the Borders, I was the Scottish Religious Adviser to Border Television, along with three from England, for Border Television's area of influence is approximately three-quarters in England and one quarter in Scotland. Every quarter we met with programme makers, producers and various boffins of the company. We would discuss coming programmes, watch video films, suggest topics for programmes that would, hopefully, be on the wavelength of today's youngsters, select places of worship, and give our views on moral and ethical issues that were coming up on "the box". We worked quite hard, and over lunch, continued discussion.

One day we were joined at lunch by two MPs... one an elderly, very humble, working class man whose braces showed! He was due to retire at the next general election, but fighting for what he believed in to the end of his parliamentary stint. He was also, it transpired, a lay preacher. The other man was a complete contrast, a young Conservative – suave, immaculately dressed, clearly upper crust, ambitious, and rapidly climbing the Conservative ladder. He asked what we had been discussing and I replied, "amongst other things, unemployment."

He immediately lost his temper, threw down his table napkin, dropped his soup spoon and snapped: "The Church seems to spend more time discussing things that don't concern it than do! Let it stick to its preaching."

I was aghast, but the humble little Labour man laughed it off and quietly said, "Oh, Ian, Ian, do you not think that He who was born in a stable is very concerned about folks who don't even have a stable but a cardboard box and newspapers under a London bridge?"

A lively discussion followed!

Now, in this instance, I completely sided with the Labour MP, not because, I emphasise, of political views or opinions, but I felt he was merely reiterating what Jesus said. At the final day of judgement, said Jesus, we would be judged on our reaction and actions to "When I was hungry; when I was sick; when I was poor, a stranger, naked or in prison"… and His words… His words, mark you, have a chilling ring about them when He sums it up and says: "If you did it *not* for one of the LEAST of these MY BROTHERS, you did it not to me. Depart from me." (See Matthew 25 if you doubt me.)

I have never in thirty-five years knowingly preached a single sermon with any bearing on party politics. Maybe I have been remiss, and I know there are clergymen of all denominations who openly state their party's case from the pulpit. This I cannot go along with, for I know there are sincere Christians in all political parties. But I have, from time to time, spoken out from Scripture, on moral, ethical and social issues, whatever the colour of the government, for if Christianity is only for our wee cosy circle, it is an unbalanced faith. As Lord George McLeod often puts it: "If Jesus Christ is not Lord of all life… He is not Lord at all."

We are commissioned, if we bear the name of Jesus, to help bring His dream come true – by prayer, love and work. This is *the* dream and as Christians we believe its coming is as certain as the dawn, when He who first came to the world as a babe, when He whom men crucified, calling Him in mockery at his cross “the King of the Jews”, will, in every truth, reign in His own world, and before Him every knee will bow. Meantime we travel on in this fair world he created and which men have defiled, believing the earth will yet be made up of a band of brothers and sisters, as it is, even now, in Heaven, where all our longings, yearnings, hopes and dreams are already gloriously fulfilled.

PART TWO

The Border Years... and Lockerbie

"I will lift up my eyes to the hills
from whence cometh my help."

SIXTEEN

Return to our Roots

It was time to go!

My doctor said so, if there was any hope of regaining my health, for the constancy of the work in a church the size of Aldermouth Old, plus a parish of believers or unbelievers, required a minister who was 100 percent fit. With the coming of big money for the many employed at the oil rig construction yard, had come also people from all over the country chasing that big money. This increased the stress load for me and no doubt my colleagues, with new problems such as battered wives, battered babies, drugs, fights, drink flowing like water. In fact in my last three years I spent more time trying to counsel people with no church connection but who (usually wives) had turned to me in desperation for help. The major problems were gambling and drunkenness, many wives not a penny better off than before the big wages, and many marriages went on the rocks. Night after night I spent with distraught wives at the manse... and little success, but felt nightly, as Jesus found, "virtue had gone out of me". I was absolutely whacked.

My mind told me also it was time to go. I had given of my best for twelve years, had seen the church grow (an average of 80 new members per year), new organisations such as the Men's Fellowship, In Betweens (a group for younger women), Mothers and Toddlers Group, Playgroup and Prayer Meeting had started and mostly were thriving. Indeed most of the twenty-two departments were thriving; 300 youngsters about the church, our premises increased, mainly for young folks and a Manse for a much needed assistant, who, after several years entirely on my own was a welcome relief. We had been instructed by presbytery we must have an assistant.

Despite these new premises, and paying another minister, the financial side was sound with never a Stewardship Campaign for funds. Certainly we had been greatly helped by a gift of £10,000, but much more was required and just came in. The church was buzzing, and its strength was not due to me, but to a great team, and on a Sunday as I looked out at often five or six hundred, I felt my heart warmed. We were one big family.

But I had nothing left to give. It was time for a new voice – probably a younger, certainly a fitter – minister, and though my heart was in my beautiful church, my mind said "Move on". To leave "Culzean Castle", as Janet's brother Alec called our gracious manse was hard, but in the end, mind triumphed over heart, and though it would mean leaving behind so many friends, for people, not architecture are the church, we went.

Janet spotted an advert in *The Scotsman*: "Eskdalemuir linked with Hutton and Corrie". We had not the faintest idea where these places were, our only knowledge being the regular weather reports that Eskdalemuir that day had been the coldest or wettest place in Britain. (Here let me state that these reports were not strictly true, but having an observatory, a weather station, as well as a seismograph centre it would be more accurate to say they were the coldest or wettest parts that had been recorded that day.) However, clearly if we went to that neck of the woods, it would be a rude awakening from the balmy, snow free, dry climate of the Moray Firth. Eventually, I sent off a brief application, something new for me, for I had been invited as distinct from applying, to both Moorton and Aldermouth. I had a very prompt reply, duly preached at Beattock before the Vacancy Committee and was appointed sole nominee.

We were scheduled to preach before the whole congregations in April. We were informed we would be staying with a farming couple, Mr and Mrs Maxwell, but we should come first, on the Saturday night, for a meal at The Closs, home of the Session Clerk, Willie Ferguson and his wife Iris. We made a bad start, losing our way on the winding country roads and arriving late, but we were welcomed like long lost friends. Willie is one of the friendliest, cheeriest men I know, with a great hearty laugh, and he and I were destined to become good friends. Iris, too, was the perfect hostess, and served us a superb meal. Along with the Fergusons and ourselves were the Maxwells and another farming couple, Jim and Kathleen Jackson, the latter the Hutton organist, and Corrie pianist, for services at Corrie were held in the village hall. All these, our first acquaintances of the new charge, were involved in farming one way or another, and despite the regular TV reports of wind, rain and snow, looked remarkably fit and healthy to me.

So they were all country folk, and as a former country vet, I was soon completely at home. After the meal we stretched our feet to a great log fire and talked. Kathleen wanted to know more about my ideas on music, and guided me in choosing for the morrow hymns known by the congregation. Soon the women were chatting about families, while the men, their pipes drawing nicely, talked about kirks, sheep, subsidies and not least their much loved last minister, Mr Lough.

Iris volunteered the statement "He didna leave us, you ken... he died".

I thought that quite a permanent way to leave! It seemed Mr Lough had been a bachelor, and from their comments about him, I realised I had a high standard to live up to as his successor. We had a grand night with typical open, country, fine folk.

The Maxwell's farm, The Gall, was like a first class hotel, and we could not have been shown more consideration. (In fact a few years later, Isobel Maxwell, who took in summer visitors, gained the award for the best farmhouse accommodation in the whole country.) On the Sunday morning, we set off down the hill to Hutton Church, a little whitewashed, cruciform shaped building on the side of a hill, surrounded by its ancient graveyard going back for centuries. In many ways the church reminded me (although smaller) of my first charge at Moorton. It was, in fact, the second oldest church in Dumfriesshire.

Janet, Jack and I walked down the brae towards the church and as I got near I stopped in amazement. It seemed as if cars had taken over the world, for there seemed to be cars lined up all along the narrow country road. Jack, however, was cautious and in his quiet way said "Mind you, we don't get as many as this every week", but it looked to me as if everybody in the parish had turned out that sparkling spring morning.

I felt very much at home in the little kirk; it was warm, homely – and ministers soon become aware of atmospheres – but what impressed me most was the tremendous singing, heads back, chests out, the folks of Hutton and Corrie were giving it big licks, Kathleen expertly handling the Compton electric organ. After the service, when I had been aware, as on all such occasions, of close but polite scrutiny, I was introduced to the elders. They were all country folks: no bank managers, lawyers, accountants, as in the town churches, and without exception they seemed glad to see Janet and me, the tongues wagged freely. I noticed a plaque on the organ stating it had been presented by Major and Mrs Tulloch, and I was interested to meet them. Major Tulloch was really the local laird, but possibly the humblest man there. One of the top brass at 121 (Church headquarters) had told me, when he knew I was preaching for this linked charge, "You will find a Major Tulloch as treasurer. He is a very fine man, gained a gallantry award in Burma, and is the laird, who with his wife, really cares for all their people. His heart is in the right place, and I am persuaded so is his soul."

I found the Major a very quiet, humble man, we had a sincere welcome from both him and Mrs Tulloch. He and I over the years became very close... also Janet and Mrs Tulloch... but he always played down the testimonial of the secretary at Church headquarters, maintaining he had as many doubts as the next man.

Then it was on to Eskdalemuir, seven miles away, and just before dropping down to the village, I paused, as I was to do every week for the next ten years, just to drink in the beauty of the lovely Vale of Esk. The church, a bigger building than Hutton, with a gallery, was also possessed of a small pipe organ, expertly handled by Miss Laidlaw. The church, though a bigger building, had a much smaller membership than Hutton and Corrie, for a reason we will come to in due course. We were welcomed at the door by a Mr Cartner, a small, seemingly shy man, though more of him too anon. The only other elder was John Dalgliesh, whose farm was practically next door to the church, and who opened the church and put on the heating every week, there being no actual beadle. John was a man with a warm smile which came from a warm heart, a real farmer through and through, as was his fellow elder, Mr Cartner, who was to act as Session Clerk and treasure for more than fifty years, surely a record. These were the office bearers, so clearly, if I was elected, I would need to see about adding to their number fairly quickly. I preached a different sermon at Eskdalemuir, just in case of any of the Hutton and Corrie folks wanted a second look at this minister. I was not happy with my performance though the people seemed please enough, and as at Hutton kirk, the congregation all crowded around to shake hands and assure us they were looking forward to our coming. I kept reminding them I wasn't in yet, there had to be a vote, which duly took place, and disaster, or it seemed to them, one person had voted against me! This was a new experience for me, but Willie Ferguson and John Dalgliesh went out of their way to explain it had been an old lady who had just got mixed up.

I had now to inform the Aldermouth Session, which I did before my next Sunday service prior to telling the congregation... and to my amazement they almost all knew already. It seemed a couple who sang in the choir, and had previously lived in New Castleton (at least forty miles from Hutton) had heard the news from friends in the Borders... and the Aldermouth pipeline had done the rest. I was constantly amazed at this word of mouth telegraph. I recalled being told at the top of the High Street that a certain man was very ill. Actually I had seen the man that very morning and knew it was a very mild condition he had. Half way down the street, another informed me the man was critically ill, and by the bottom of the street, he was dead!

Since there was much to do at the Hutton manse, most of it by voluntary labour, for money was tight in our new wee kirks, and also because the Aldermouth Session hinted they would be grateful if I would stay on for the summer when all the visitors came, and in addition they didn't want a vacancy at that time of the year, it was finally decided we should leave in September... so, oddly enough, all my three inductions were in that month. The summer really seemed to fly past, and almost before we realised it, I had come to my last Aldermouth Sunday. I did not want a farewell social, so it was decided my last evening service would be a mixture of worship and goodbyes.

It was a moving occasion for us for farewells are never easy, and I knew I would not see a good many of these, my people, for twelve years. There were tears here and there... so at least some were sorry to see us go... and we both had lumps in our throats, especially when our matchless, blind organist who could make the organ speak better than anyone before or since, allowed us to choose three of our favourite anthems which our wonderful choir had sung, as they always did every Sunday. Our joint favourite was *Seek ye the Lord* with Billy Foley's fine tenor voice taking the solo part, this anthem conveying in song for the last time for us the message I had tried to preach every Sunday: the invitation to come to Christ and know

Him as Saviour and Friend. Various people spoke briefly... our quiet, gentle, humble Session Clerk, Alastair Taylor, who had meant so much to me; one of our very best elders, Arthur Marshall, editor of our magazine, fellow golfer and good friend, whose home I had visited perhaps more than any other because of his wife Cath's frequent illness; and a surprise, one of my former assistants, Peter Humphris, who had come up all the way from Dundee and said some kind things about his old "Bishop" – and I had always thought my preaching curled Peter's hair! Sorry, Peter! I appreciated greatly his kind words, and also the generous gifts from the congregation, with one of which I am typing this (with one finger that doesn't always do as I want it!). Finally, my faithful beadle John showed me out for the first time, we shook hands with everyone and the busiest years of my life were over.

We left Aldermouth as we had arrived, pulling our much used old caravan which had covered thousands of miles, and given us, as a family, and many of our friends, a great deal of pleasure. We were now, however, minus the poultry which had been with us when we first arrived away back in 1968, but they, and their descendants were now no more, but they had played their part (as well as laying eggs), for even today, someone will say to me "I mind when you had poultry in the pulpit. I'll never forget that children's address... in fact I got more out of it than the kids!"

We arrived quite late at our new home in Boreland, our tiny little village (Hutton being the old parish name). We were tired, the manse felt damp and unlived in, so I lit a fire while Janet put down some cushions from the caravan for Neil, our oldest boy, to sleep on. He was just out of hospital following a particularly dirty appendix operation, and while the caravan cushions were not the most comfortable bed, with our furniture not yet arrived, it was the best we could do, then we all fell into bed, whacked, after 250 miles pulling our caravan.

By morning light we saw there was still a deal of painting and papering to be done... but a lot of people had been very busy, each district decorating a room, we learned. Jim Harkness, a former footballer and professional painter and member of Hutton, had expertly done several rooms.

The house was big, though not on the scale of Aldermouth's huge manse, but despite the size and age, had a homely, family feel about it, and in time we felt it was our happiest home.

We had arrived about a week before the induction by Annandale and Esdkale presbytery, but it took us the week to get everything in order and arrange accommodation for various friends and family who were coming "to see us in". Three things I remember in particular about the final induction of my ministry, which, with the following social, was to be held in Eskdalemuir, it having the biggest building for the occasion, although as I have said before, the smallest membership.

The first was the thing for which Eskdalemuir was nationally famous – the weather. I have never seen such rain… in fact I thought the Lord was going back on His word and we were in for a second flood! The rain poured from leaden heavens, as if every cloud in Britain had heard there was something on at Eskdalemuir and they should be there for the day, and especially the evening, but bless them the folks turned out in their hundreds. What was a spit or two of rain to them, they lived with it regularly.

The second was the actual induction, which is always a special event in a minister's life, the vows sacred and solemn, no matter how often he has said them, especially his affirmation to the question: "Are not zeal for the Glory of God, love for the Lord Jesus Christ and a desire for the salvation of men, so far as you know your own heart, your great motives and chief inducements to enter into this ministry?" No man can answer that without a deep searching of his soul and a clutch at the throat. The devotions were conducted by Rev Jack Owen of Lochmaben, whom I honestly could not recall, but who said publicly we had met before (he was quite a few years my junior), and was kind and generous enough to say I had been an influence on his becoming a minister in my Moorton days, when he had been in an Irvine Youth Fellowship with which we in Moorton had special ties. That moved me. The Moderator, Geralo Moulê of Moffat, inducted as a senior minister, Andrew Rae of Annan, a kind and gentle man with deep sincerity and understanding gave the best charge I have heard to the new minister. I shook hands at the door, and the folks girded up their loins and faced the deluge. Some didn't know where the village hall was and asked me. I didn't know either, but understood it was just a little way along the road, and some set off walking. In face it proved to be two miles away, and there must have been some none too happy with this new minister, but fortunately most got lifts. There are no strangers in the country! When we reached the hall, various soaked bodies were steaming in the heat but I have never seen a happier crowd. I don't know how many the hall was supposed to hold, but it had twice its number that night. Herrings in a box! Sardines in a tin! Folks climbing over chairs or crawling under tables to find a place. It was utter bedlam until Major Tulloch arrived when he, a very quiet speaker normally, used his parade ground voice, and some sort of order resulted, with everyone somehow getting in. A fire would have resulted in the total extinction of three parishes – maybe that is why the Lord sent all these clouds, just in case!

The final thing I recall was, of course, the social itself. It was my first experience of a scattered rural community's catering and they clearly had as their model the feeding of the 5,000. There just wasn't space on all the tables for the mass of food, something I was to see many times thereafter at every function. It was also my first experience of scattered communities getting together and out to enjoy themselves. Tongues clattered, there was much happy laughter and the women kept everybody supplied with tea and urged you to try Mrs so-and-so's pancakes, or Jean's cream sponges. The amazing thing was (again like the feeding of the 5,000) there seemed to be as much left at the end as at the beginning. Then we came to the entertainment, with instrumental music, some fine singers and a special request from Ian Ramsay, the Interim Moderator, that the tiny Sunday School of Corrie be allowed to sing, which they duly did... the only song the infants knew was *Jesus Loves Me*. I have never felt so welcome. It seemed as if everybody there wanted us to be sure they were glad we had come.

Also there were Alistair and Margaret Taylor and John, my Aldermouth beadle with Elizabeth. John spoke for Aldermouth, beginning with the words, "I'm just the beadle", my right hand man for twelve happy years. John spoke despite a shocking cold – evidently the Border weather had got to him! He spoke humbly, for he is a humble man and I am sure everybody there realised that one of the reasons our twelve very hectic years at Aldermouth had been so smooth and good was the bond that existed between these men and their new minister. Ben Johnstone, my first assistant at Aldermouth, was there with Annette, his wife, and he was generous in his praise, which recalled the three happy years which we shared. The main speaker was my closest ministerial friend, Bill McPherson, who features in the article *Goin' Home*. There were local speakers, but unusually at such do's, nobody spoke too long. There were presentations to Ian Ramsay, a gem of a man and everybody's friend, and also gifts to Janet and me… until at some unearthly hour, it was all over. We had been well and truly welcomed, and while everybody told me their names, I have to admit that my brain simply couldn't cope with the deluge of well-wishers. I think it doubtful if there was a happier gathering in Scotland – and still some ill-informed critics say Christianity takes the joy from life.

We reached the manse eventually, saw our guests to their beds, then went outside into the wood of more than 100 trees which surrounded our new home, just to get a breath of air before turning in. The rain had cleared, a glorious harvest moon was riding majestically across the sky, owls were hooting, a soft breeze rippling the leaves, and all around us was the stillness that belongs to lonely places. Janet and I stood side by side, soaking up the quietness after an eventful evening, and feeling, like Elijah of old that God was not in the noises of this world but still spoke, as of yore, in a still, small voice. It had been an eventful night, and we felt good. There could be no doubt whatsoever of the welcome of these country folks. For twelve years I had given my all to Aldermouth, as had my beloved spouse. This had been our big ministry. Now God had taken us back to how it had all began, and entrusted to me, and to my charge, the souls of such warm hearted folks, fewer by far than Aldermouth, but just as precious to God, just as much in need of the Gospel of Redeeming love.

We had begun our lives as country children and young people. Our first home together had been in a farm; I had been a country vet; my first charge had been a country one at Moorton, though much bigger and more compact than our new charge. Now, for my last ministry, we had returned to our roots. It seemed to round it all off neatly. It felt right. We smiled at each other in the moonlight, and hand in hand climbed the stairs to bed, lulled by the soft rustle of leaves in our very own wood. Somehow, we seemed to have come home.

SEVENTEEN

Happy Valley

"I mind when there were nae trees an' a' the hills roon here were covered wi' sheep" said Mrs Pringle to me on my first round of the village, visiting first, as I have always done, the elderly and frail. She went on, "Some ferms had as mony as six shepherds, an' maist o' them had big families, so there were a lot of folk in Eskdalemair" (as the locals always called it).

"Was your husband a 'herd, Mrs Pringle?"

"That he was an' a guid yin. We stayed away up in the hills an' some o' the hooses had nae roads to them."

"Was it not awful lonely at times?" I enquired.

"Tuts, no! We had gran' times. When it wisna lambing, clipping or dipping time, often your neebors would come ower an' we would hiv a gran' nicht at the dominoes. Sometimes mair than one lot would come an' we would hiv a rare sing or a wee dance." She paused, looking back over the years. "Aye, it wis a happy valley then. Noo, maist o' the sheep are gone an' it's a' covered wi' trees. Mind you, the trees are richt bonny tae."

"What did you do if anybody took ill?"

"Och, the doctor would whiles walk up into the hills, or get a lift in a horse and cairt frae the nearest ferm... one had his ain horse. Once I had to go to hospital an' fower men cairted me in a chair across the hills doon to the road where an ambulance wis waitin'. We aye managed; we were never stuck."

Mrs Pringle was in her eighties and stayed with her daughter, Helen Young, or Nell as most called her. She kept the village shop. I was enjoying my crack (chat) with the old lady and learning something about my parish at the same time. Then, realising I was her new minister, she obviously thought I would be interested in the church so went on "You ken, there used to be two kirks an' two ministers in the valley. At sacrament time folks would leave early in their best claes (clothes) an' tramp across the hills in their bare feet an' just pit their boots on when they got to the road."

I had a grand time with the old lady and her daughter, drank a cup of tea, asked a simple house blessing, and went on my way.

My next call was at The Holm, where John Dalgliesh, our elder, and Nan farmed. Nan also did bed and breakfast and was kept busy with visitors. I wanted to speak with John about the glebe. Once, as with most country churches, ministers farmed their glebes... it was part of their stipend, but now virtually all glebes are let out and administered by the general trustees at Church Headquarters. John had rented twenty-three acres, and the trustees were proposing to put up the rent considerably. Although the minister had no power over rents, and gained nothing from them, the rent merely helping to make up his stipend, he was always informed of proposed changes and asked his views. I felt the proposed increase too much as sheep farming was no longer the lucrative business (far from it), that it had once been, but I wanted to hear John's views. I told him of my talk with Mrs Pringle and the hills being covered with sheep, something that was now hard to visualise with the miles and miles of trees.

"Mrs Pringle's richt" said John, "the hills roon here were reckoned to be about the best in the Borders, an' Eskdalemair sheep aye fetched a guid price."

"How many farms would you say there are left now, John?"

He thought a bit, then started to name them, counting as he went. "Oh, I would say about six or eight. The rest is trees."

"But why did this change happen?" I wanted to know.

"Och, there were different reasons, but farmers were being offered huge prices for their land by the Forestry Commission and the EFG, and some made fortunes. You could say a lot of it was just greed."

"What happened to all the 'herd's houses?"

"Oh... some are holiday homes and the folk come in the summer an' some o' them come to the kirk. But maist have been taken ower by the Boods".

I had learned by now that the latter were the Buddhists of Samye Ling, of whom more anon.

John went on: "You see, the trouble noo is when a young couple in the valley want to get mairrit, the Boods, or ither outsiders come an' offer a ridiculous price for the hoose, an' the local folk canna afford it, so one by one they're leavin' the valley."

We talked about the glebe rent and I promised I would try to get 121 (as Church Headquarters were invariably labelled) to lower their increase, and make these mandarins sitting in a city realise what a struggle farming had become to make into a living. I have to confess that while I had a little success at Eskdalemuir and also the Hutton glebe, it was pretty minimal. There is bureaucracy even in the Kirk, or so it sometimes appears.

There was still time so I decided to go to Langholm to see Mrs Young, probably our oldest member, who lived with her unmarried son Willie in his house there. Another son, Tommy, was Nell's husband. Mrs Young was a frail old lady, but still had a sparkle in her eye and a ready laugh.

She too talked of the old days when she had lived in the valley. "It was hard, especially after I lost my man, and a family to rear. But I worked hard at whatever job I could get, folk helped one another in these days and we managed."

"Was Eskdalemuir a happy place to live in?" I enquired of her.

"Och, the very best. Everybody kenned everybody else and we had some good entertainment in the hall... dances, concerts, plays. But, Mr Cameron, you shouldna' bother to come a' this distance to see me. It's a long way, twenty miles."

"But I want to see you, it's a lovely run, and I like to hear about the old days."

"Well, you see and look after yourself an' no' be doin' too much."

Again, we had a wee word of prayer, she thanked me, and all the twenty miles back home I thought of this happy valley as it had been and now was. I realised very early on it was going to be hard for the church, for there was a slow, but constant drift to the towns, most of the foresters even came out each day lorries, and as the old folks passed on, they were being replaced, in the main, by the steady invasion of "Boods".

Mind you, in my early days of my new charge, there were some exceptionally fine people in the valley and I found it still a happy place. How utterly wrong is the picture many city dwellers have of country people, almost regarding them as a lesser species in every way. We had people like Miss Laidlaw, our fine organist, which she had been for over twenty years, a music teacher who had at one time been a teacher in South Africa. There was Dr Kathleen Webster, who had retired to Eskdalemuir with her surgeon husband, she had lost him early to a heart attack, but she herself had stayed on a good many years and was a tremendous asset to the parish. There was the manager of the Forestry Commission, Mr Cameron, a clever and kind man who was in church every week with his wife and three children. Tragically, early in my ministry, he died of a brain tumour, while still a young man, his poor wife in fact losing husband and father within ten days. Some folks get it very hard in life. Mrs Cameron coped wonderfully, though with a sore heart, but was a living testimony to Sir John Arkwright's *O Valiant Hearts*:

> Long years ago, as earth lay dark and still
> Rose a loud cry – upon a lonely hill.
> While in the frailty of our human clay
> Christ our Redeemer – passed the selfsame way.

Then there were newcomers such as Mr and Mrs Cass, a retired Yorkshire farmer, who worshipped every week, and sometimes Mr Cass took the pulpit. After Miss Laidlaw moved to Kippen, Mrs Cass took over the organ, and when, after a few years, they also moved on, Mrs Coles became organist, she and her husband (who became church officer), having come from Somerset. A number of these were folks who had chosen to make their homes in our Happy Valley, but there were other folks who had lived there all their lives; like the Richardsons of Kilburn who farmed a Forestry Commission holding, were again a church family, people of real quality, the son Robert having had the harrowing experience of finding his father lying dead of a heart attack by the side of the road. Yes, life can be hard and cruel. None found this more than Jock and Jean Scott whose only son was killed in a horrific way by farm machinery. Jock was an outstanding shepherd, he and his wife country folk born and bred. It has often been said that tragedy either drives us to or from God. The Scotts found solace in their faith and coped with great courage, still coming back to the valley church in my later years when they had moved a considerable distance away. Their life and work was hard, but they loved it, holding to the old ways. It was there in their home, I recall, that I first saw a pig hanging from the rafters, to see them through the winter for meat.

One of the biggest remaining farms was Glendearg, right at the top of the glen. Wattie and Mrs Scott had four daughters who were as expert as men at lambing, and in my ten years there, I married three of the girls, one of whom had married the boy next door, young Ronnie Rose – next door being four miles away! I had also the joy of baptising several of the young people's children. The Scotts had been away up there all their lives, but distance meant nothing in the valley.

Then there were the Observatory workers, whose manager, Ernie Scott, I had the pleasure of ordaining as an elder shortly before I retired.

There were still numbers who had lived in the valley all their lives, and knew every field, burn and almost everything that moved. One of these was Geordie Bell, who had been the postman, and his sister the postmistress, both natives of the valley, and Geordie the handyman everyone sent for whenever any kind of job was to be done. In his younger days, Geordie was part of a band called *The Eskdallonians*. They were booked to play at the wedding reception of Jack and Isobel Maxwell in Glasgow. Unfortunately the bold Geordie had forgotten the name of the hotel, but nothing daunted, when the band reached this wee place called Glasgow, they stopped the car and Geordie enquired of the first man he saw if he knew where Jack Maxwell was being married! Sadly, Glasgow was slightly different to Eskdalemuir where everybody knew everybody else, but somehow they did at last find the reception hotel.

Willie Anderson was the oldest man living in the valley, an old soldier of the Great War, a cavalryman with still a great love of horses, and not for the first time, my former profession as a horse doctor became useful in giving an interest to an old man, and many chats we had.

Geordie annually helped Willie to lay the wreath, Geordie being a survivor of World War II. Willie's wife, Madge, well into her eighties, never missed Sunday worship, loving her kirk dearly. Oh yes, there were people of real quality in Eskdalemuir, very different from the country yokel picture so many city dwellers had.

One could go on mentioning these genuine, fine people, whom I quickly got to know, people like the Robertsons, Mr Walker a shepherd poet, Mrs Johnstone, old Mrs Elliot, Mrs McPherson, and many others too numerous to mention. We may have been thin in quantity, but we were rich in quality and I recall them all with deep affection. There was one other notable family, the Roses, but more about them anon. Suffice to say they had three children whom it was a privilege to marry, and in time baptise some of their babes. Six grandchildren when we retired. Eskdalemuir had been Happy Valley indeed and in many ways still was. But the days the older folks loved were gone forever, not because of the trees, but because of something else that had grown up. In this chapter there is one notable family I have not mentioned, but will soon... and also apologise to any others I have inadvertently omitted.

When China simply walked into the mountainous kingdom of Tibet and annexed it in the early sixties, there was much killing of these peaceful people, and many others fled. The infant ruler, the Dalai Lama, was smuggled by faithful retainers over secret mountain passes to safety. Many other monks also fled, one of them a young man called Akong Rinpoche, accompanied by perhaps half a dozen other monks. They came to Britain, and after much searching for a suitable abode, settled on Eskdalemuir, which they thought was the nearest place they had seen resembling their former home. They bought a large house, just fractionally larger than our manse, and with it a portion of ground. There they started a settlement with a twofold aim: 1 To practise their Buddhist faith... and propagate it; 2 To preserve Tibetan culture, literature and philosophy.

They even brought two yaks with them, but these hardy animals of the snowclad high peaks found Eskdalemuir too much for them, and died of pneumonia.

Samye Ling, as their centre was named, was run as a sort of guest house and anybody was welcome, whatever their religion or none, provided they paid the going rate. I believe in the early days (which were long before my time) it was a pretty wild place, not infrequently visited by the police, for it was the swinging sixties in Britain, when there were many rebels against authority, and traditional British values were being cast overboard, and many of these rebels arrived at Samye Ling, some complete with drugs, which were just becoming a major worry in our land. Very many of those who gravitated there were from upper class families, sons and daughters of politicians, high ranking army officers, and of aristocratic background... young folk who were rebels against authority, and their parents' way of life, the swinging set, and the place got a bad name. One could imagine how it affected quiet little Eskdalemuir and its inhabitants, as these angry, and wild young men (many of them), dressed in weird clothes, threw all convention to the winds and arrived like a whirlwind in the quiet, traditional type of Scottish country village. All this of course I learned from others… the folks of the valley, but also doctors and police. I do not for one minute think the founders of the settlement encouraged this, but this somewhat weird settlement in the heart of the Border hills was something new and, like a light bulb, for a time attracted every variety of moth. There were, of course, many other genuine seekers after truth, and hearing the story of this Buddhist settlement, I was reminded of Paul's words about those who were "ever learning and never coming to the truth".

Most were vegetarians, and those who stayed permanently, set to work, grew their own vegetables, kept some animals, and tried to be as self supporting as possible. Others who had skills in printing or pottery stayed on, extra prefabricated buildings were built to accommodate the permanent residents, and in many ways it became somewhat like a kibbutz.

By the time I arrived in 1980, by and large it was only genuine Buddhists or those still seeking a philosophy in life who remained, those who called themselves Seekers after Truth, and almost without exception had cast overboard all western culture and values, the influence of the home and of course Christianity. I believe there were about 300 Buddhists in Scotland, and for them all, Samye Ling, with its prayer wheels turning in the wind, was their centre and guide. I met many of the regular or sporadic inhabitants from America, England, France, and a variety of European countries… very few Scots, and not a single convert from Eskdalemuir. I felt sorry for many of the youngsters, for it was patently clear they were on a constant journey for the truth, and for many never arriving at their goal, but others appeared to have found for what they were searching. How I longed for them to find the One in whom all truth is embodied, and can still the restless, seeking soul.

I tried to maintain a good relationship with the leaders, and found them to be courteous, peace loving, quiet people, and some of them very gifted in painting, printing, pottery, and in time they had craft workshops. As I have already noted, they were almost 100 percent vegetarian, though there is nothing wrong or pro-Buddhist in that. They had, of course, that great plank of the Buddhist and Hindu faiths – reincarnation. In other words you kept coming back to the world again and again, though in what form, none could say, and the great goal of the faith was to break out of the cycle and reach Nirvana, their Heaven. A vet friend, who had been a student with me when I was a young assistant, told me he had been asked on one occasion to inspect a large consignment of British birds which, for what reason I do not know, were being exported and required a vet's certificate stating they were free from disease. He found them covered in lice, but said cheerfully, "Never mind, I'll give you some powder which will get rid of them."

His offer was declined, as they explained politely, and sincerely, one of these lice might be a grandmother or other relation. It might have been laughable if this did not also apply in many of the homes, and Eskdalemuir School consistently have the highest lice rate in its pupils in Dumfriesshire.

This belief in reincarnation could also have its tragic side. One day a Lama (or monk) committed suicide. Now the poor man had periodically had mental illness, and constantly pined for his old mother and his beloved Tibet, neither of which he would see again. I called briefly to express my sympathy to the community, and have never experienced such a feeling of blackness, helplessness, and utter despair.

Now, in the course of my ministry I have officiated at the funeral of a number of suicides, and whilst there is always deep sorrow, which can linger in the hearts and minds of the relatives for a long time, and know how desperately hard it is, never have I had such an overpowering sense of total, complete despair. The reason being, I understand, that by this act the poor man had condemned himself forever to the wheel of reincarnation, and could never reach Nirvana. I was deeply sorry for the poor Lama (and the community) and longed to be able to give them the assurance of eternal life, given to us by the only One who came back from death and said: "He that believeth in me, though he were dead (no matter the method of his dying) yet shall he live".

As I get older and see many of my friends depart, how precious has become the certainty that in the presence of the conqueror of death, we shall meet again. Of that I do not have a shred of doubt.

In the eighties the great venture of the Centre was to build a temple, which they did, a huge structure with its own grandeur, built almost entirely by voluntary labour, but still costing £1 million, the largest temple in Europe, but to me an alien, out of place building in the quiet and beauty of the Scottish countryside. Although I am well aware we are now a multi-ethnic land with many religions, and even though I admire the great achievement of a relatively small group, it is an eyesore in what is still classed as a Christian country. On one occasion when there was a notable visiting Lama, a scholar of Buddhism, my Session and I were invited to meet him, which we did in (I believe) their most sacred room. We spent an evening of discussion on the two faiths, and although we were treated with the greatest courtesy, the only common ground we had was a desire for world peace. On another occasion there was a visit to the Dalai Lama himself... a gentle, peaceful man still hoping to return to his own land one day. I came away, as I am sure did many of the hundreds of others invited, only with a feeling of pity for this homeless, globetrotting figure.

There were, so far as I could see, two distinct types of people who were associated with, or claimed association with Samye Ling. Very much in the doubtful category were a goodly number who really had no religion, no money and (even before the recession) no apparent desire to work, but happily live off the state (but that is not confined to Buddhism). Many lived in caravans or semi-derelict property and the council perforce had to house them. When I left in 1990, the new council houses were occupied almost 100 percent by these so-called Buddhists. Also almost 100 percent were occupied by one parent families. It appeared to me that this class was not so much immoral, as amoral. All that seemed to matter, as I shall touch on again, was the happiness, not of the family, but of the individual, no matter who might get hurt. We had in the school three children with the same mother, but all different fathers... but sadly that too in a once Christian Britain, is not confined to other religions, or more accurately, lack of them.

The other class were fairly well off people who were genuine Buddhists and had bought or built homes to be near the centre. Indeed amongst the whole mixter maxter of searchers for the truth were numbers of genuine people who had found their Shangri-La, and for them Eskdalemuir was indeed Happy Valley, but the unhappiness of the local residents has increased in direct proportion to the increase in people from all over the world who, as I have already mentioned, have taken over almost all the available properties, and folks whose forebears have been in the valley for many years, are being forced out.

The fact is that the two cultures are so different they can never work or socialise together, only co-exist, for this is an alien faith that has been implanted against the wishes of the residents of the land, and, as with all implants, the body can sometimes reject it. One very good thing we can, however, learn from this eastern faith, is the importance, indeed the essential nature of prayer and meditation, but over all, my heart bleeds for many friends who have been forced to stay on and work in the midst of all this when they have seen their Happy Valley, if not quite taken over, certainly seriously invaded. But they say: "Why should we move? This is our valley." What the future will bring to the little church, I know not, but whilst I may have fears for the Church as an entity, I have no fears for the faith of its people, for they are folks of great character, strong conviction, whose house of life is built on a rock which cannot be moved.

Mention has been made more than once of the trees. They covered a huge stretch of country, stretching many a mile, and away beyond Eskdalemuir. But in the valley of the Esk, a remarkable man has brought about a miracle of conservation, and in the great world of nature, it is still Happy Valley. This outstanding man is Ronnie Rose, warden and manager of the Economic Forestry Group (EFG), plantations and wildlife officer for a vast stretch of country. To see his slides, and hear him speak is a fascinating experience. EFG was, of course, largely a tax dodge, and Ronnie, son of a gamekeeper, and in many ways a self taught man, was engaged to make sure the trees would grow, take charge of the wildlife, and ensure each was in harmony with the other, and his work is beyond praise. For example, when he came to the valley, there were only ten different kinds of birds, most of them scavengers such as carrion crows. Now he has well over 100 species, including the osprey, living and breeding there. His plan, in essence, has been simple: to let nature control nature, but it has been a masterpiece of planning and involved years of hard toil and fighting to convert others (the majority of nature "experts")j, to his way of things and to his ideas. For example, instead of massive spraying of young trees to kill predatory insects, he has, by creating the right conditions for them, brought back to the area the birds which feed on these insects. To control voles, mice and such like which nibbled and killed seedling conifers, by providing the right kind of nest boxes and other devices, he has enticed back the different species of owl and birds of prey, and they in turn have put paid to the voles. In area after area, in varieties of ways, he has carried out his plan... seemingly simple, but unbelievably involved in planning and carrying out. He has, at times, been a lone voice crying in the wilderness, for university graduates and self-styled experts on nature have been reluctant to listen to the son of a gamekeeper. It has been hard, unremitting work over a huge area and over many years, and it took its toll, Ronnie requiring a few years ago heart surgery, for he never spared himself. But more and more are listening and being convinced, and his son Ronald, whom his dad made certain had a university degree, with a team of trained young men, will, I am sure, continue the work father Ronnie has begun. The farmers trust him, for he keeps down the foxes far more effectively and humanely than any hunt. The forests are now filled with roe deer whose shooting annually under strict supervision (culling, really) brings in much needed revenue, and visitors come from the continent for the shooting, thereby boosting the income of those who do B&B. Yes, a remarkable man whom it has been a privilege to know, with a wonderful wife, Florence, and a lovely family.

When I first went to Eskdalemuir, I recall Mr Cartner, my Session Clerk, naming people in the parish before I had met them, describe Florence Rose as a wonderful woman and a real Christian. She certainly proved this description to be true. She supported her husband in every way in his long hard battles to create a Happy Valley of nature. But she did more.

When I first met Ronnie Rose, he told me he had been, while still a young man, an elder in Aberfoyle Church, but he had no time for the Church now. A terrible fatal accident to a loved brother had driven him from God. I never sought to argue with him, or re-convince him, but now he is right back in Christ's Church, and he, Florence, and son Ronald are all elders and mainstays of the valley's little kirk. It was none of my doing, though I am proud to know him as a friend, but the quiet, consistent, sincere witness of his godly wife have brought him back. God never stops working, and works through different agents, sometimes it may seem slowly, but it is also sure. Ronnie one day in the not too distant future will retire, and he and Florence plan to stay on in the valley. The wealth of any area is its people, and with folks like Ronnie and Florence and the living testimony to his life's work all around them in nature which is the handmaiden of God, why, with the other true believers who plan to stay, Eskdalemuir will continue to be Happy Valley.

EIGHTEEN

Weathering the Storm

Taking advantage of a visit by two of our big, husky sons, I suggested a session of chopping blocks of logs into suitable sizes for the manse fires, of which I was the regular stoker (practice for the life to come, my wife occasionally suggested!). We had no central heating then in our large manse, but in our last two years there we luxuriated in it, thanks to a suggestion from Tom Carruthers, an elder and later Session Clerk... and I hadn't even dropped a hint. So eventually our home was as comfortable as The Ritz. However, the boys' visit was in pre-central heating days, and we had to keep several fires burning each day – a costly and dusty business. But thanks to the willingness of another elder, Tom Bell, a forester, who with muscular arms and a power saw annually took down two or three full grown but dead or dying trees which had become dangerous, and then aided by other willing souls, sawed them into suitable lengths to be chopped into fire sized blocks... an unco task for the ageing minister. So, without admitting it was getting beyond me, and to show I was not yet senile, every visit I coaxed our lads round to the large pile of logs, swung a stylish axe for a few minutes to show how it should be done, then extolling the virtues of manliness and muscular arms, suggested they have a go. It must be said they were always willing to help the old man out, and encouraged by the dog, who always took a new lease of life when any of our sons were at home, and who dashed around barking and fetching sticks, they warmed to their task with a will, competing with each other. When I saw them going hard at it, I surreptitiously slipped away and wandered through our large wood.

Actually the tree that day had not been cut down but struck by lightning which had ripped off one leg of its Y shape and sliced a huge area out of the trunk of the sycamore. This had happened in early winter and I had thought the tree could not survive such an amputation, so I was greatly surprised now in early spring to see it covered with its beautiful green foliage as of yore. It was alive and lovely as ever, despite its massive "surgery".

I wandered on to the edge of the wood, from which I looked over our little hamlet of Boreland, thinking of other trees which had suffered in winter gales. The first was in my first church at dear little Moorton – to be accurate a very large white lilac tree which we were sorry to lose for it was our only white one – and there it lay, broken completely, its roots sticking up in the air. I kept meaning to clear it away, but never got round to it, and was glad I didn't, for it taught me a lesson. When spring came, the fallen bush was covered, as always, in beautiful blooms, even though lying apparently dead. How had this come about? I looked more closely, poked about in the ground, cleared away some earth, and found one solitary root still going into the ground, and drawing up from the earth enough sap and nurture to supply the whole plant. It was as beautiful as ever, even though now recumbent.

The other tree was even more amazing. It was the main branch of an old gnarled plum tree at Aldermouth, a tree which annually had a huge crop of the most delicious Victoria plums, and the branch lay on the ground, seemingly broken right off. But yet when spring came, the branch blossomed... and I looked at it in wonder. How could this be? I examined it carefully and found just one bit of bark still attached to the parent tree, and through that tiny channel, food and water was flowing, and in due course there was a magnificent crop of plums.

The lilac and the plum, and now the sycamore, were still doing their job... and looking beautiful and fruitful in the process. How could they do it? I was reminded of Jesus' words: "Abide in me and I in you. So shall you bring forth much fruit, for without me you can do nothing." The damaged trees were still abiding in the roots.

There are times in life like that, don't you think? We are jogging along happily when suddenly a gale gets up, often without warning, and hits us. It may be a gale of illness whisking us to hospital for surgery. It may be a gale of bad news, perhaps a youngster we love kicking over the traces, going the wrong way, getting into trouble, causing us terrible worry. It may be a storm of sorrow, perhaps the loss of a parent, or life's partner or someone very dear to us, perhaps a life long friend. The wind can get up very quickly and flatten us, and it is not always predicted by the Met Office! But if we can learn the lesson of the trees and stay attached to Christ, we can weather the storm; we can still be beautiful for God and others like the sycamore or lilac, and still be fruitful, like the plum, still, come what may... abiding.

By now I had reached the edge of our wood and was looking over the village, where I knew every home, and it suddenly dawned on me how many of the folks down there had known the storms of life – some very violent storms – some continuous gales. I looked right across the valley to Gillesbie, and I though of Major and Mrs Tulloch. Alec Tulloch had been up and down in health and sometimes life was a struggle, Adele Tulloch had frequent stays in hospital, and they had lost while she was still young a loved daughter-in-law to a disease whose very name frightens people – cancer.

Below them was The Mill where lived all the Rae family. Bobby told me proudly when I first came to Hutton that he was the oldest resident there, but Mamie Graham his sister didn't let him off with that, informing me she was actually the oldest in the village, she just didn't happen to have been born there. Now Bobby was gone, after a long weakening illness and Bella, his wife, had poor health. Mamie Graham had experienced several years of indifferent health, and at times very serious and painful illness. Her husband Charlie, though well into his seventies, never missed a day's work, and his cheerful, ebullient personality and marvellous pawky sense of humour went a long way to his beloved Mamie's healing. Their son and daughter-in-law lived just next door, and Margaret, their daughter-in-law had illness after illness.

My eyes moved on to young Bob Rae's farm, and I thought of his wife Marjory's father, who had for years been confined to a wheelchair... a hard cross to bear for an erstwhile active farmer.

Moving up the village brae, there was the McTurk household where, in quick succession, I'd had two funerals. Just across the way were two sisters, Cathy and Christine Hunter, two village stalwarts, faithful church attenders and always deeply involved in some good cause – Christians whose lives showed real Christianity – expressed in deeds, not words.

My eyes moved on to the four council houses where was Mrs

Taylor who also had spent many years in a wheelchair, and who had but recently lost her husband in an instant, a heart attack while watching his favourite football team, Queen of the South, accompanied by Rae Graham, Charlie and Mamie's son, Margaret's husband. At the other end cottage was Mrs Grieve, whose father had also been taken. Then on again up the other side of the village brae, and I could see the two sisters Hunter busy in their garden, and I recalled how tenderly they had nursed their elderly mother... as I said of them, Christianity expressed in deeds, and mindful that not only charity, but care and compassion begin at home, and their care for their bedridden mother had gone on for years. I had looked at almost every house in our tiny hamlet, and almost every one had known "the tears of things". "Aye, life can be gey hard whiles", as an old shepherd said to me.

My eyes had now moved on to the top of the village, where in a little cul-de-sac were half a dozen houses. The first one was the abode of Tom and Jean Bell, whose children Peter and Lesley were stalwarts in the Youth Fellowship Janet and I ran on a Sunday evening in the manse, something almost every youngster in the parish attended, some coming many miles. We had a serious study portion, then table tennis, carpet bowls and other games in three rooms... and the manse shook with these enthusiastic youngsters, most of them eventually being confirmed as Church members. Tom Bell was one of the most willing men I have known, and helped in a great variety of ways, while Jean, his wife, a lovely, kind woman, despite having a strange disease which affected her balance and frequently caused her to fall, ran our thriving Sunday School, assisted and finally succeeded by Mrs Robson and Mrs Middleton. Next door was an empty house, but a house too which had seen much suffering where had lived Mr and Mrs Coupland, the husband with an artificial leg which caused him much discomfort, the result of a horrific tractor accident years before, an accident where he had been trapped for a very long time... but he still did much of the housework, for his wife had been poorly for many years. Just two doors along was the lovely Carmichael family with two bright, ever present at Youth Fellowship youngsters, Ewan and Hazel. But that day, Hazel, a clever and cheerful lass with brilliant red hair, was in hospital, where she was eventually to have many stays, and Bill and Hilary knew great and continuing worry and without doubt, it was their strong, sure faith which kept them going. They knew in their own family the comfort of God's word which said: "Lo – I am with you always."

As year of illness succeeded year for their lovely daughter, and they were frequently at their wit's end, a verse from THE WORD at least helped them to go on "a day at a time".

As I gazed at this, but one tiny corner of my parishes, it occurred to me as it has many times, how many good homes had known the storms of life... sudden, unexpected gales, or continuing wind and rain, but along with the thought came a feeling of gratitude that I was a country minister, and could know everybody and at least try to help my little flock.

My gaze went further up the Boreland Brae, and I thought of one or two folk beyond my gaze. Just a little way along a side road lived Mr and Mrs Lorimer, a grand, solid, dependable, loving couple, who rain, hail or shine never missed a Sunday in church – real country folk – Bill had been a shepherd on Major Tulloch's estate, their son Brian had taken over from his dad when he retired, but in the most tragic circumstances their other son John had lost his life. Further along the road was the beautiful home of Commander and Mrs Hill where, out of a quarry behind their house, they had created a great area of breathtaking loveliness, masses and masses of azaleas and rhododendrons. Mrs Hill had been in hospital a very long time, had many operations, at times her life hanging by a thread... and not long after she got home her husband, a man held in the greatest respect, passed away. As the old Shepherd said: "Life can indeed be gey cruel"... and all this catalogue of the storms of life in just one tiny corner of one parish.

Of course folks get through the storms of life somehow. Couples help each other; neighbours do what they can, and this is one great advantage country folk have over city dwellers – in a village everybody rallies round, nobody is forgotten. Frequently when there was illness, or somebody had gone into hospital, I would have three phone calls telling me about the illness, just in case I hadn't heard, while my colleagues in city charges often were never told and might be in total ignorance of an illness or a problem in a home where an early call by the minister could help. There was real camaraderie in rural areas, and it was rare for somebody to be left to struggle alone. I remember seeing this sharing in a problem one day up in the hills. As I drove along, I saw a sheep on its back, and as every countryman knows, this can quickly lead to death. I stopped my car, and started to climb the fence when I paused and witnessed something I had never seen before. Another sheep with its head was pushing the helpless one. Again and again it pushed, but always the poor sufferer rolled again onto its back. I watched fascinated; this was something I had never even heard of before. At last the rescuing sheep got the helpless one on to its feet, but it was still wobbly. The strength had gone out of its legs, but the good Samaritan stood beside it and held it up until the helpless sheep was able to walk away. Every shepherd knows that a sheep cannot be left on its back long and at certain seasons he has constantly to be on the lookout for "a coupit ewe". But that day in a lonely place the sheep on its back would have died soon, but for its friend coming to the rescue. I was reminded of a verse in the book of Psalms which is a great comfort: "Fear though not for I am with thee, be not dismayed for I am Thy God. I will strengthen thee... I will uphold thee." (Psalm 41 - 10)

But to all of us in the journey of life comes suffering or sorrow, and we can get to a very low ebb and feel like the trees lying, seemingly helpless or even lifeless, on the ground. Then is the time for faith, for abiding. Even the greatest saints have experienced what St Theresa called "the dark night of the soul", when they felt so low, so flattened like the trees, that they would never rise again; and have even reached the ultimate depths when they have felt that God – if there was a God – had totally deserted them. But as one saint put it: "when you come to the bottom you find God", and these very saints have gone on to testify that it has been in the darkest moments of life they have been most conscious of the presence of Jesus who experienced what no one else has: utter loneliness when His Father, the Holy God, turned His back on His dearly beloved son as on the cross He bore the sins of all mankind and there was wrung from Him that terribly cry of dereliction: "My God, my God; why have you forsaken me?" None of us will ever know that. So when the gales come, hang on to God for no storm can shake Him.

A very small part of this story of the trees was published in the women's magazine *People's Friend* in a feature column *Through the Manse Window* to which I periodically contribute. Purely by way of examples of the storms we can experience in life, I had written: "It may be you have recently lost your mother or your mother-in-law; maybe you yourself have known much illness, and are in hospital awaiting surgery; or of course there can be storms in the family circle, especially when our youngsters are going through the 'rocky' teens." Six months later I received a letter from a lady in Australia, from a poor soul who had experienced gale after gale, and the faith in God she had once held was now all but gone. She wrote to me from hospital where she was awaiting surgery for the umpteenth time. She said that on that particular day when she wrote to me she was so low in spirits that when her husband visited her she could not speak to him but just cried solidly for three hours. She had, just very recently lost her mother, to whom she was very close, and her husband had brought her news that her mother-in-law (his mother) had died that day, both mothers of cancer. She herself was a very ill woman with a very doubtful future, and to crown everything, their teenage son some weeks before had, after a thundering row, left home and they had no idea where he was. Finally, her husband, unable to comfort her, left, and a little later she picked up the top magazine from a pile on the table. It was a six months old *People's Friend.* She opened it at random and read the story of the trees weathering the storm and how they had produced life again. Of course I recognise it could have been chance, coincidence, or whatever we like to call it, but the point was, in exact detail her problems had been mentioned. She wrote to me and said how comforted she had been by the flattened, or damaged trees bearing fruit because they were still abiding in the parent plant, and for the first time in weeks, she had just quietly prayed and left all her problems in His hand. She asked me if I would write to her and help her, which in my own stumbling way I did, enclosing a little booklet which has often helped me (for ministers can get down too), and which I had given to many folks struggling to survive in their own particular storm. She replied almost at once and asked me to keep in touch, told me she had come through her operation successfully, and best of all, the prodigal in the family was back in the fold. She told me she had learned the secret of the trees, just to abide, let go, and let God take care of the future. What a difference there has been in her letters... the tree is beginning to blossom again because, and I quote her, she has found the secret of victorious living: "the wonder of just abiding, resting, and leaving it to God." God certainly works in mysterious ways!

But life is not all storms and Jesus' word about abiding, resting, and leaving it to God is a good recipe for life... after all, it is His recipe.

I recall many years ago when I was a young vet, going to hear a

Scottish missionary speak about his life in India. He was called Tom Wilson and he had gone out with all the enthusiasm and world changing plans we all have in youth. But it hadn't worked out that way... oh, he had worked, flung himself into everything, but saw not a single result for his labours, and became down like the trees, utterly discouraged. What more could he do? Where had he gone wrong? He decided to seek the advice of Sadu Sundar Singh, at one time a famous name across the globe. He had been a Hindu holy man (Sadu means holy one), and been converted to Christianity. He was a calm, serene man, and his wisdom was so legendary that the leaders of several nations had consulted him. He listened to the young missionary's tale of woe and seeming failure and said, "Let's go into the garden". It was a beautiful, peaceful place, with against the wall a glorious peach tree, the peaches golden and succulent.

"What a struggle these peaches are having to grow" said the Sadu.

Tom Wilson looked at him in amazement... a strange man, this Sadu. "Oh, I don't know" he replied, "they just seem to be hanging on the tree."

"Exactly!" said Sundar Singh, "and that's the secret of life and of peace... and our function as Christians. No struggling... no rushing about... no fighting... just abiding in God and a day... nay an hour at a time drawing power... and peace from Him." He laid down his hand on the missionary's shoulder and said, "It's the Master's own recipe for all life. Abide in me and I in you; so shall you bring forth much fruit."

We live in a hectic world, and I am persuaded there is, in most of us in life, and certainly in living the Christian life, too much trying and not enough trusting. His way is the way of peace and calm of spirit, whether weathering a storm or in the daily run of life.

NINETEEN

Crossed Lines

Considering the small population of Eskdalemuir, there were a considerable number of outstanding people some of whom I have mentioned, but probably the best known were the Cartner family, who had farmed the very large farm of Clerkhill for generations. They also had a haulage business and the contract for keeping the roads of the area gritted and snow free, or at least passable, for the snows came, often very heavy falls, every year.

Naturally, because Irving Cartner was Session Clerk and treasurer of our little church, I got to know him very well and held him in high esteem. He was at the church door every Sunday as he had been all his life, holding office, as I have indicated, for well over fifty years. So he was in his seventies when I first knew him, but still fit and athletic and, like the former rugby player he had been, could and did still run after the sheep, and did a lambing every year. A remarkable man. A kindly, caring man. He was blessed with an equally lovely wife, Winnie, a London girl originally who had come to the area to teach, and when there were many more children, was headmistress of the local school for many years. She knew every child of course, but also kept an interest in them, all when they moved out into life, and was held in veneration by them, and in time, their own families. The Cartners had two sons and two daughters, the sons and some of the grandsons working in the family business. Mr and Mrs Cartner were amongst the first people I visited and on that first occasion, as always, the welcome was warm and sincere, and their home a delight to enter. They always seemed pleased to see me, no matter how busy they were. They were also two of the most deeply spiritually minded people I have known, with their lives bedded down deep in God, so that to have a prayer in their home was but talking to the One who was always there. Great Christians. Great people.

Their granddaughter Yvonne's wedding was coming up soon, the first I had to take in my new Border charges. Irving and Winnie recalled to me their own wedding all those years before. As they drove off in their car for their honeymoon, they became aware of a peculiar and far from pleasant smell in their car, apparently coming from the engine. Irving stopped and opened the bonnet to find a pair of kippers on the radiator... certainly by then well and truly kippered! There is no doubt that this man, respected by all, including the Buddhist community, would have been Provost if Eskdalemuir had boasted such an official, but he was chairman of the community council and though reticent and not given to long speeches, generally managed to make his will known, always for the good of all in the valley. I wish I had known them in the halcyon years of the valley, when everything revolved around sheep, everyone knew each other, there were many functions in the village hall, and both Mr and Mrs Cartner trod the boards in plays.

Knowing that Yvonne's wedding to a pleasant lad called Frank Smith would be a big occasion – and my first – I was naturally anxious it should go well. I saw the couple, of course, and went over everything with them, and to my delight they opted to repeat their vows instead of merely affirming "I do", as every couple had done when I began my ministry in Moorton. I felt making their vows in full to one another added to the beauty and completeness of the ceremony, though I always gave a couple a choice of vows. Now at that time I had taken something upwards of about 400 weddings without a slip on my part, so far as I knew. Mind you, I'd had about everything a minister could have: crying brides, crying mothers, a fainting groom, flower girls weeping for Mummy, children being surreptitiously smuggled out to the toilet, babies yelling so loudly I had to shout the wedding service, frequent late brides – one an hour and twenty minutes late because when she had put on her gown for the first time, it had burst (which her strung up bridegroom almost did too), and one piece de resistance I will never forget, away back in my early days in Moorton. Well through the ceremony, the church door opened, a man marched in, very obviously clutching a handkerchief, kept marching purposefully behind the wedding party, handed his large hankie to the person at the end of the row holding the bridegroom's relatives, who were all unknown to me. The hankie bearer whispered something to the person receiving the handkerchief, who nodded and passed the garment on to the next in the row, until it finally reached the bridegroom's father, who was sitting in completely the wrong place, the inside. I was intrigued by the wedding version of pass the parcel, and out of the corner of my eye watched proceedings while still carrying on with the order of service. The father took the hankie casually and unconcernedly and put it to his mouth and all was revealed – literally. His formerly toothless gums were now occupied! I believe weddings should be happy affairs, but had not expected slapstick comedy.

On wedding mornings I always went over the whole service, even though I could repeat it blindfold, and this I did on Yvonne's great day. As I recall it was a fair, bright sunny day, and the church full. Everything went fine till we came to the couple's vows, when I said to Frank, a phrase at a time: "I, Frank, to take thee, Yvonne, to be my wedded husband..."

There was a deathly hush, I was aware of some gasps and hard stares and the groom said to me "wife".

I stared at Frank... what was the fellow saying? I said "beg pardon", and Frank, with a grin repeated "wife"... and the awful truth dawned on me. I stammered, blushed, and asked "Did I say husband?"

Frank was a good natured chap and he just grinned again and said "yes".

So we had to begin the vows again, but not before I had looked round for a hole to crawl into. After hundreds of weddings without a slip, in *this* wedding to do that! I was mortified, humbled and at the reception afterwards apologised profusely, but folks couldn't have been nicer or more understanding. Indeed they were highly amused and Margaret, the bride's mother said "It shows you are human just like us."

I felt pretty sub human and miserable and some must have thought that this minister from a big kirk, as they still regarded me a bit, should go back to being a vet when he couldn't do a simple wedding without a mistake. If Yvonne was one of these wives who were, as they say in Ayrshire, "going to wear the breeks" in their marriage, it might have made sense calling her "husband" but she wasn't like that. I had not even realised what I'd said at the time. Anyway, they forgave me, and still send me a Christmas card every year. So far as I know, for the rest of my ministry, I never got my lines crossed... but thanks, all you good forgiving folk!

The other crossed lines were very different. We had in our church nearly every Sunday a man in his forties who was a sincere, devout Christian, an American who was living and working in the valley. His parents had been missionaries in, I think, China, but now, well up in years, and somewhat frail, were retired to their native land. Ted, their son, went to see them most summers in the States, and when we had a congregational vote for additional elders, he was elected and along with the others, Willie Young, Miss Laidlaw, Mrs Webster, Mrs Rose and Mrs Cartner, was duly ordained. These were my first women elders... indeed years before when in Irvine and Kilmarnock presbytery, in my Moorton days, I had voted against women elders. But these four women, and others who were later ordained at Hutton and Corrie, proved me wrong, and no minister could have wished for more devoted, committed, whole hearted Christians and were among the finest of the almost 100 elders I ordained in my ministry. But to our story of the crossed lines.

One evening Ted came to see me and tell me he wanted to marry a woman who was a whole hearted Buddhist. I was deeply unhappy about the whole proposition, knowing what the Bible says about being yoked together to unbelievers (or non-Christians). I explained what the scriptures said to Ted, but it was clear they were going to be married anyway, probably in a registry office. I thought and prayed much about it all, and finally, with the greatest reluctance, agreed to tie the knot, feeling it was better to maintain one foot in the door than lose Ted altogether. I went over the service, the Christian view of marriage, and the vows they would take, and Susie, who was an intelligent and thoughtful girl, felt she could truly take and would keep the vows, so, after many meetings and discussions, more than with any other couple, I agreed, largely because Susie assured me she would happily take the Christian vows, including the promise to be faithful for life to each other. The wedding was to be in Samye Ling, but the only part the Akong would have was to ask a blessing at the end.

It was before the massive temple had been completed, and the ceremony was to be in the Shrine room of the house, which no one was allowed to enter with their feet shod in any way. As always at such occasions, I was in my ministerial robes, as the Akong was in his. When I kicked off my shoes before entering, I had a quick peek at my socks to make sure there were no holes. There was no singing except by the Buddhist guests, who sang several pieces, one of them which had about twenty verses in it being, I understand, the story of the Buddha's lie. They took their vows, so far as I could tell, with deep sincerity, then as was my custom always, I emphasised that they had taken these vows before God, and made their promises for better or worse, in sickness in health, to each other for life, and these promises were for complete faithfulness to each other. They listened intently… then the Akong laid his hands on their heads and in Tibetan, which only he understood, asked what was presumably a blessing. It too seemed to go on for ever, and I felt my shoeless toes beginning to curl. Afterwards the bride said, in all seriousness to me "it must have been a very strong blessing for he pressed harder and harder on our heads."

That was supposed to be it and what had been agreed. But it seemed the representative of Buddhism was not done and proceeded to give his advice to the couple. I remember it well: "The goal in life is happiness for each, individual person. If you find happiness with one another, that is good, but if you do not, don't hesitate to seek your own happiness alone or with someone else."

I gasped… at a wedding advising perhaps a quick separation or a life with somebody different. No one else, apparently mattered… only the happiness of the individual. No wonder there were so many one parent families, I realised, and so much for my love for life and loyalty to one another. And these, mark you, were two clever, well educated and in their own way, devout people.

However, for some years things moved along reasonably well and our couple were even interviewed by Sir Harry Secombe as an example of how two totally different religions could get on happily together, when he did a *Highway* programme from the valley. Alas, it was not to last. After a few years together, Ted, the husband who was, incidentally a thoroughly nice fellow, returned from a visit to his aged parents to be more or less turned out at the door by Susie. She informed him she felt happier without him, and had not the Akong said it was one's *own* happiness that mattered, and was the goal of life.

The poor fellow came to see me, and I offered to do all I could to bring about a reconciliation, but he didn't want me to intervene at that point in time. He wandered about the valley for some time, still hoping, for he loved his wife, and staying with various friends. He looked utterly lost and I felt deeply sorry for him, but finally he realised it was hopeless and returned to the States. This example, at any rate, of two totally different cultures and disparate religions simply did not work. It may be others have... but I know of none. The old, wise book had been proved right again, and in retrospect, as any colleague reading this story probably has felt all along, in an attempt to bring happiness to a couple I had in the end caused heartache.

I am bound to say that having observed Buddhism at close quarters for ten years, however it may work in Tibetan culture, it is, despite the wisdom of the east, an alien thing in our way of life. While I do not doubt for one minute the sincerity of those who genuinely follow it, I found it, as practised in Scotland, a very selfish, self centred philosophy. Only the individual's happiness at any given moment mattered.

So these two very different wedding had definitely crossed lines – in different ways – and when lines cross you can often get a short and everything goes dead, as with our second couple... or you blow a fuse which I certainly did in the first.

TWENTY

The Moderator!

There was a buzz in my four parishes. For the first time in donkey's years, the Moderator of the General Assembly of the Church of Scotland was going to visit us. For the benefit of those unfortunate enough not to be Church of Scotland, let me explain who this dignitary is.

It is really easier to say who he is not. He is not the equivalent of the Archbishop of Canterbury, a Cardinal of the Roman Catholic Church or some other high ranking official who holds the post more or less for life. In fact there are no steps and stairs, no ranks in the Scots Kirk. All ministers, male or female are equal. True, some are paid more than others, depending on the size of the church in large measure, but there is a minimum stipend below which no minister – the great majority in the Church – can be paid. The Moderator is merely a senior minister who is appointed by a committee representative of all Scotland. The Moderator, in turn, represents the whole Kirk as a spokesman and ambassador for a year. Many men have accepted the post with great reluctance, but some, contrary to Jesus' words about seeking high places, from early on in their ministry have set their sights on the position, and have worked their way through a variety of important committees to reach their goal... climbers, we call them. If this seems a harsh judgement, so be it... it is, sadly, true. Until comparatively recently the Moderator was appointed without first being approached, but after Professor William Barclay turned down the invitation as I have said elsewhere, an irate committee decided it would be better to approach the man, or woman, first and sound them out to avoid such an unthinkable disaster again.

Here let me say that Professor Barclay, whom I knew very well, felt honoured to be invited, but he was not a committee man and felt he would not do justice to the pose, and the Church, and many were more suited. I am sure his assessment of himself was wrong, but it was honest.

Having, I hope, cleared the air, let it be said there have been many outstanding Moderators who have travelled far and wide at home and abroad, represented the Church at all sorts of occasions, encouraged many ministers labouring in lonely or difficult places... and usually aged about ten years in their diligence to their task. The man coming to us was Dr William McDonald, known to most as Bill... a humble man and neither climber nor authoritarian, albeit an outstanding scholar and preacher. I knew him slightly, but he always treated me as an old friend. He was a man of the people... all people, whom I knew in advance would lift our morale in our wee Border kirks and give a message we would remember. He was also a man to whom I was greatly indebted for a tremendous kindness one terrible night.

It all began with our phone at Aldermouth ringing at 2 am. I galloped down the stairs to answer it, thinking it must be a sudden death in the parish, but to my surprise I heard the voice of one of our sons, apologetic for disturbing us, which was typical of him, but also very agitated. He was working in Edinburgh at the time where he shared a bedsit with several other lads, each, of course with their own bedroom. One of the young men was a big, strapping teenager, a blacksmith, but also an ex-borstal boy. Our son had wakened to find this fellow in his bedroom, with much drink in him, and threatening our lad, who was, of course in bed, with a knife. Our lad hastily got up, pulled on a pair of trousers, and managed to get the knife off the fighting mad aggressor. None of the other lads seemed keen to be drawn in... our boy was on his own, and trying to talk sense into the drunken youngster. However, when his attacker broke a bottle and came at our son with it, he wisely decided it was time to clear out, which he did, only half dressed, and phoned us for advice.

"You must phone the police," I said, but this he refused to do for it would certainly mean jail for the aggressor, and our boy was unwilling for this to happen, particularly as the tough had a record, and was also I believe, an orphan. I tried to persuade our boy, but he refused, so finally I said, "Give me your location, the number of the phone box and stay there till I get back to you."

So I phoned the Edinburgh police, explaining the situation, but they could not have been less helpful, refusing to do anything unless our lad would bring a charge against the other, which he was unwilling to do. So the police did nothing!

What could I do, in the middle of the night, 160 miles away? I have seldom felt so helpless. I did not know anyone in Edinburgh… then I thought, Bill McDonald, whom I had met two or three times. I phoned him very apologetically, explained the position, and he could not have been more helpful or understanding. He explained that he could not rescue our son himself (there was no way that a peace-loving, gentle lad was going back to be attacked with a broken bottle), for Bill was just that day out of hospital after surgery. "But leave it with me. I'll get help" he said, and he did.

He got one of his elders to go and pick up a cold and frightened laddie from the phone box, took him to his home, where he and his wife gave him a hot drink for shock and a bed for the night. That elder also went the second mile, for next day, he took our son back to his bedsit, gathered up all his belongings, and saw him settled in a safer abode. Of course, I wrote thanking Bill and the elder for their considerable kindness and understanding, but I had not seen Bill since that night. This then was the man who was coming one Wednesday evening in 1990 to visit us and preach in our humble wee kirk, but a church just as important to our Moderator as a cathedral.

Quite a few months before, our Kirk Session at Hutton and Corrie had decided that it was time the church had a facelift in the interior. When we learned of our important visitor, we were naturally anxious to have the painting done in time for his coming, for although his visit was to all my parishes, the service was to be held in Hutton as the most central of the four. On the Saturday before the visit I was to have a father's great pleasure in marrying our youngest son Alan, to Jill, a Yorkshire lass. We had asked Mrs Spence, a wizard at flower arranging, to see to that side of things, we kept our fingers crossed that the painting would be completed in time, and it was – just!

I must say that though I have seen many churches decorated… hundreds, for a wedding, I have never seen one more beautiful than our little old kirk on the hill, the oldest in the presbytery. The wedding passed off happily, and then by dint of daily watering, talking to the flowers, snipping off anything that was wilting, we managed to keep the church just as lovely for the Moderator and his lady.

On the big night Janet and I went to pick up the Moderator and Mrs McDonald from the hotel where they were staying in Lockerbie and he greeted me like an old friend even though I was but one of hundreds of minister he had met, and Mrs McDonald was equally gracious. On the way over to our church, I thanked him for his great kindness to us that dreadful night, especially when he was far from well, but he dismissed it as nothing. Now he had been worked very hard in our presbytery, and ours was very likely the smallest church he was visiting, but he treated it as just as important as any of his bigger engagements, then surprised me as we drove by asking: "What do you want me to say to your people tonight?"

Who was I to tell a Moderator, and I stammered a bit, having assumed that he had his address all prepared. All I could do was give him the background of our churches, which he clearly already knew... he had done his homework, so all I could suggest was that as we were so small, we sometimes felt small, and perhaps just to make our country folk feel they were really part of a worldwide Church would help their morale, and I assured him he would have as attentive and knowledgeable a congregation as the biggest kirk, and the welcome would come from the heart.

It was an unforgettable night. The atmosphere was warm, the singing, a mixture of old and modern hymns, as always, tremendous, and I felt very proud of my flock, and also felt we were just a big family gathered in worship. Bill spoke to them as a friend, and because he knew that life could be hard at times, and faith harder, he just wanted to pass on three qualities that a fellow citizen of his in Edinburgh had desired for himself and others, and prayed for – a man who sometimes soared on the wings of faith and at other times had the most dramatic plunges into the pit of doubt – the man Robert Louis Stevenson, author of *Treasure Island.* His three wishes for them? 1 Courage; 2 Cheerfulness; 3 A quiet mind.

I have no doubt the Moderator had used that theme before, but it came over fresh, it instructed the mind, it touched the heart, it found an echo in everyone there, and Bill, without a note, spoke to them as one of them, not someone talking down in any way, and as the folks leaned forward to listen, a pin could have been heard dropping, and we were caught up in a real worship. Afterwards, of course, there was tea in the village hall, prepared by the Guild and elders' wives, and as always in our country charges, far more than could be eaten. Bill and his wife moved among the folks, and there was a smile on every face. A night, indeed, to remember.

Two evenings later Janet and I were at a reception for presbytery ministers and their partners given by the Regional Council in a Lockerbie hotel for Dr and Mrs McDonald. It proved to be a veritable banquet. I have never in all my life seen or tried to consume such quantities of food – enormous portions. By the end I felt it would take a block and tackle to lift me out of my seat! The Moderator evidently had a greater capacity than me, or had been sparing himself, for, as always, he had to get up and speak to the whole gathering, which he did with that gift he seems to have of drawing everybody into a big family. As Janet and I headed for our car at the close, completely overloaded in the abdominal region (us, not the car), our presbytery elder and Session Clerk of Hutton and Corrie said "Was that no' tremendous! Aye, you'll be groanin' in your beds the nicht."

Tom was right... despite Rennies and milk of magnesia when we got home, it was *not* a comfortable night!

The Moderator was busy preparing to go to China the next week and I did not expect, or look to hear from him, but he wrote, a letter as to an old friend, a letter which I have cherished, in which he said: "I shall long remember the service at Hutton. There was a warmth and intimacy which meant a lot.

Every Blessing,

Yours ever,

Bill"

Yes... a people's Moderator who warmed the hearts and instructed the minds of all our folks.

TWENTY ONE

Wonders Beneath our Feet

I was standing in the village hall of Corrie, accompanied by my wife one October day. Also there were Archie and Isa Carruthers, and Tom and Anne Carruthers (no relations) and Kathleen Jackson. Everything in Corrie centred on the hall. There had been a time till very recently when the little one teacher school had been another focus of events. There were not many children, so, of course, I knew them all and visited them fortnightly, as I did with my three other schools The teacher was superb, ideal for a country school, with a genuine love for the kids, and a realisation that the school meant much to the whole community of this hamlet perched right on top of the hill, catching every wind that blew. But the inhabitants of Corrie loved it, despite the wind and weather. Every year the teacher wrote a pantomime performed by all the children and all the mums. It was a great success annually, as were the sessions of Scots poetry and other events. The local people were always afraid the school would be closed, but since the education authorities had spent £60,000 renovating it, it was considered safe. However, having spent all that money on the building, in next to no time they closed it, to general mourning all round, and also anger at the waste of the nation's money.

So now the hall was the only place people could gather, which they certainly did in number for badminton and carpet bowls in winter, and a very popular, and well run summer show of sheep, flowers, fruit, jam, vegetables and so on. They had a big Burns Supper every second year when the hall was always packed, and almost as soon as we arrived in the parish, learning I had come from Burns' Ayrshire (and indeed having been born beside the river Afton and done much of my courting beside "Ye banks and braes o' bonnie Doon"), I was roped in to do the Immortal Memory.

Virtually everybody attended everything in Corrie, situated about six miles from Lockerbie, and part of the huge Castlemilk estate. And so there was hunting, and a clause in the farmers' agreements that they would allow the hunt to go over their land, in complete contrast to neighbouring Hutton, some four miles away, almost all downhill, but still 500 feet above sea level when you arrive, and the folks of Hutton were dead against hunting. I said everybody attended everything which was almost the case, and they all attended to one another. If anybody was ill or incapacitated, they could be certain neighbours would rally round and help. There was no loneliness, as there seldom is in rural communities, so different from the soul-less multi storey flats of the cities. When old folks did move away to sheltered housing in Lockerbie, while they liked their modern facilities, suitable for walking with zimmers, and with all mod cons, they would still bemoan their little village on the hilltop and say "Ah, Mr Cameron, it's no like Corrie." While most of the folks in Corrie had grown up there, and many lived there all their lives, some retired people made their home in the village, and if they joined in the life of the village, they were at once accepted and roped in to all the ongoings. Folks like George and Ethel McNeil, who had chosen to make their retirement home there, were an enormous asset to the life of the village. Every fortnight a service was held in the hall, but here, sadly, not everybody joined in, and about half the worshippers generally came up from Hutton. Although lacking somewhat in numbers, these services were lively, homely, informal, friendly, warm hearted, cheerful gatherings and with Kathleen at the piano, I was constantly astonished at the vigour and volume of the singing. I joined briefly in the chit-chat which went on at length after the service, but it went on long after the minister was on his way to Eskdalemuir for their hour of worship. Archie, who had seen to the heating, seating, hymn lists and so on prior to the hall service, would clear everything away at the end. We were just one big family who enjoyed one another's company and worshipping God together, an integral part of the life of our scattered community.

But to return to the day in question in October, we knew there would be a packed hall the next day for it was Harvest Thanksgiving, still an important and meaningful day in the country, and we were viewing the marvellous display at the front of the hall, on the stage and all round the walls. Mostly it was the work of Archie and his wife Isa, though the others mentioned and periodically farmers' wives popping in with their gifts would add to it. Though in his seventies, he was the village handyman, nothing was too much bother and whenever some problem arose the cry went up: "Send for Archie!". Every year for our harvest display he scoured the countryside with his car and trailer and came back with masses of greenery, rowan berries and so on and arranged it all around the hall. In addition he had the best chrysanthemums in the village, and willingly brought them to our display. As if that was not enough, he had made a miniature corn stack, whose big brothers I had helped to build in my youth before the days of combine harvesters – for all my spare time was spent on farms where I gained my love of animals which led eventually to vet college and my Devon practice – as I've said several times in this diary.

As I looked at Archie's magnificent flowers, I recalled a story I had just heard, and knowing his keen sense of humour, passed it on.

Three clergymen died and went to their celestial abode. One was an Anglican, one a Roman Catholic and one a Church of Scotland. At the Pearly Gates they were interviewed by the duty angel of the day. He took them one at a time, as it happened, the Anglican first, to whom the angel explained he had to pass a small test: "Spell God". This the vicar did easily and was admitted. Came the Roman Catholic's turn, and he had the same test, and likewise passed and was admitted. That left the Church of Scotland minister, and he was asked: "Spell chrysanthemum"... so in spare moments, I'm studying the dictionary and brushing up my spelling!

Archie laughed heartily, clapped me on the back, and pronounced "That's a gude yin. I can aye ca' them crysants, so tell the angel that's the Scottish way."

We stood silent for a moment, then, hesitantly he asked, "Are you pleased wi' the hall? Is it a' richt?"

"Archie, you don't need to ask. It's magnificent. Thanks again for all this work. We do appreciate all you do for the kirk, you know."

"You can aye rely on Archie to get it richt" said Tom Carruthers (our Session Clerk in our later years), who ran a builders' business with his sons Frank and Tommy, and saw to it that the manse was kept in top class order. His wife Anne had been a most capable and loving Sunday School leader at Corrie until there were no young children left.

There seemed to be everything on display: bags of tatties (potatoes), leeks, cabbages, onions, turnips, apples, butter, eggs, jam, a glass of milk and one of water, coal and logs which the minister had once asked for, a lovely bunch of grapes, as always, hanging on the lectern, and of course flowers of all kinds.

"Well done, Archie boy" I said, "you've done it again... but you've forgotten one thing."

"Whit's that?"

"The commonest crop in Britain... including Corrie."

Archie scratched his head and asked "tatties?"

"No... they're there."

"Turnips?"

"No."

"Barley?"

"No."

"I gie up," said Archie, something he had not done at the Battle of Arnhem, and all the others in the hall confessed themselves beaten.

Just then a very large man and his little wife came in the door, Mr and Mrs Willie Bell, a couple well up in years, and Willie, a real character, known to everybody as "The Deil" – an apt description, for you never knew what he was going to say next, including to his minister, but a workaholic with a heart as big as his frame.

"Here's the man to tell us" said Archie. "Willie, whit's the maist common crop in Britain?"

And the Deil immediately said: "Weeds!"

There was general laughter, then I said "I'm going to talk about it tomorrow and it would be nice to have some on show. What do all the beasts in the field eat? Can be made into hay or silage."

"Grass" said Archie, "man, you're richt!"

"Grass is not a crop" maintained the Deil. "It's... weel, it's just grass."

"We'd be lost without it, Willie, and I'm sure when you were looking after your milk cows, you saw many a one stawed at the end of winter, sickened with cattle cake, and just wearying for some grass."

"I'll have a turf richt in the middle the morn" said Archie.

He was as good as his word, and no doubt to the surprise of a full hall of worshippers, as Kathleen, our skilful, enthusiastic and most willing organist and pianist struck up *We Plough the Fields and Scatter*, and the congregation let rip (for as I've noted already, they could certainly sing at Corrie), there was the unusual sight of a turf of grass surrounded by apples, oranges and all the rest, they must have wondered what grass was doing there. It was a cheerful, happy service, as these country folk truly and sincerely gave thanks... no formality, this service, as it often is in towns... but thanks to the Great Creator of everything there for another year when "seedtime and harvest" had not failed. At the end, everybody had a good blether, and the elders got busy packing the produce into boxes and bags for the sick and elderly. I felt good as I looked out at the great throng, everybody knowing everybody else, my people, I felt with pride, every one of whom had listened carefully to every word, joined in all the proceedings, nodded encouragingly when a farmer and a farmer's wife, with quaking knees, had read the lessons. Eventually, they drifted off home, having truly "thanked the Lord".

Now what is there to say about grass, someone may wonder? So just in case anyone is curious enough or a busy brother minister is looking for an idea (as I always was), let me stick my neck out and give "the heads of the sermon". I used as a text some words from Psalm 147: "Sing unto the Lord with thanksgiving who maketh grass to grow on the mountains."

First, we are talking of something that is *sure*.

As I write this, the sun is beating down from a cloudless sky as it has done much of this summer, and the grass has grown lush and green, but even in a wet summer it grows... perhaps even more. There are more than 100 different varieties of grass... Timothy, Ryegrass, Cocksfoot, Sweet Vernal, and so many more, but we don't need to understand it to grow it, for it comes up of its own accord. As sure as the seasons, as certain as day and night, glorious when you see a field of long grass rippling in the breeze, restful to the eye, soft to walk on, safe for our children to play on. Whatever else may fail, in our land every year the lovely green grass grows.

Hudson the naturalist writes: "When I hear people say they do not find the world interesting, and have nothing to be thankful about, I am apt to think they have never seen a blade of grass." Year after year it comes, even if we do nothing to it, fulfilling God's promise that "While the earth remaineth, seedtime and harvest shall not cease." The harvest of grass, something that is *sure*.

Second, The Psalmist tells us of something that is *surprising*.

Grass... on the mountains. Of course we expect it in the valleys, along river banks, or on our rolling Border hills, but it is only the highest peaks of Scotland that have no grass. You find it clinging to ledges of the mountain sides, providing a bite for the Blackface sheep, the red deer and the mountain hare.

Years ago my wife and I climbed a mountain at beautiful Plockton in the Highlands, and after scrambling up a rocky face, right on the very top of the mountain we had a lovely surprise. There was a little loch with water lilies blooming on it and all around it soft, green grass... a surprise indeed.

God is a God of surprises. He takes a timid girl frightened to cross the street (long before motor cars), and makes her into a great missionary who faces up to witch doctors and native chiefs, and saves the lives of countless twins who were considered "bad medicine" and killed... and we call her Mary Slessor. He takes a rich young nobleman with everything the heart could desire, and turns him into a poor friar with a love of all created things... and we call him Francis of Assisi, with a prayer the whole world badly needs to heed *Make me a Channel of your Peace.* He takes a young pop star, the idol of millions of youngsters, and we call him Cliff Richard. Surprising! Like grass upon the mountains. Most of all, long ago, when men looked for a mighty king, He sent a babe to Bethlehem, and instead of hob nobbing with the rich or religious, He was found at a carpenter's bench and mixing with humble folk and outcasts. When His nation looked for Him to lead an army against the oppressors, they heard Him preaching peace and love. *Surprising.*

Third, and finally, this wonder beneath our feet is *simple.*

No doubt grass has a complicated chemical make up, but we don't need to understand it to grow it. Throw a handful of seed into the ground and it comes up, we know not how. And you know the heart of the gospel is simple like that. Once there was a little rocky hill and there cruel, blind men crucified the Prince of Glory. But that was not the end – and there will be no end – for in three days He walked alive on the dewy grass and is alive for evermore. All we have to do is believe, trust, receive Him... and over the whirling centuries millions have found the faith that transforms life in the Man of Calvary and who is the conqueror of death and the assurer of Eternal Life. As the old Scotswoman put it: "Was it no' a wunnerfu' thing that God should come the way He did so that an ordinary body like me could grup Him". I like that "grup Him". *Simple.*

So the next time you walk across a park or field, or even sweat over the lawnmower, think for a moment of the wonders beneath your feet... and give thanks.

TWENTY TWO

Memories are Made of This

That Magic Night

They were streaming into Hutton kirk as we sang our warm up, gathering carols. Some folk we had not seen since last Christmas Eve, but no matter – on this special night of the year, this most magic of occasions, the Watch Night Service – somehow we were all one. On every face there seemed to be a smile. Pews meant to hold four had six in them and nobody complained. We sang the old carols and some new ones. Jim Jackson, one of our many farmer friends, and husband of our organist, read in the Doric the matchless story of the shepherds. Then the lights were dimmed, except the Christmas tree, as I led "my family" in pilgrimage to a stable manger, and we thought of Wise Men following a twinkling star to a little town in the long ago. At midnight the lights went on again, we greeted all around us with a warm handshake or a kiss and voices everywhere were saying "Happy Christmas". Then the finale, as we sang every year, surely the loveliest of carols: "Silent night; holy night; all is calm; all is bright"... and a peace that is quite unique seemed to enfold us all together for "Christ the Redeemer is here"

A ray of hope flickers in the sky,
A tiny star lights up way up high.
All across the land dawns a brand new morn,
This comes to pass when THE CHILD is born.

Born in our world, the Mighty God... born in our hearts the Saviour of the world... peace wrapping us round... for once again it was Christmas.

The Prince Drops in

The folks of the valley had turned out in force, old and young. There was security in the shape of Allan Irving, a Special Constable, and all eyes were raised heavenwards at the first rattle of the helicopter. We knew it carried Prince Charles, and also that he was piloting it. It was a month before his wedding to Lady Diana, and on that day of bright sunshine, we all watched as the helicopter landed, the Prince and his bodyguards stepped out to be greeted by the official party, and made their way up to our field. There most of the inhabitants of the valley were lined up in two rows behind restraining ropes, in one corner the schoolchildren dancing about in excitement. He was officially there to see the work of the Economic Forestry Group and the progress Ronnie Rose, the warden had made, and Florence, Ronnie's wife, was to give them all their lunch.

He walked between the lines of smiling subjects, stopping every now and then to have a few words with a group. To their great disappointment, he didn't stop at the children – I don't think he actually spotted them in their little corner – but to my delight he stopped at us. Delight because my aged mother was with us, leaning heavily on her two sticks. I thought she would be thrilled, and while she was undoubtedly pleased, she took it all as a matter of course. He asked her if she'd had an accident or an operation and she replied without a "Your Highness" or "Sir": "No! It's just this old rheumatism. Could you no' get me a pair of new knees?"

He laughed, but then was all concern and said, "I think they can fit new knees now". He then asked her age and when she told him he said "Why, that's the same age as my grandmother."

Then he spotted my dog collar, asked about the church, and when I told him I was an odd minister, having been a vet first, quick as a flash and with a twinkle in his eye he said "Same job... different flock!"

Everybody around seemed awed by this notable visitor except my mother who had simply spoken to him, and later of him, as if he was just one of Jock Tamson's bairns... but then aren't we all?

A Joyful Noise

The Hutton choir was in full voice – all two of them – as they gave *Onward Christian Soldiers* big licks. It was amazing what a lead the two sisters Mamie and Bessie gave to the singing. Mamie had the stronger voice, but Bessie was, in a way, a greater marvel, for she was deaf, yet she managed to keep the tune perfectly.

Eventually we decided (we being Kathleen the organist and yours truly) to try to enlarge the choir, big enough for singing in parts. People were approached, an appeal was made, and lo and behold, we got fourteen, scarcely one of them who could read music. Practices were started on a Thursday evening, and some peculiar noises emanated from the church for a time. But very quickly our new choir settled down – mainly sopranos, two contraltos, two tenors, and one bass – and me. I have a light baritone voice (though some would say I have no voice at all!), and I would augment tenor or bass, whatever one needed help. Having sung in a choir in my youth, as had Janet, where we first met in my father's junior choir, we had some basic knowledge and were able to explain the symbols – ff (very loud), pp (very soft) – and so on. It was all great fun, there was plenty of leg pulling, and Kathleen at the organ was delighted with our progress, and her skill and patience gradually moulded us into some kind of shape.

In no time we were ready to sing our first anthems. We began with *Crossing the bar*, which sounds like something from a football match or hostelry, but went over surprisingly well... and the congregation was delighted.

At Christmas and Easter we produced a veritable bevy of pieces, everybody getting well into the spirit and swing of it all. I don't think we could have entered any "new choirs of the year" contests, but there is no doubt it enhanced greatly the worship of our wee church. The choir, I think surprised themselves in what they could do, and produced several surprises like Tom Woodcock, a gardener aged 60 who had never sung before, but proved to have a good tenor voice, and scarcely missed a practice, even when he retired and went to live in Dumfries, twenty miles away. When Willie Ferguson, the Session Clerk, was able to come, his great booming bass voice resounded all round the kirk.

Of course, it was Kathleen's enthusiasm that moulded us together, and being a glutton for punishment, she also started a guild choir which was very good indeed, and soon being invited to perform at other guilds or churches. We introduced several new items from *Songs of God's People* and other modern books, and in time the congregation loved them, especially when they heard their choir could sing many things they heard on TV's *Songs of Praise.*

"Make a joyful noise to the Lord" said the Psalmist – and we did just that. Noise was right at first, then it became tuneful, and it was always joyful.

The story is told of a minister who was preaching in a holiday town one summer Sunday. In the congregation were many visitors, one of them being a Salvation Army member. He was a happy soul, and whenever he agreed with the minister or appreciated what he had said, he called out "Praise the Lord". Eventually an elder bore down on him with solemn tread and with even more solemn voice informed him: "Look here, my good man. We dinna praise the Lord here!"

Well, we praised the Lord, gained much pleasure and I think gave much. Well done, Kathleen and the choir… Praise the Lord!

Country Camaraderie

The snow had fallen all day, and it was hopeless to try to do any visiting, for the roads were blocked. I had been to Lockerbie in the early morning, and slipped and slithered my way the seven miles home along the main road the snow ploughs were battling to keep open. But we still had not collected our milk from The Gall farm, only a mile away, but up a minor road. The snowflakes were large, wet blobs of ice blown horizontally on a howling wind… a complete white out. I knew I couldn't walk against that Arctic wind to the farm so tried the car. But the wipers were helpless. I tried driving with my head out the window and was immediately blinded; the sides of the road were blotted out, the car slipped and slithered, and the inevitable happened… I went off the road into a ditch. What now?

My murmured prayer was almost immediately answered as an angel called Ian Roxburgh was sent to my help. He came down from the farm driving a large tractor with a snow plough on the front of it… and a big smile on his face. Ian was the son-in-law of the Maxwell family at The Gall, and though an industrial chemist by profession, loved farming. He was also one of the most cheerful, willing and helpful men in the district.

"Spot of bother, Mr Cameron?" he greeted me. "But don't worry,

I'll soon get you out."

He did exactly that, and went in front of me with his snow plough tractor and cleared a way to the manse.

"Now don't worry. I'll bring down your milk with the tractor"... and he did.

We were snowed in for about a week, but it was really quite cosy. The outside world was one white mass, sparkling in the sun. We had plenty of coal and logs, so were warm in our large manse; the deep freeze had enough food in it; the birds came every morning to the back door for crumbs and nuts; a hedgehog strolled along each night for a saucer of milk; the dog went mad, diving into the deep drifts and having the time of her life and over all was that special silence that only comes in a snow clad world in the country.

On the first day the roads were clear, our grown up sons visited us, looked out their sledge, and flew down a steep hill next to our home at break-neck speed, the dog galloping beside them barking with excitement. Even the old man was persuaded to go back to his youth and had a go on the sledge... but once was enough!

There was no panic anywhere in the parishes such as would possibly happen in towns with families cut off for days. People kept in touch by phone, made sure everybody was alright and stocked up with food and fuel, especially the old folks, and running short of supplies could be sure of neighbourly help. It was the typical camaraderie of the country.

It is a truism to say the loneliest people are in the big cities... in a crowd. In the country, folks truly care for one another in a very companionable way. I get angry when still in this day and age I occasionally hear those who should know better and live in cities or suburbs refer to country people as if they were an inferior race. Why, they are the salt of the earth.

Ambassador for Peace

There was an air of expectancy and excitement among the Buddhist community of Eskdalemuir, and even the non-Buddhists were touched. The Akong sent out invitations far and wide, including one to me, and I think most of the people of the area, to see, hear and meet the Dalai Lama: spiritual head of Tibetan Buddhists. He was a world figure, honoured wherever he went.

So, along with a large crowd of others (as I have previously mentioned), I went. The folks of Samye Ling had worked hard to make the visit a success. For them it was a bit like the Pope visiting a Roman Catholic country. It appeared that while the Samye Ling Buddhists revered the Dalai Lama as leader of their mountain kingdom of Tibet, he was not, in fact, head of their particular order of Buddhism. Only then did I realise, something I confess I had forgotten, that Buddhism was actually fragmented like Christianity, with different denominations, so to speak. The Dalai, nevertheless, impressed me. He appeared in his eastern garb, and I remembered how he had been chosen, a boy child who had been born at the moment the old Dalai had died, and his spirit, they believed, entered into this child at the precise moment of departure of the old leader. He had been still but a child when the Chinese simply stole Tibet, and they were most anxious to get hold of the Dalai, for to him the millions of Buddhists worldwide, looked up. I recalled how he had been smuggled away by faithful retainers across secret mountain trails and escaped from his native land, the land of which he was, in effect, ruler, and to which it was extremely unlikely he would ever return. So there was an air of sadness about the occasion, whatever our faith, for this was a leader without a country, a monarch without a throne.

Now he was a world traveller, still hoping one day to return to his own land. But despite his circumstances, there was an impressive air about this eastern figure. He seemed a man at peace… and indeed that was the theme of his address – world peace – and there was too (and not because of pomp or glory), a certain attractiveness about him. He was an optimist, with a ready smile and joke. He spoke to us, Buddhists and non-Buddhists, as friends, and each of us, all in our own particular way, a world traveller. I felt the pathos of the situation, this homeless great man visiting the leaders of the countries of the world, none of whom will ever help him get rid of the Chinese from his land. And yet, despite his situation, very much a world figure, and unlike so many of those he met, preaching peace – world peace, peace in heart and mind of all of us. He seemed to me the epitome of all in this cruel, unequal world who had suffered, and who had power thrust upon him… just by being born.

Glorious Mother Nature

I was humming to myself in the car as I made my way home to Boreland from Eskdalemuir. I had been on a round of visits, and, as always, had a warm welcome everywhere, plied with tea, and truly made to feel I belonged.

The road was quiet, as it always was at 10 o'clock at night, when I seldom saw another car, and it stretched before me, an undulating ribbon, brilliantly illuminated by a huge full moon hanging away out there in open space. On either side of the road were thick, dark forests where I often walked Sheba, our boxer bitch, and my companion on many journeys. Suddenly, bounding out of the forest on my right came two deer, heading across the road to the other side. I braked hard to avoid hitting them, and breathed a sigh of relief that I had stopped in time. This kind of thing happened often... there always seemed to be a pair, but not this time, for immediately I had stopped, a third came racing out and thumped into the side of the car. It was such a wallop, I was sure it would have broken its neck, and the car be badly dented, so I leapt out to see the damage to deer and automobile... to find all was well. There was no sign of the roe deer, and there wasn't a mark on the car. Relieved that none of the participants in the boxing match had apparently suffered any damage, I drove on. Within a few minutes another of our wildlife came out to keep me company... a fox, which raced on ahead of me up the road for a considerable way. Daft creature, when all it needed to do was swerve into the wood, but apparently it was having its evening constitutional. Eventually it dived into a wood and I wondered which of God's creatures would be next. It proved to be a hedgehog, which was strolling across the road just over the Eskdalemuir–Boreland boundary. Then I was in rabbit country, when hosts of them skimmed out in front of me, playing a dangerous game, but that night I didn't hit any. I wondered idly how God who marked the sparrow's fall kept a tally of all the rabbits!

Eventually I reached home and our own private wood and as I went up the drive, a beautiful barn owl floated silently across my bows, as if to inspect me that I belonged there, for this was his wood, many nights we saw him, and almost every night heard him. I was glad he had made our wood his domain, for we were mightily plagued with voles, and without him we would have been over-run.

We lived our lives with the great world of nature all around us, and as I fell asleep, lulled by the swishing of the trees and the call of night birds, I felt something rare... that I should really be paying the Church, instead of getting a salary... just for the privilege and joys of being a country minister.

The Boreland Bus

It was one of the sights of the district and an institution in the village: a large bus belonging to the Rae family and driven by Sandy Fleming, in his sixties, a former shepherd, who had married Bessie Rae. Sandy was a thoroughly nice fellow, but a very canny driver so that if one got behind the bus on its way to Lockerbie, it was as well just reconciling oneself to the fact that it might be some time before one could pass on the narrow road. Occasionally the dashing Charlie Graham, in his seventies, took over the wheel, and progress was generally somewhat smarter. Charlie was also married to a Rae, Bessie's older sister Mamie.

There had been a time before cars were plentiful when the bus had travelled far and wide and taken crowds to dances or other functions over a wide area, in the various village halls. But these days were long past and now the main function of the bus was to take the children to Lockerbie's secondary school in the morning, and bring them back in the late afternoon.

But it made other trips and picked up regular passengers and to travel on its morning return journey from Lockerbie, as I did a few times, was an experience not to be missed. For it was also the delivery vehicle, and at many isolated cottages Sandy would slow down, slide open his window, and the *Daily Record*, *The Scotsman*, *Farmer's Weekly* or *People's Friend* would soar through the air in a neat arc to land on the doorstep. His aim was perfect... he never seemed to miss the target! Here and there he stopped and left bottles of milk or other items at the gate. I lived in the hope that one day he might have a sheep or wee pig as passenger... but alas, that was an ambition I never had fulfilled.

There can't be many "Boreland Buses" in the country now, but where they still exist in isolated areas, they provide a real service for country folk. Well done, Sandy and Charlie! You did a good job.

Rose Red

After the dreadful Lockerbie air disaster (which is referred to elsewhere) there were thousands of articles scattered over an enormous area, and all, however small, had to be handed in to the authorities. One of our Corrie farmers, Willie Halliday of Capelfoot found a passport in one of his fields with the name Flora Swire on it. His wife Ruby and daughter Lynn took it to Lockerbie and handed it in. Lynn, who was a very gentle, caring girl felt this was very cold and formal and that they should do something, anything, but what? They finally bought a single red rose, wrote a message of sympathy on the card and their name and address, and put the rose with the *thousands* of flowers heaped up outside Lockerbie Town Hall.

Some days later, Dr and Mrs Swire visited Lockerbie, and astonishingly, found the single rose for their daughter. Dr Swire, who was to become the leader of the British relatives of the deceased – and indeed proved a doughty fighter for greater security at airports – got in touch with the Hallidays. He thanked them for their gesture of sympathy. He told them that, quite unknowingly, they could not have chosen anything more apt for their beautiful and clever daughter. Why was this? The girl they had lost in the disaster was known to all in their family as Rose Red.

Just one of the remarkable things that can happen when love and compassion, even in the darkest night, can bring their cheer.

Welcome – the Marriage Bureau

The first talk I ever gave as a young minister was to a Young Farmer's Club, and I have always had a high opinion of this organisation. In my many contacts with these youngsters (though a few seem to manage to stay on past the age for leaving!), I have admired the work the organisation does, the enthusiasm of its members and the immaculate way its affairs are conducted – far, far superior to many more senior organisations. Whilst the principal aim of the YFC is to instruct young farmers, keep them up to date in their work, and in general make them good, competent farmers, it has also been a kind of marriage bureau, and many hundreds of couples first met in the YFC, and they good naturedly accept their second title.

But although they were planning to meet in a church, I don't think any of them had marriage in mind, when the Annandale YFC through their president, young David Paterson, approached me and asked if we could have an evening Harvest Thanksgiving in Tundergarth Church, principally for the YFC... but with everyone welcome, regardless of age. I was delighted in this day and age when God has little part in the lives of many people, that the club should want to meet in God's house and thank Him for another harvest. David's father Alastair of Paddock Hole was one of our elders, and I was very happy in due course to ordain David too.

Most of the young farmers were not regular church goers, and it was an occasion when I felt my former life as a vet was an advantage, for most of the young folks, even if they did not think too highly of ministers, respected vets… except when the quarterly bills came in! So it proved that night. I could not have wished for a more attentive congregation. They sang well, they listened carefully when David and another committee member read the lessons in expert and reverent fashion, and no man could have looked for a more interested audience. They were all at that stage of life when the mind is malleable and very much thinking things through, before they get set in their ways. Furthermore they seemed to be enjoying themselves – something that is not always the case, but should be – in real worship.

One who was not noted for his love of the kirk said to me years ago, "Christians! When you see them going to the kirk they all look like folk going to the dentist… and when you see them coming out you're sure they've been at the dentist!"

Well, all I can say is if my YFC congregation were like dental patients, they must have been given laughing gas. It was refreshing to have such a large, youthful congregation as they gave thanks, joyfully and sincerely, for another harvest time.

The older folk present, many of them former YFC members, enjoyed it too; including the material side of things when, having dealt with the spiritual needs of us all, they got cracking on the sumptuous tea the girls had provided.

One never really knows if a seed is planted in some young mind on such an occasion will in time bring forth a harvest, like the symbols of harvest around us that night, but all in all, it was a refreshing and joyful occasion for me.

Thanks for the opportunity, David, and your YFC. It was a night that made an old boy like me feel quite young again.

Women of Faith

"Could we come to Eskdalemuir Church for our Eastern Star service?" asked Margaret Scott. "I'm Worthy Matron this year, the service is usually held in the Matron's church, and the members are looking forward to coming to the country for a change; especially on a summer evening."

Now the Eastern Star is a Masonic organisation for women. As a young man I had been asked to join the Masons but declined; none of my relatives had ever been Masons and my parents were dead against the organisation. There were ministers who were Masons, but the great majority were very anti-Mason. But as far as I was concerned this was simply a group of people who wanted to worship God in my church... and I was not going to discourage worship or an opportunity to preach the Gospel. Besides, two of the leading lights in the movement locally (their meeting place was Langholm, twelve miles away), Margaret Scott and Florence Rose, were two women of whom I had a very high opinion.

I was informed of the four women in the Bible who were most venerated in the Eastern Star, and decided to preach on Ruth, something I had never done before, and I enjoyed both the preparation and delivery of the lovely old story.

The church was full with members of many branches present and also many men. The singing was quite tremendous – there were smiles everywhere – they were indeed a happy band of worshippers and it was as warm hearted a congregation as I had known, and preachers are very sensitive to atmosphere. Some had come a considerable distance, old friends met up, they could not have been more friendly or appreciative, and the "townies" in particular among them were clearly delighted to be in a country kirk on a glorious summer evening. Some years later the occasion was repeated (no, I didn't use the same sermon), and as I noted with the report on the Young Farmer's Club service, the cheerfulness and obvious joy all round gave the lie to the gloomy picture so many have of Christ's Church.

After church, of course, on both occasions, as always in the country, there was a "bean feast", and the cheerful chatter of old friends meeting up with each other in our village hall.

I am still not a Mason – and won't be – but I am glad of the two contacts I had with people who, whatever else they may have believed, clearly believed in God – and worshipped Him the way the Bible tells us He likes to be worshipped – with cheerfulness and joy.

Goodbye

"Parting is such sweet sorrow" says the poet. I had known it a number of times in my life, but for the last time it would be very hard, for I loved these kind folks of my Border parishes, and we could not, for ten years, have been shown more consideration.

Goodbye was modified somewhat for me by the fact that I was now quite ill and only being kept going by the grace of God and masses of painkillers. So while on the one hand I was wearying for a rest, on the other I was... we were... so reluctant to go and leave so many lovely people.

So what does a man preach on his final sermon of his ministry? I had long decided that... it was given me by Paul in all his letters at their conclusion.

So on 24 June 1990 I preached on, "THE GRACE OF THE LORD JESUS CHRIST BE WITH YOU ALL."

I felt I could wish nothing better for my people than that they know, what I had tried to preach for ten years: the riches of Christ stemming from a deep faith in God.

Grace... G.R.A.C.E.... God's riches at Christ's expense, as a schoolboy put it. I don't think any theologian could come up with a better definition. It was, naturally for us, a moving service, but it was not, as I had asked at the beginning, a "greetin' meetin'".

True, I had one more address to give on the following Saturday when I was to dedicate the Tundergarth Memorial Room, but this was, in reality, my last address as a placed minister of the Gospel. The singing was good (the minister had chosen his favourite hymns!), Jill Porteous and I sang a few verses as a duet of the *King of Love my Shepherd is*, which is a paraphrase really of the 23rd Psalm, and I felt apt for the congregation, so many of whose lives were lived among sheep. We sang it to a special and most beautiful tune, which we had done several times over the years, and the congregation seemed to enjoy.

The folks had been considerate to the last and decided that on my last Sunday I should only have one service to take, with all congregations gathered together at Hutton and Corrie Church, the most central point of this vast charge. At the end of the worship, we were inundated with gifts; flowers and a lovely ring of dried flowers for Janet; a painting of me (which didn't exactly flatter me, but it was really a cartoon cleverly done which brought in my variety of interests and the different parts of my life and various places I'd been), it was a mischievous piece of work, the brainchild of Kathleen Jackson, and sits in my little study, giving me a smile each day. The main gift was a pair of handsome Clydesdale horses made in the magnificent Border Fine Arts workshop, a really lovely gift. Janet and I named the horses... I thinking of the first horses I had worked in my teens, and Janet giving the names of the pair her father had worked, and our good natured difference of opinions had the congregation highly amused. They sit proudly in our sitting room of our little bungalow home, flanked on each side by two collie dogs in the same workmanship, all of which must have cost a pretty penny and are much admired by all who visit us. The dogs had been private gifts which, knowing the price they would be, as well as their beauty, touched us greatly. Then Sir Rupert made a very warm and generous speech and a kind tribute to us both, and handed over a cheque, the size of which made me gasp. Such generosity! Right to the end.

Then it was the final blessing on *my* people, friends every one, handshakes all round, goodbye had been said, which all know means, "God be with you".

In the afternoon, as it happened, we all met up again for an Ecumenical service by a visiting group at Eskdalemuir, at which, gladly, I could just be one of the worshippers. If any of my former parishioners ever read this, let me just say again, "Thank you. For ten years you made us very happy amongst you all".

What rubbish! No, not for ten years, but for more, much more, for memories are made of this.

TWENTY THREE

Hands Across the Sea

In the course of history, and in our own individual experiences there occur from time to time events of such magnitude that we know we will never forget them, and years later can recall these happenings as if they were but yesterday.

Such a happening was the assassination of President John F. Kennedy, the new hope of the west and of democracy as the Cold War rumbled on in the world. Not so long ago there was a TV programme when many Americans from many walks of life, were asked if they could remember what they were doing when the news of the President's killing was announced some thirty years before.

In like manner 21 December 1988 will be remembered to their dying day by many people in different parts of the globe, but most vividly by those in south-west Scotland, for at 7 o'clock that evening, PanAm flight 103 was blown out of the sky by a bomb smuggled aboard by evil, corrupt, devilish people and 270 people met their death in horrific fashion: eleven in the pleasant little town of Lockerbie and 259 in the plane. Its mark has gone deep into many lives, of those who lost someone from the plane; in many cases several loved ones, and I am certain all who lived in the area, like the Americans, questioned about President Kennedy, will remember clearly, for such a disaster has left its mark in very many lives. In fact, as I write this some five years later, I have learned that over 200 people in the Lockerbie area are still being treated for a variety of nervous disorders dating back to 1988.

I recall clearly what I was doing in our manse seven miles away. I was in bed with flu, and my wife came up to our bedroom saying she had received two phone calls from relatives in Ayrshire, for they had seen a flashed announcement on TV and were anxious as to our safety.

"I think we should go to Lockerbie" Janet said, "and see if we can help in any way."

We set off at once, an attack of flu in the face of this disaster a mere pin prick.

We got to the town hall in record time to find it mobbed with people. We saw no panic, but much bewilderment and shock, for the picture was still far from clear... news was coming in all the time, and many people evacuated from their homes were in the town hall till somewhere could be found to house them, at least for the night. The magnitude of the disaster was not yet realised. It had been thought for a short time it was a RAF jet which had crashed, but very soon the magnitude – and the horror – became clear. The four local doctors were just about to go out to the centre of the holocaust. My own GP, Dr Hill, the duty doctor for the night, seemed to be in charge. I had a quick word with him, emphasising we did not wish to get in the way but could we help in any way.

He replied, "We don't know yet what we are going to find but it looks as if there will be many casualties who will come here initially. But meantime maybe you can help to reassure the old folks and others who have been hurriedly evacuated from their homes dressed just as they had been sitting, and others who, in the confusion, have been separated from their partners and feel totally lost."

In no time the doctors were back – there were no casualties to treat – all in the area where the plane came down were dead. In fact it was not the plane that came down on Lockerbie, but its blazing fuel tanks and those who had seen this enormous fireball come hurtling from the sky at an incredible rate, in the process lighting up the whole sky, had watched paralysed with fear and wanted to run away... but where? And what was it? Something from outer space? A bolt from Heaven? ... at first they didn't know. Some thought it was a blazing RAF jet. I was friendly with the young man who normally served me with petrol and he described how he felt it was coming straight at him and he was riveted to the spot with terror as the fireball just missed the garage and landed just behind on Sherwood Crescent, an area of bungalows. All in them, and the houses themselves, were incinerated in almost an instant, such was the ferocity of the heat. The disaster was terrible enough, but one shudders to think what might have happened if it had ignited the garage's petrol tanks. The plane's tanks finished their journey of destruction buried deep into the high earthen bank of the A74, the main road south, but also leaving an enormous crater where the houses had been. Parts of the plane fell scattered around the town, mainly the council houses of the Rosebank area where one of the plane's large engines landed in the garden of a house. Another house had its roof ripped off, and when the terrified occupants went upstairs to investigate, they found themselves looking out at the sky, and horror of horrors – a body hanging from one of the rafters.

The word came through to the town that the remains of the giant Jumbo, the nose cone and part of the fuselage had come to earth just 100 yards from Tundergarth church, some three miles from Lockerbie. Mr and Mrs Beattie, two of our church members whose cottage was practically directly opposite the church told me afterwards how, standing terror struck in their garden, they watched the plane just miss their home and end up just beyond in a large grass field. Little imagination is required to understand their feelings and fear. In fact, none of this trauma and destruction had been intended by the bombers, but this in no way mitigates their evil deed. They had intended the *Maid of the Sea* to go into the sea just as an Air India plane had done not long before, but the reason the Jumbo jet came down on land was it had been half an hour late leaving London.

Dr Hill went out to Tundergarth to see if anyone was in the plane, and bravely aided by one of the Wilson girls whose parents' farm was just behind the church, climbed into the cockpit while she guided him with a torch on that pitch black, bitterly cold December night. The courageous young doctor found the remains of the plane was full of bodies, while others lay around the field – all of course dead. Horror piled upon horror that dreadful night, and bit deeply into the minds of all who lived through it in that quiet little corner of Dumfriesshire. The picture of the plane that always appears on television was, in fact, taken from just in front of our little church of Tundergarth to which we will return shortly; for along with the little town of Lockerbie, it was at the heart of the disaster, and my story is really about how the disaster involved and affected Tundergarth. The little hamlet a mile beyond the church is, in fact, called Bankshill, but the old parish name of Tundergarth was always used.

We did what we could that awful night, trying to comfort many people numb with shock, and succeeding in reuniting some old couples who had been hurried from their houses as the whole Sherwood area was evacuated by the police, and numbers had been separated from their partners and families in the first desperate hour. No one, of course, had experience of such a disaster, and the town hall was filled with many bewildered people, but considering the massive nature of the whole disaster, people came through it remarkably well, and there were many willing helping hands, and offers of homes for the night. Janet and I concentrated mainly on trying to reunite and reassure the elderly who had been hastily plucked from their homes, but what we did was little enough.

The next day I went searching for an elderly couple, brother and sister, whose house had been destroyed. I eventually found them staying with friends, and heard their story. Sitting at the fireside watching television, just after 7pm a huge ball of fire burst through their window. For foot comfort, they had been sitting in their stocking soles, but just as they were, they headed for the back door. Before they reached it, more flames came through it. They were trapped, but grabbing a coat each and draping it over their heads, they somehow got through the flames to safety. One minute more would have been too late in the tremendous heat. The couple, though retired to Lockerbie from Corrie, were still members of Hutton and Corrie Church, hence my involvement with them, but all the other local clergy were caring for their folks, many of whom have similar stories to tell.

But to return to Tundergarth. For many years this little church had been attached to Lockerbie St Cuthbert's, but when the minister of both – the scholarly, highly respected Dr Griffiths – had retired, it was decided to unite St Cuthbert's with the other Lockerbie church, for St Cuthbert's was a very run down building which would cost an enormous sum to repair and the congregation was small and not really able to support a minister. The question then was what to do with Tundergarth. The Kirk Session was consulted and they asked if they might be linked with Eskdalemuir, Hutton and Corrie. It was a natural marriage, for both Corrie and Tundergarth were part of the huge Castlemilk estate. The villagers, though a good many miles apart, were neighbours, and the farming folks of both parishes knew one another well. So I was asked to take over Tundergarth about half way through my ten years in the Borders. I was happy to do this, though it gave me an enormous, though sparsely populated stretch of territory, the largest I believe, in southern Scotland.

I had never been in Tundergarth Church and confess to some dismay to find it too was badly run down. No blame is attached to anyone for this unless perhaps presbytery for linking a little country kirk to a much larger town one, for in my experience, the country kirk nearly always suffers and feels itself a kind of second class citizen, for most of the minister's work, naturally, is with the larger town parish. The church building was in need of much repair; there was a hole in the roof, the tower was crumbling, the heating system had broken down completely, and the old harmonium, which the uncomplaining Mrs Black had faithfully pedalled for more than forty years, was on its last legs. What made me raise my eyebrows, however, was the discovery that the four elders did not have districts for visitation, which is one of the great strengths; is an essential part of the Church of Scotland, and indeed laid down as a must for the elders. There had therefore been no visitation carried out for many years. The four elders were all first class men: the laird of Castlemilk, Sir Rupert Buchanan-Jardine, who had been a Major in the army, a quiet, courteous, thoughtful, well loved man; the Session Clerk, Andrew Spence, who was a human dynamo and did an enormous amount for the church, a farmer by profession with a great love of, and breeder of horses; the treasurer, Jim Sloan, also a farmer, brother of Mrs Black, who handled the church finances for many years, and Alastair Paterson, farmer at Paddock Hole, and the only one I really knew initially, for he had frequently come with his energetic and cheerful wife, Beth, to some of our Corrie services. There was an active, well attended Women's Guild, but that was all, and the little church had slumbered the years away, so that now there were but few attending it, sometimes, I was told, as few as half a dozen.

I felt it was a real challenge to try to do something about the situation, and since I have always believed (as in the early days of Christianity) that a church is its people, rather than its buildings, I got the church roll and spent about nine months visiting all on the roll, plus numbers who were not, whenever I could fit in my visits with the work in my other three churches. We doubled our number of elders almost at once, with four very good men, all were given districts, and they too started visiting their district regularly. On my rounds I was frequently told I was the first person they had seen from the church in twenty-four years. Mrs Mortimer, the very fine schoolmistress who clearly loved her children and their work, invited me into the school, and I visited fortnightly and got to know the children. Janet, enthusiastically supported by some of the young mothers, started a Sunday School, which quite quickly she handed over to the willing Mrs Mortimer. We had a Communicant's class, with an encouraging attendance. Gradually more and more people came back to the church, some for the first time in many years... in fact we saw a mini revival. It was not any of my doing, but, as with all revivals the work of the Holy Spirit, and as the song puts it "a little bit of loving". The folks felt the church *really* cared for them, as indeed it did, and they should care for their church, a real sense of belonging together, of fellowship, and it thrilled my heart on a Sunday to see sometimes the biggest congregation of my four.

The various repairs were carried out in time... the roof, the tower, new heating (an absolute immediate essential), and eventually, last of all, a new electric organ. Life was flowing once more through the whole church and the enthusiasm of the people grew month by month. It meant more work for me, of course, but if a minister is not prepared to work and get to know his flock, then it is high time he should be examining his ministry and recalling his vows. I was loving it all, for the folks were so welcoming, the numbers kept increasing, and I was just grateful I had seen the hand of God at work in bringing life back into what had been a somewhat discouraged little group of Christians... and this was to prove vital, as we shall perhaps now see.

For at much the same time as the fuel tanks of the plane were falling on Lockerbie (as I have already stated), the nose cone and a small part of the fuselage, with the co-pilot, Ray Wagner, still at the controls, came down just 100 yards from Tundergarth Church, which within a few hours, was to become the centre of furious activity by a variety of agencies. The next morning, the police set up their Incident Van just outside the church and also used the church building. Likewise many soldiers, some of them mere boys, used the church as a centre. Their task was to search the area and hills for bodies, a gruesome business, which proved too much for some of the younger lads. The search dogs and their handlers were also there, and both men and dogs did a wonderful job. The world's press was there en masse, radio and umpteen television companies were everywhere. PanAm officials arrived from America, and other groups concerned with air crashes swarmed around the plane. I was glad our church was available for such a practical use as giving shelter and warmth to soldiers and police in very biting, cold weather. In the midst of all the destruction and desolation around, it also provided something else – a sense of peace and beauty – for it was dressed for Christmas. The Christmas tree, with its lights, and the old church itself, almost 100 years old, gave a feeling of permanence. It had stood there weathering many storms for all these years, and was a reminder that there was another dimension to life than man's inhumanity to man. I had a word with the assembled searchers, sympathised with them in their grim task when they saw so much that was horrific and assured them we were only too glad to help in any way we could – the church would be open, the heating kept on for as long as was required. I did make one request, which, as we shall see later, was to get me into trouble. I asked with complete courtesy that they would not smoke in church, for with so much wood around and padded seat cushions, there was a very real danger of fire. I apologised for this but hoped they would understand, and also reminded them it was still the house of God. Seeing the strain on many young soldiers' faces, I made enquiries about their own Chaplains who were accompanying them and was assured they were watching every man carefully, and only that day had withdrawn three at breaking point from the search.

Whilst some bodies were found many miles away, clearly sucked out of the plane at the moment of explosion, a large hole being blown in the giant plane, 70 percent were found in our scattered parish which went away up into the hills.

The search in time moved on, and then the relatives of the victims started arriving, coming from many parts of the world; some unexpected like Latvia, Turkey and others, but again 70 percent were from the USA, for 70 percent of the passengers were from there. They came to Tundergarth in great numbers. Some even tramped up into the hills to see the spot where their loved one's body had lain, and most of them came into the church, whatever their religion or none. Outside was the desolation of man, inside the timelessness of the ages and the peace of God. Many a sore, grieving heart found at least a measure of peace when the heart is broken. Janet and I and sometimes one or two of our church folks were there to greet them. We did not intrude, leaving people to sit in the stillness, but if we say anyone in great distress, we sat beside them, and tried to console.

Many, as soon as they came into church, seeing a dog collar, just threw themselves into my arms and wept... and cried sore on my shoulder. We felt terribly helpless in the presence of so much grief, but did what we could, and were amazed again and again at the courage we saw – an old man in his eighties, erect like a soldier, who had lost six of his family – a granny from the Manchester area who had lost her daughter and four grandchildren, but could still, somehow, smile through the tears.

Some we got to know personally, especially the co-pilot's wife, Norma Wagner, and a young woman, Cathy Segal, who both came from the same small town in America, but had not previously known one another before their mutual sorrow brought them together. Cathy Segal's husband had been a very brilliant University professor, and the girl was in deep shock. They spent a little time at the manse with us, and it was infinitely touching to see how the older woman, her heart breaking, took Cathy under her wing, and sought to share and comfort. We later had some literature from Norma, a copy of their local paper, which was largely devoted to a tribute to Ray. He had been one of these larger than life characters, involved in much in his home town, but especially active with young people, able to get alongside teenagers and looked up to by them. As I read his story, I thought what an enormous amount of brilliance and future potential for good in the world had died at the hands of unbelievably wicked people in snuffing out, practically in an instant, 270 lives.

For example forty students from Syracuse University had been on that plane. What might they have done in time, for the good of mankind? Of those who came into our little church which had really become a place of pilgrimage, the wrecked plane just outside (for it was some time before it was removed), some just wanted to be quiet, and in the silence of the old beautiful place of worship, find, like Elijah of old, that God was not in the storm, the wind, the fire, the earthquake, but in a still, small voice – or as one translation puts it – in the "sound of a gentle stillness". Others just wept quietly, others again were totally overcome. All I can say is that Janet and I did what we could, day after day, and we would go home at night knowing, as Jesus did, virtue had gone out of us, and we were totally exhausted... but to whom can a person in need turn, if not to a minister or priest?

Every single person who came into the church asked if they might take something home with them, to remind them of the parish in which their loved ones had died, and the peace they had found in our little church. All we had related to the church were the Bibles or hymn books from the pews, and these were readily given and most gratefully received. I had also obtained a supply of two little booklets. Now there are many such things about, but these were the best I had seen: *A Day at a Time* and *Thoughts on the life to come* compiled by Mary Oakley, a minister's widow. The first one is beside my own bed all the time, and I know what a comfort these booklets are. The folks were invited to help themselves. These were laid out on a table at the back of the church, where we also had a placard in big print of Abraham Lincoln's famous words: "LIFE IS ETERNAL" (It doesn't end here) "LOVE IS IMMORTAL" (it too goes on...) "DEATH IS BUT A HORIZON AND A HORIZON IS ONLY THE LIMIT OF OUR SIGHT"

The press and TV were there every day, looking for some comment or other, but we refused them entrance to the church when mourners were in it, and tried our utmost – for the most part with success – to shield the relatives from the media. The relatives kept coming for weeks, and long after Christmas, when the tree was eventually removed, the church was kept very beautiful with flowers, thanks to Mrs Thornwaite, our gentle, caring, flower convenor, Mrs Martin, Mrs Spence, and others.

Many, I know from what they said, and just the look on their faces, felt that God was there to comfort and console, and their dear ones were safe with Him. Many times I marvelled that the disaster had happened when it did (though it was emphatically not an act of God, as the insurance companies describe disasters), for if it had taken place two years earlier, when the little church was at such a low ebb, it could not have coped. But the revival of the church was God's timing.

The rush of relatives gradually thinned, though they kept coming for many weeks. Janet moved her operations to Lockerbie which was the central point for everything, and she opened a canteen for the various workers to use. But the church remained open for any to visit, and a young Swiss couple were so taken by its beauty and peace, they planned to have their wedding there.

There was one jarring note which only concerned me. Right in the middle of the turmoil, with soldiers departing and relatives arriving, when I was working flat out (as was Janet) I had a letter from a lady, who, though not a member of Tundergarth, sometimes did worship there. That letter was written in acid, and in my tired, emotional state, trying each day to comfort the broken hearted, and giving of my best, it bit deep. The lady began by calling me a complete and total hypocrite, but did not specify why. She accused me of merely seeking personal publicity and doing anything to get on TV... of rebuking young soldiers using the church as a base... of not going with these young lads up into the hills to search for bodies... of deserting my post at a crucial time to give a Christmas message on Border Television at Carlisle. It was the most bitter, hurtful letter I received in my whole ministry, and I have only mentioned the bare outline. Every line dripped hatred, and in my tired, drained state, I confess I wept when I read it. Was that what people *really* thought of me?

I have had very few letters during my ministry of a critical nature, and these few have been anonymous and gone into the bin. But while maybe I should have done the same with this one, having slept on it, prayed about it, and pondered it, I decided to answer it point by point. I could not say anything about the hypocrite accusation for my correspondent had not specified in what way I was a hypocrite. But the other points I did answer. The accusation that I had rebuked young soldiers, I have already mentioned. I had welcomed them warmly, sympathised with them in their gruesome task, and merely courteously requested they did not smoke in church for the reasons given. That was apparently my "rebuke". As for searching the hills with the soldiers, quite simply I was not well enough to do it, nor were civilians particularly wanted. So far as seeking to appear on TV, I did my best to avoid this, but in a church with only two doors into it, it was impossible to slip in unnoticed. I tried to sneak in the side door but was caught by the BBC who wanted a comment or opinion on some point, and when I had answered them and turned round, it was to find no fewer than *five* other TV channels waiting for me. Anyone who has tried to avoid the media when they are hot on a trail will know it's nearly impossible. The Christmas broadcast? It had, in fact, been recorded a month before the air disaster. But my letter made no difference, I had no apology. In the eyes of that lady there were two disasters at Tundergarth – PanAm 103 and me.

But life goes on and what a comfort and strength to have a wife who understood and shared, as Janet always has... and to recall that even Jesus, when seeking to help and heal, even when He raised Lazarus from the dead, had his critics that his motives were ulterior. Perhaps most of all, I just had to meet some poor mother from

America who had lost two sons, or a couple who had lost their only daughter, and realise what real hurt was... and mine was not even a pinprick.

At Easter Janet spoke to the women of Tundergarth and asked if they agreed with her that it might be a nice gesture and comfort (especially in the time of year when we remember Jesus dying at the instigation of blinded, evil men... and rising from the dead, thus giving us hope, the great Christian hope of eternal life), to send an Easter card to all bereaved families. The women thought it was a good idea and enthusiastically joined in. A card with an etching of our church on front was made, inside a message of sympathy, and bearing in mind not all the recipients would be Christians, or might call God by some other name like Jehovah or Allah, we chose a verse that could not give offence: "God is our refuge and strength, a very present help in trouble." The cards were given to about thirty women who were asked just to put their name and address, nothing more, inside. There was, however, difficulty in sending them, for we had no names or addresses. The police were reluctant about the whole idea, wishing, understandably, to preserve the privacy of all the families. Several high ranking policemen, led by the man in overall charge of the hunt for the killers, came to see us at the manse and asked why we wanted to do this. We explained simply that at the season of Christ's death and resurrection, and the time of resurrection and new beginnings in the world of nature, we felt that a card showing the bereaved families they were not forgotten by us might be a comfort to them. They explained they alone had the addresses and they could not release them, and departed. However, they returned again quite soon and said that after thought and discussion, felt our action was a kind gesture and the way round the question of privacy for the families was for us to give the cards to the police and they would send them, and this was done.

I recall in conversation with the police over a cup of tea saying their task of finding the bombers would be enormously difficult. The chief of police acknowledged this, said they had visited several countries and been in touch with others, and they were 90 percent certain who had done this terrible deed, but there might be difficulty about extradition. He, rightly, gave nothing away, but it was really a very considerable achievement for the smallest police force in Britain to have made such progress in three months.

So the cards were sent by the police, privacy was maintained, but all over the world, though principally in America, those who lost someone have a correspondent in this country, a home where they will be made welcome, someone to whom they will not be strangers should they visit the Lockerbie area. Hands have been joined across the sea, and friendships have sprung up between families that previously were total strangers to one another.

There is much evil in the world, but Tundergarth reminds us that there is also much caring and love, and love in the end is always stronger than hate.

That was the theme of the memorial service we held exactly a year later in Tundergarth. A large, open air, united service was to be held in Lockerbie at 8 o'clock, and although for some reason, the authorities were not keen we also should have a memorial act, we decided to go ahead, at 6.30, so that all who wished could still go to Lockerbie for the big ecumenical act of remembrance.

Our church was crowded, people standing at the back, and I felt deeply moved as I led the service, for there was a great silence and feeling of expectancy. At the very back of the church were some little green lights which were twinkling, and this puzzled me for I could not see exactly what they were in the darkened church, practically the only lights being those on the Christmas tree. I have always regretted not realising what these green lights were, only at the close finding out that they were the little lights on the search dogs who were there with their dog handlers. My biggest regret is that I, who love dogs so much, and spent a chunk of my life caring for them, somehow in the service, when mentioning other groups who had done so much, sadly omitted to mention the dogs and their handlers... and there they all were, helping to light up the church. I still regret it to this day.

The service was short and simple, and in fact taking place not only a year to the day of the disaster, but at the very time the plane had crashed, whisking 270 people in an instant to Eternity. The address was given by Rev Mary Morrison, Church of Scotland adviser for evangelism at that time for the Borders area. I knew her to be a fine, sympathetic speaker... as well as a good friend. She took as her theme the Celtic cross she always wore, which, if you are not familiar with it, is a cross with a ring or circle at the top. Her two points were those I have already touched on – the evil people who had caused this disaster exactly one year before, bringing so much sorrow to so many. But just as when other evil men nailed the son of God to a cross, there was the ring of love, the love of God encircling them all, surrounding them all as it had been manifest too on the Cross of Calvary, when Jesus' thoughts were for His mother, His friends, the dying thieves beside Him... and astonishingly a prayer for forgiveness of those who had so brutally done Him to death.

I have nearly always felt the presence of the Lord with me in church, but never in such a way as that night. I believe too that was the feeling of most who attended. There was a tremendous hush and we felt in that deep silence God was still there – right there with them – evil could not defeat Him – and His love would never leave them.

I had laid out an enormous stock of the little booklets I mentioned earlier – *Thoughts of the Life to come* – and every one went. Indeed I could have used double the quantity. I like to think that somewhere and somehow in all our efforts, sore hearts were comforted and the little church that had been so run down was at the centre of hope, assurance and peace. As St Paul put it long ago: "Love suffers long, and is kind; bears all things, hopes all things, ENDURES all things. LOVE NEVER FAILS".

Many hundreds came into our little Tundergarth Church in these first terrible weeks – and many are still coming to the Memorial Room beside the church. It is a peaceful place, a place of healing. Those who came in the early days, and for perhaps two months after were from different branches of the Christian Church, from other faiths, or from none – united in a common grief. As a symbol that darkness would not last or evil conquer, many lit a candle (or candles) for each one they had lost, and these little flickering lights seemed to me to shed their rays triumphantly into the gloom... and fulfil the words of John about Jesus, reminding us of "the true light which lighteth every man that cometh into the world"... and adds John with ringing confidence "darkness can NEVER put it out".

Light and love have triumphed... even in very thick darkness.

TWENTY FOUR

When the Curtain Parted

Someone once said "the only sure thing about life is death".

It is certainly true we must all "shuffle off this mortal coil", most of us at the end of a long life. But for 270 people on 21 December 1988, as has already been stated and as all the world knows, death came with a terrible suddenness when PanAm flight 103 was blown apart by a bomb planted by cruel, evil, devilish men, transferring innocent people in an instant from time to eternity, as I have already written.

The various proceedings went on for a very long time, while the search for the murderers became a worldwide thing. It was finally decided the official mourning and various proceedings in an around Lockerbie and Tundergarth would end on 30 June 1990... a full eighteen months after the crash, during which time a vast crowd of people from all over the world had visited, as well as Lockerbie itself, our little kirk at Tundergarth, which had become a real centre of pilgrimage for relatives of the dead. A very beautiful little annexe building has been built as a permanent memorial from the old Session House, with inside its simply but tastefully furnished room, a large book of remembrance containing the names of the dead, each on a separate page, with beside it another book in which relatives could write any message they desired. The date of the dedication of the memorial was fixed by the various authorities, and I was asked to plan and conduct the proceedings and give a suitable address. This service was to take place at 11am and in the afternoon of that day, I was already booked to take a wedding – the two events seeming typical to me of a minister's life, all of life – sorrow and joy. This was also to be my last day as an active minister, since the rare blood condition from which I suffered was making it impossible to carry on.

Now in my thirty years' ministry, I have taken at least 1,500 funerals, each of which brought its own sorrow and sense of loss, and one tried to bring the comfort of our Heavenly Father in each case. But this dedication, and remembrance of 270 deaths was very different and quite outside my experience. As well as local people attending, relatives were coming from all over Britain and Europe, and a special plane load from America, to which the whole service was to be televised live. As I have already noted, some coming had lost as many as six of their family, but every single soul was precious to some family. I was awed by the courage and faith I saw and desperately anxious to try to speak a word of hope, comfort and assurance... but what? I was deeply conscious of the poverty of words on such a day, and in the midst of my other work which still had to go on in my parishes, preparing weekly talks, taking other funerals, I tried to think of what I could say and how to express it. I had many ideas and discarded them. The whole thing had to be prepared some time in advance, for programmes had to be printed, so hymns, readings, the words of dedication and all those taking part had to be considerably pre-planned. I wanted to keep the ceremonial to a minimum, and this was done. Whilst our MP and the Lord Lieutenant of the county were to be present and take part, for the most part the planning was left to me, and I felt very inadequate, for few in their ministry have experience of such an occasion. I enlisted the help of my friend and neighbour, Rev Jack Stewart of Beattock, who would take the prayers, and I planned also to give him a photocopy of my address, in case at the last minute, I was not well enough to carry out my poignant task – a distinct possibility, for by now I was very far from fit. The RC priest from Lockerbie was to round off proceedings with prayer and pronounce the blessing.

Of course all this had to take place in the open air around the little memorial room, and anxiously we listened to weather forecasts, and on the morning itself looked fearfully to a grey sky, for we had experienced a miniature deluge all week, but miraculously, for the duration of the service, the rain held off. The electric organ had to be carted out and a cable led to a plug, and shelter arranged for the organ, microphones and participants. It was just not possible to provide shelter for the large crowd... but praise the Lord!... astonishingly for that brief hour we did not need it. The whole thing was a considerable masterpiece of organisation which the Disaster Committee and counsellors, who had been involved in all the events following the disaster, handled efficiently and thoughtfully.

After much pondering and praying for the right line to take (if there is such a thing) and the right words to say, bearing in mind the congregation would be composed of different branches of the Christian Church, different religions, or none at all, I remembered Dr Hampson and his experience, and rightly or wrongly, felt this was the theme I should take.

Dr Hampson was a young house doctor doing his training in a large hospital. He had started with faith in his heart, but in the presence of so much suffering and death, had lost his belief in a loving, caring God, and indeed had become hard and cynical. In the day of our story he was feeling weary and defeated, for, like most trainee doctors, he was expected to work ridiculous hours, and during almost a whole night of treating patients, had lost a little girl with meningitis. Death had won again, and he very much feared there would soon be another – a Mr Hilley who was in an oxygen tent and had a rapidly failing heart. On his rounds, the doctor saw his patient was very far through, and only managed to whisper "Send for my family". The doctor nodded, the family were contacted, and Dr Hampson continued his rounds. Some half an hour later he was called hurriedly back to Mr Hilley's bed. One look told him it was too late... his patient was dead. There was no pulse, no heart beat, of course, no respiration.

Angry that death should conquer again, the young doctor pushed the oxygen tent aside and began artificial respiration. He kept going until the sweat was dripping off him. His senior doctor came along and said, "It's no good. That kind of heart never revives."

But the young man kept going on and on, till, after a very long time, wonder of wonders, he was rewarded with a gasp... and breathing started again, and Mr Hilley swam back into consciousness. Just then his wife arrived, pale faced and frightened. Her husband reached for her hand, and whispered, "I just wanted to tell you Mary, that I have faith we will meet again."

She gripped his hand tightly, smiled through her tears, and said, "I know without a doubt we shall."

Now Mr Hilley had technically been dead for a considerable time, and the young doctor was curious as to what he had felt. He asked,

"Do you remember seeing or hearing anything just now, while you were… unconscious?"

The sick man looked at him and said haltingly "Yes! I remember. My pain was gone and I couldn't feel my body. I heard the most peaceful music. God was there and I was floating away. I knew I was dead but I wasn't afraid. Then the music stopped and you were bending over me."

The doctor looked at his patient unbelievingly, then asked, "John, have you ever had a dream like that before?"

Emphatically, the sick man retorted… "It wasn't a dream."

The doctor went on his way, leaving the couple together, but three hours later he was called back to Mr Hilley's bed. One glance told him there would be no return this time.

I am aware that this experience poses many questions which I cannot answer, and there will be many sceptics, and doubtless many medical theories. One question, for me, surpasses all others: "why had the curtain of death parted for a time?" for there was no doubt in the mind of an unbelieving, cynical, matter-of-fact doctor, that this had, without question, happened. So certain was Dr Hampson of what he had seen, heard and experienced, that it led to a rediscovery of faith by the young doctor.

As I look back over almost a lifetime of visiting the sick and dying, whilst I cannot claim to have had that doctor's experience, I have seen and heard enough to confirm the doctor's experiences, and emphasise the words of Jesus that come ringing down the centuries, the words of the One who was dead and lived again: "He that believeth in me… though he were dead… yet shall he live."

I cannot say, as I write this some years later, whether the theme of my address was the right one to adopt for the occasion… one is never sure and always conscious of the poverty of one's words. I can only say that it *seemed* the message and emphasis to which I had been guided, and certainly, from their remarks, many grieving souls seemed to find comfort and reassurance that their loved ones were not gone from them forever… merely gone on ahead.

So, my dear sorrowing friends who know deep grief now and the bitterness of parting… grieve not overmuch, for death is but the door to a more wonderful, fuller, more glorious life, where our loved ones in the Lord await us, and the One who took the sting out of death by His victory over death, is there to welcome us Home. *Himself* is there: "This is the victory that overcomes the world… even our faith."

TWENTY FIVE

Goin' Home

I switched off the television with a sigh. I had been watching a horror film, though it had not been billed as such. It was in fact the 6 o'clock news, but almost unbelievably, every single item that night had been about war, fighting, bombing and killing. There was Romania, Somalia, Sudan, Sadam Hussein having another go at the Kurds in their so-called "save haven", civil strife in South Africa, fighting in the Ukraine, rumblings of the horrors to come in Rwanda, and of course the almost daily murders in Northern Ireland. There were pictures from different parts of the world of suffering, starving children, hundreds dying daily with no food, no safe water, and no medicine of any kind in some places. I almost wept as I watched the latest examples of man's inhumanity to man and unbelievable brutality. As I looked at the world's need unfolded before us and thought of the rich west – and we *are* rich compared to vast millions across the globe – and thought of the gallant souls; doctors, nurses and many others; gallant souls of many charities such as Save the Children, Christian Aid, Tear Fund and many representatives of the United Nations providing in many places, at risk of their own lives, the only help and hope for these pathetic souls; and then thought of Britain's contribution of much less and one percent of its GNP to this vast need, I felt ashamed… and angry. Was this the best the so-called Christian west could do?

Even the weather forecast that night should have had an X certificate with news of storms, gales, thunder, and rivers that had already burst their banks, flooding thousands of homes, about to have a top up that night. No, it wasn't a programme to cheer us up!

I went on thinking of the folly of fighting, and like most folks getting on in years, I looked back over the way I had come from my boyhood, and for the first time realised that there had not, in fact, been a single year in my life when there had not been a war somewhere. A verse of Scripture floated into my mind: "God saw everything He had made... and lo... it was very good." I wondered idly if He was feeling as depressed as I was that night at the unholy mess this creature man – the crown of his creation – had made of the beautiful world He had given us. I marvelled that He didn't, as He had once before, wipe out the lot of us. But there was that wee word Love, which despite our stupid follies, greed, hatred, ambition, desire for power and so much more, still goes on down the ages from a Father God who loves everything He has made, for it is His very nature.

But to return to the wars. I was, to my parents' great relief, too young to be called up at the start of the last World War, but in its final year I was of age, and had in fact, put forward my name for the Marines. But I had also started studying to be a vet, and because there was an acute shortage of vets for farm animals at the time, and would be for some years, and also because the war in Europe was in its death throes and clearly Hitler and his evil minions would soon be no more, it was decided for the sake of the country's agriculture to grant deferment till one had completed one's course and review the position of each student then. But there was the occasional person who thought I had decided to become a vet to escape National Service, which was just not true and I remember an acquaintance who despite his fine uniform had seen no active service saying to me with a sneer, "Knew what you were doing, eh?" and turning his back on me. That stung!

My mother used to say, "Nothin' good ever came oot o' a war" – and very few would dispute this, though of course, as in all of life, someone has to stand up against the bullies, and if countries had not stood up to men like Hitler and Mussolini... and for a time, of which we can be proud, little Britain standing alone, the world would have been enslaved.

What had particularly shocked me in the news that night was the enormous numbers: hundreds of thousands, who were in refugee camps, people without home or country, and seemingly without hope, particularly children, large numbers with ghastly wounds, many of them orphans who had seen their parents killed before their eyes, and as I have said, pathetically few people from the various organisations to help them, and a totally unknown future for them.

By a natural process of thought, as I looked back over the years, I went back to Hitler's war and the Japanese part in it, the biggest world conflict of my time, and probably the greatest slaughter of all time. Seeing these camps took me back to the numbers of our own country and its allies who had suffered in similar camps. I have numbers of friends who were POWs and I have found that, without exception, they scarcely ever mention what they experienced and how they survived.

My Session Clerk at Aldermouth, Alastair, a kind, gentle, wise man, as a young officer, had been part of the last line of defence as the bulk of our troops headed for Dunkirk and rescue in what has become famous as "the little ships deliverance". France had surrendered, Hitler's Panzers were sweeping all before them in the low countries, and Alastair's contingent and others had been instructed to halt or slow the German advance to France so that the bulk of our men could be rescued. At all costs they had to gain time to save their comrades. They were expendable. Their losses were frightful, but they carried out their task, and because of their sacrifice, many of our troops who would not otherwise have done so, escaped.

Alastair was crawling across a field from one trench to see his men in a neighbouring trench were alright when he was badly wounded, his leg shattered and bleeding profusely, death staring him in the face. It's a long time since he told me just a small part of his story, and Alastair has gone to Glory some years ago, but I believe I am right when I say it was a German, an enemy, who found him, stopped the bleeding, and had him transported to a German hospital and then a POW camp. Alastair was a brave man, one of many such men, but he was also a modest man, for although we worked closely together for twelve years in Christ's Church, only once did he refer to his experiences. For the rest of his life he was to suffer much pain, having of course an artificial leg. The amputation had been a crude affair, and as well as pain in the stump of his leg, he frequently suffered this strange but very real phenomenon – phantom pains in a leg that was no longer there. But his wound affected his life in many other ways. He had been no mean sportsman, but apart from the occasional game of golf which he could still manage, all his other sporting activities were not possible.

Also in Aldermouth, to which we have retired, I have been invited to be part of what we jokingly call "The Koffee Klub", when we meet, seven OAPs, twice a week for a coffee and a chat. Although I am the baby of the group, I very much enjoy hearing of the experiences of the others over the years, and am grateful for being invited to join them. Two of that number were POWs but they virtually never speak of it. One is Robbie who was a prisoner of the Germans, but he dismisses his experiences, saying he was much better off than others, and certainly those in Japanese camps. While no doubt the latter fact is true, I suspect it wasn't the cushy number he implies.

Our host is Peter, who is also the oldest of the group at 84, and he was a prisoner of the Japs, and suffered much, but never says so. He spends much of his time visiting old folks on his bike or on foot. Most of those he sees are, in fact, younger than him and I know how very much his visits mean to "the old folk". When I was his minister and he was one of my very best elders in our band of 70, back in 1980, the year I was to depart to the Borders, his wife Betty was fighting a brave battle with cancer. They had no family... though he has a huge family of friends, many of them old Scouts, for which Peter has a lifelong love, but together Peter and Betty fought this disease whose very name strikes terror. They fought it matter of factly, and knowing that in time she must leave him, Betty taught Peter how to cook, bake and run a house. Peter was... and is, a marvel, for there is virtually nothing he cannot do in the culinary line, laying on marvellous spreads. Though Peter, like Alastair, is also a quiet, unassuming man, I know the faith he and Betty shared was a tremendous strength to them in these grim months. Their house was built on a rock and it stood firm. One of the few things Peter has said of his dreadful experiences in a Jap camp was, quietly, to me: "Without my faith I could not have come through." He and other Christians in the camp built a little church, held Communion, and without a doubt that shared fellowship gave him the will, when often ill, to carry on. And eventually, though down to seven stone, he came home, and what a blessing this quiet man has been to so many, and from his own experiences of suffering has helped countless others.

Thoughts of Peter took me to another Japanese prisoner – and a turning point in the life of one of my longest ministerial friends... Bill McPherson, and it was his experiences in a Jap camp and something good that did come out of war that moved me to write this piece, and give it its title as this book nears its end.

Bill, like Alastair, lost a leg in the last stages of the fighting for Hong Kong – a bloody, cruel business, where Japanese soldiers went into hospitals and bayoneted every patient. One brave British nurse threw herself on top of a patient to protect him, but the bayonet simply went through her and the patient she was protecting. Another group of gunners, told to surrender and they would be spared, were simply lined up with their backs to their captors and bayoneted to death. Yet another large contingent of British troops were promised they would be spared if they surrendered, which they did – but were not spared, like their colleagues killed by bayonet. Among them was a certain Corporal Leith who had a blow on the back of the head, not by a bayonet, but an officer's sword. The force of the blow caused him to pitch forward into a ditch, into which the Japs threw the bodies of the dead… so Corporal Leith was saved by the bodies of his comrades. He dodged about for eight days, mainly hiding in ditches, until he was captured and sent to Bill's camp in Hong Kong. Bill makes the comment, "What could any officer write to next of kin in such cases about how their loved ones died?" Though Bill and I were very close, he never told me about this almost unbelievable brutality on the fall of Hong Kong – but he told his sons of his experiences, and they have put it into print, a manuscript that perhaps should be put into book form – "lest we forget" how near to the surface is the beast in man.

But Bill told me much of his experiences in prison camp. None of the Japanese camps were good, but some were unbelievably bad, and Bill was in one of them. It was a huge camp and prisoners died in their hundreds. Diseases of every kind were rife: beriberi, pellagra, malaria, TB; they all had worms; but the big killer they all feared was diphtheria. Yet probably the most lethal killer of all was just the loss of hope. These men could see no way out… no future. There was a hut called the hospital and two doctors who did what they could, but for a long time had no kind of medicine, not even the humble aspirin. There was also a padre, but it needs no imagination to realise what these men suffered, with none or nothing to aid, and many, like Bill, were to carry the relics of their years in camp for the rest of their days. Bill's heart was damaged, and I doubt if he knew a day without pain all through his life. Bill was never a critical man, but he told of how he nursed one of his officers called Le Mesurier till he died, the officer saying Bill was to have his clothes after he was gone. But when the officer died, another officer whom Bill, uncharacteristically called "a bit of a pompous ass", well kitted out with clothes, ordered Bill to give Le Mesurier's clothes to him. Bill had nothing but pyjamas and a dressing gown, so, probably for the only time in his life, he "stole" two shirts and two pairs of shorts and tucked them under his pillow, for he had no kind of cupboard. Life was hard, primitive, cruel, and Bill says that in the early days, the Japs kept no names of any prisoner under the rank of Captain who died. But enough of this life of suffering and hopelessness, and I turn to a little miracle... and the good thing that came out of war.

Bill had been brought up in Glasgow, a home typical of thousands of the time. He attended Sunday School, Bible Class, was confirmed as a Church member because the minister said it was time he joined the Church, but it really meant nothing to Bill. He felt that Christianity was just a matter of being good. There were not many bibles in camp, and prisoners caught reading one of the few were sometimes beaten. But Bill fell in with a small group of men, about a dozen, who met most days and discussed problems like "Is this all there is to life?" and "If so, why bother going on living?" They decided there must be more to life than this hopeless existence. Bill was impressed by these men, some of whom, despite sufferings and beatings, read the Bible. So Bill asked the padre eventually if he could lend him a Bible, which the padre was happy to do, told him to keep it, and Bill cherished that Bible to the end of his days. He decided to leave out the Old Testament and Paul's letters and concentrate on the four Gospels. The more he read, the more convinced he became that Jesus was either the greatest liar who had ever lived, or He was what He claimed to be, the Son of God. Day by day he read, studied, thought, discussed with his companions, not all of whom were Christians. Then took place what Bill was to call his conversion, not in a blinding flash of light, but with absolute certainly. To quote his own words: "I came to know I could only find life in all its fullness if I gave my life to Jesus Christ. The surrender was made. Once more I was a prisoner... a prisoner of Christ."

The little group built a church with whatever they could lay their hands on, as Peter and his friends had done in their camp... all to the amazement of the Japanese guards. One day Bill and his friends also had a Communion service and that Communion remained vivid in Bill's memory all his life. The bread was baked somehow from rice and for the wine representing the blood of Christ, they had water. Again, to quote an old friend, "That was the most wonderful and meaningful Communion service I have ever shared and it was in that crude, rough and ready camp church. No choir, no vestments, no organ, no candles – none of the trappings that seem to glorify man more than God. If I never take Communion again, it would not matter. The memory and joy of that simple act will remain forever."

That he was truly Jesus' man completely, and not merely seeking a shelter in the storms of his life in that appalling camp was emphasised by his decision, if he survived the war, to become a minister.

He did survive terrible privations, had several brushes with death, but eventually came home, mere skin and bone. He kept his vow, studied for the Congregational ministry, but never forgot the wonderful free, open fellowship he had enjoyed in camp when not only his own denomination but Methodists, Presbyterians, Baptists, Roman Catholics and Episcopalians met as one – the richest fellowship he ever knew – as indeed it will be in Heaven.

There is a well known legend of a man who went to Heaven and was conducted round by St Peter. They met a procession dressed in rich vestments and he recognised the Roman Catholics. In a corner were some sombre men in black meeting in committee, and he saw the Church of Scotland. A cheerful band was brightening the Heavenly streets... the Salvation Army for sure. Then they came to a high wall and Peter went on tiptoe, the man doing likewise. When they were past the enclosure, the man sought the reason for the secrecy.

"Oh, said Peter, the _ are in there," naming a very exclusive group, "and they think they're the only ones in Heaven."

A ridiculous, but ludicrous story, for we know that it is a complete parody of the Heavenly abode where, thank God, there will be but the one fold and one shepherd.

For a time Bill and I were neighbours in our churches and our four and Bill's five bairns were friends. But he and Sheena experienced great sorrow, for when only two years old, their youngest, Graeme was killed in a ghastly accident at their back door. Yet, if anything, Bill's concern for and compassion with his people grew even more. He was a born pastor and comforter, a shepherd who knew and loved all his flock. J.M. Barrie said: "It was because of the loss of her son, his mother had 'soft eyes' so that those in sorrow would turn to her."

So it was with Bill. Folk turned to him for comfort and were not disappointed. But you would never have known that Bill's life was such a continuous struggle with sorrow, sickness, and daily pain. Always there was his smile and ready joke. Their home was a place of joy.

In due course he came over to the Church of Scotland and served in three parishes, probably the most notable ministry being in the

Gorbals in Glasgow – a far from easy billet. But Bill and Sheena, as Glaswegians, were on the wave length of the Glasgow folk who loved Bill and his constant helpmeet in everything, Sheena, and they loved the Gorbals folk.

Bill McPherson was not famous, nor ambitious for the highest places. He never climbed the ladder of power which some seek; he wasn't a TV personality, did not have friends in high places, but he exerted a most faithful ministry in all his charges. He was all his life "content to fill a little space that Christ be glorified". The seed planted in that Japanese prison camp brought forth much fruit, despite a lifetime of pain with his leg and damaged heart.

A few weeks into 1991 he was hospitalised and it was quickly discovered his condition was terminal. He refused chemotherapy, and was told he had just a few weeks to live. As I would have expected of him after nearly a lifetime's friendship, he took the news as calmly as any man can take such a death sentence, supported by the love of Sheena and a very close knit family of sons, their wives, and grand-children. He was cheered by his Major son who phoned his dad from the Gulf where the land war was about to begin... and went home to die.

Hold on, you say, this is all too sad and harrowing... not something for a book. Maybe, but then as I have said before, the only certain fact of life, my friends, is death. We all have to pass that way. We sometimes refer to "life everlasting", but the phrase in the Apostle's Creed is *the* life everlasting. That *the* is important for it refers to a different kind of life, a richer quality of life that any of us can know on earth. Bill had no doubts about its reality, its certainty, so death for him was but Goin' Home... and in a few days he slipped away to the place where there is no more pain or heartache, and where all our questions are answered. His family were round him to the last and Stewart, the youngest son, and a minister who had been looking forward to his dad preaching him into his first charge, quietly and naturally led the family in prayer. Just one life of a humble, fine man. As the poet put it long ago: "Only one life, 'twill soon be past, only what's done for Jesus will last", and certainly something good that came out of war, for who can measure the value of a human soul, and Bill influenced many souls.

So goodbye, and thanks old friend. No, not goodbye ... au revoir... till we meet again. At Home.

TWENTY SIX

When Day's Work is Done

About a year before I retired, my wife and I attended a conference arranged by Church Headquarters for ministers nearing retirement. I was not quite due to retire since the retiring age for ministers was not 65, as it now is, but 70 for those of my era. However, my old enemy, that rare blood condition, had come raging back and every day was a struggle, so I knew I would have to go for my own sake and the sake of my churches. I felt it my duty to stay on till all the affairs of Tundergarth related to the air disaster were officially ended, though of course, there really will be no ending, for relatives and their children will come for many years to see where their loved one, or in many case, loved ones, died or are buried and they will come – to remember that dreadful night.

Our pre-retirement gathering was in Crieff Hydro – we had an executive suite, were lapped in luxury – and felt like kings. I had not expected to enjoy the conference, for having worked hard and played hard all my life from the age of twelve, retirement seemed to me a bleak desert stretching ahead. I expected all the other ministers of the course to be as mournful as me, but not a bit of it! It was one of the brightest, most cheerful gatherings I have attended. We met old friends, though it was a little difficult at first to recognise some of them without hair. Tongues wagged freely, experiences were recounted, jokes told, pictures of families passed around, and all in all we were like a bunch of youngsters, or sailors on shore leave, determined to enjoy ourselves.

We had a host of speakers who told us what pension the Church would pay (gey low!) – how we should invest our money (what money?), what sports or hobbies we should take up – with photography, bird watching and bowls strongly fancied. I had always played more active games – football till well into my forties, golf with a swing a friend described as "a good baseball player wasted – and tramping away into the hills to some lonely loch to fish. Gardening was also a lifelong love of mine, ever since, as the eldest son, I had helped my father break in fallow ground of considerable size to "dig for victory" in the war. As I have stated more than once, as both vet and minister, I had inherited gardens that gave a fair imitation of the wilderness in which the Jews wandered for forty years! The Church doctor gave us much advice on exercise, diet and soaking our false teeth in Domestos.

We had a very moving, but realistic talk from Dr Gray, whose husband had been minister of Dunblane Cathedral, been Moderator, a man whose name, John R. Gray, was known throughout the Church. He had died of cancer and his wife had nursed him as long as she could. That one solemnised us for it reminded us we were into the last lap of life's journey, and should at least be prepared – as husband or wife – for living alone.

Then came Uist McDonald and he was a ray of sunshine. He had been retired a number of years and was obviously loving it. He told us to take care of our car for we probably wouldn't be able to afford another, and many other practical things, but what has remained the lasting memory of that whole conference for me was how his face shone as he said, so matter-of-factly, at the close of his address: "You know, brethren, when day's work is ended, we don't sit around and mope. There will still be plenty to do, but there is now time – life's pressures are off – we can have outings, trips and do things together we never had time for before. We have time for our grandchildren. Friends, we are privileged people FOR WE ARE IN THE ANTE-ROOM OF HEAVEN – and what better place is there on earth."

The ante-room of Heaven, I thought. Maybe it sounds a bit final and bleak, but it is the ante room to a fuller, more glorious life beyond our richest dreams. As old Sir William Mullock (the Chief Justice of Canada) put it on his 90th birthday: "I am still at work, my eyes towards the future. The best is yet to be, hidden from our eyes beyond the hills of time."

I have now been retired for four years. It has not been an easy time with health problems, weakness and considerable pain. Yet it has been a good time too. Janet and I take each day as it comes and don't plan much ahead. As a little booklet I keep by my bedside puts it, we live "A Day at a Time", which really is the only way to live. We love our little home and the garden we have created from another wilderness. There are walks with our beloved dog, an old lady now, along our glorious beaches or majestic woods. There are short trips into the country, there is time for our children and grandchildren, and a glorious feeling of freedom. The stress is over. Life in the quiet at close of day is calm and sweet, and the sun in the westering sky of life I have found very beautiful and a place of great peace, and when the sun fades, the sky is filled with glittering stars. It is a breathtaking prospect!

I have no active ministry now but I have learned deeper reaches of prayer, and always, but especially in the hard days, I have known the presence of my great Friend more real and precious than ever before. I have also had numbers of letters to write to people who have written to me, sometimes desperate, asking for help or advice; folks who have read my first two books or the little thoughts in *The People's Friend*, so I still have a ministry of sorts. I also visit numbers of people, mostly old now, who were members of my Aldermouth church and I have found that to visit someone else who is suffering makes one forget one's own. Janet has become a bona fide Reader of the Church, and she tries her sermons out on me. Mind you, as I tell her with a twinkle, she has been preaching at me for nearing fifty years! She is also a Samaritan, and in considerable demand to speak at various groups... so she is far from being retired. When it is my turn to take the hospital or church Home Service, we do it together. I enjoy that. So, although life is sometimes tough and pain filled, it is nevertheless good, and while we look back with so many happy memories, and think of the wonderful people we have known who allowed me to be their minister or care for their animals, what a grand life I've had. Not everybody in this world has the job satisfaction I have had – I've been a lucky fellow – with tremendous variety in both my lives. The other day, too, I realised I now had a bonus. I went to see my son David playing football in the Highland League, and for the first time in my life I got in at half price. We're special people, you know, us OAPs!

On the day before we moved house from Boreland to our new home, I was phoned by Radio Solway to see if they could interview me next day for their version of *Desert Island Discs*. I said, "Impossible, we're flitting tomorrow".

But these interviewers are persistent. "It will only take half an hour" she said, "and we can find a corner somewhere. Meantime, think of your choice of four pieces of music."

Well, rushing hither and thither, packing boxes, clearing up and all the preparation for house moving (something I wouldn't wish on anyone!) I had little time to think of music. The lady duly arrived with her tape recorder and microphone, half the furniture had been loaded, but we found a corner which still had two chairs in it, and she took me through my life and certain specific incidents. The music was to be added later. In fact, she took two hours, and I had visions of us sitting in the furniture van finishing the thing off. Having said this much, you may just be wondering about my musical choices, which might have been different if I'd had longer to think about it all.

My first choice was *True Love* from the film *High Society*, which I have seen many times, with Bing Crosby and Grace Kelly singing together. I felt that summed up the lives of Janet and me... still in love after a lifetime. Our sons get very embarrassed when they hear this one! Secondly, I chose Burns' last great poem, a love song written when he was a dying man, and part of which I have quoted in the dedication of this book, but I am, and always have been, a sentimentalist.

Oh, wert thou in the caul blast, on yonder lea, on yonder lea;
My plaidie to the angry airt – I'd shelter thee, I'd shelter thee.

Then, turning to my Church life, but with a look back to youth when I was still a student vet, I chose *God so loved the World* from *Stainer's Crucifixion* – and the conductor emphasised to the choir (which contained my father, my twin brothers Graham and Fergus, as well as me) that we, in turn must emphasise the little word SO... "God SO loved the world... as much as that, allowing His Son to be crucified." The whole Gospel is wrapped up in that word, our organist made clear to us.

But what for my last choice? I wanted it to be a hymn, but I have dozens of favourites – but finally I chose a great hymn of victory, making clear that no matter the unholy mess the world He created may be at present, the end of all things is still with God – the

Kingdom WILL come, a Hymn of certainty which I felt summed up all I had tried to say as a preacher of this glorious Gospel. It may not come in our time, but if it doesn't, there is a whole new Kingdom awaiting us when the time comes to leave the ante-room and be ushered in to the presence of the King.

> At the Name of Jesus, every knee shall bow.
> Every tongue confess Him, King of Glory now.
> 'Tis the Father's pleasure, we should call Him Lord,
> Who from the beginning was the mighty Word.

As I draw this *Dog Collar Diary* to a close, I look back on a wonderful life, full of action and interest for a very plain, ordinary man, but enriched with the companionship of my Lord all the way. Nothing has ever removed that... nor will it. At the end of his ministry, the apostle Paul could say: "I have fought a good fight, I have finished my course, I have kept the faith." Ah, Paul! If only I could say that but I can't begin to.

William Booth, founder of the Salvation Army, as he neared the Golden Shore, could say sincerely "He has had the whole of me."

I don't doubt it, for Booth was a saint, but I can't say that either, for often I feel my personality, faults and failings have got in the way of Christ. Long ago I heard a wise old minister say, "As Christians we are not necessarily promised success... but we are called to be faithful."

But I rejoice far more in the promise God gives all His children... that HE is faithful, no matter our faults, failings, doubts and wavering. It's an almost unbelievable promise that no matter how we may have fallen short, or our downright failures, His faithfulness and love never falter.

So life goes gladly on in this fair world God has given us. The ante-room is a good place to be but we don't sit around reading back numbers of *Country Life*, *Homes and Gardens* or *The Scot's Magazine*. Just to be alive in this wonderful world the great Creator has given us... and it IS a wonderful world, should make our lives filled with interest and joy. So let me end with a story I imagine every minister has told at some time. It comes from George Borrow's *Lavengro*.

Borrow had attended an open air service on a wide moor, and he came away thoroughly depressed, for the preacher's theme had all been about preparing to meet God in death. He wandered across the moor and came on old Jasper the gypsy sitting in the heather watching the sun setting.

Borrow asked him, "What do you think of death, Jasper?"

The old gypsy replied, "Life is very sweet, brother", with no mention of death.

"Do you think so?" said a somewhat doubtful Borrow.

"Think so? Why there's day and night, brother, both sweet things. There's sun, moon and stars, brother, all sweet things. There's likewise a wind in the heath, brother. Life is very sweet."

The old man is right. Why should we hang about, preparing to meet God in death, when we can meet Him every day in His world, and have as a constant companion the One who is stronger than death, and drawn its sting by His victory over it?

Some time ago I happened to meet one of my former parishioners, a bright woman who always has a smile, but though a widow, and that fairly recently, while sorrowing, is anything but morbid. "I'm looking forward to going Home for Geordie (her husband) is there, Jesus is there. Is that very wrong of me, Mr Cameron?"

Her face was beaming. She truly meant what she had said, so I replied, "I understand your feelings, lass, and of course it's not wrong. It's natural for a Christian, and Geordie was a lovely man."

Then I thought, "You know, we don't often refer to a man as lovely", but it was the word, the right word, the mot juste for this man of great kindness, warmth, understanding, patience and love for all mankind... and late that night as I thought of what we had said, I recalled that what first captivated me in the Christian faith was not fear of judgement, or the need to build up a good league of points to pass some heavenly test, but what Samuel Rutherford used to preach, even though living in the hard, grim, cruel days in the Covenanting period, "the loveliness of Christ".

This he did too through much illness, sorrow in his family and the constant danger of execution – "the loveliness of Christ", "a lovely man", and when a person experiences that loveliness and all embracing love, we *know* that nothing life can do to us can separate us from Him in time or eternity. We are secure.

So on with the sheer joy of living – in His world – in His company, and when summoned from the ante-room to the presence of the King and the One who is... oh so thankfully... a Father who understands us, and we will be able to sing the old Sankey chorus the fisher folk loved.

Oh that will be glory for me, glory for me, glory for me
When by His grace I shall look on His face;
That will be glory… be glory for me.

To sum up

From the flowing of the tide to its ebbing;
From the waxing of life to its waning.
Of your peace provide us;
Of your light lead us
Of your goodness give us
Of your grace grant us
Of your power protect us
Of your love lift us
And in your arms accept us
From the ebbing of the tide to its flowing;
From the waning of life to its waxing.

A Celtic prayer